929

WRITING FAMILY HISTORIES and MEMOIRS

KIRK POLKING

BETTERWAY BOOKS

CINCINNATI, OHIO

Writing Family Histories and Memoirs. Copyright © 1995 by Kirk Polking. Printed and bound in the United States of America. All rights reserved. No part of this book may be reproduced in any form or by any electronic or mechanical means including information storage and retrieval systems without permission in writing from the publisher, except by a reviewer, who may quote brief passages in a review. Published by Betterway Books, an imprint of F&W Publications, Inc., 1507 Dana Avenue, Cincinnati, Ohio, 45207. 1-800-289-0963. First edition.

99 98 97 96 95   5 4 3 2 1

Library of Congress Cataloging in Publication Data

Polking, Kirk.
    Writing family histories and memoirs / Kirk Polking.
        p.   cm.
    Includes bibliographical references and index.
    ISBN 1-55870-394-2
    1. Genealogy — Authorship. 2. United States — Genealogy — Handbooks,
    manuals, etc. I. Title
CS16.P645   1995
929'.1 — dc20   95-3559
                                                                              CIP

Edited by Tom Clark
Cover and interior design by Brian Roeth

The permissions on page 242 constitute an extension of this copyright page.

ACKNOWLEDGMENTS

In addition to my editor, Tom Clark, and the sources already mentioned elsewhere in this book, I extend my thanks and appreciation to the following for their help in researching and writing this book: Deborah Auffart, Naomi Barnett, Jennie Berliant, Joan Bloss, Bernice Canady, Mary Cassidy, *Cincinnati Enquirer*, Cincinnati Historical Society, *Cincinnati Post*, Cypress House's John Fremont, Deb Cyprych, Erica Decker, Dewey Decimal Classification Editor Joan Mitchell, Family History Library's Kory Meyerink and Jayare Roberts, Helen Botsford Faucher, Virginia Felson, Jean Fredette, Ottmar Friz, Jane Heimlich, Kathy Heinz, Todd Johnson, Melissa Lanier, Luella LeVee, Sharon Lee, Dave Luppert, Dr. Jacob Marcus, Ohio Genealogical Society's Jean Morrison, Carol Mahan, Kenny and Nancy Burck, Pat Overbeck, Lynn Perrigo, Press Community Newspapers, Rob Portman, Colin Pringle, Mert Ransdell, Bernice Rudney, Linda Schmalz, Ruth Stechschulte, Bill Strickland, Betty Wettstein, Ethel White, Mike Willins.

TABLE OF CONTENTS

INTRODUCTION

A number of years ago, as editor of *Writer's Digest*, I conducted a little essay contest for readers on "Why am I a Writer?" The winner got an all-expense-paid trip to the national writers conference we held in Cincinnati, but the letters told us from people's hearts why they were infatuated with the world of words.

In answer to "Why am I a Writer?" some said:

- Because I have to, have always wanted to; when I write nothing else matters.
- Because I have had an interesting life and want to record it.
- Because I can be whatever I want to as a writer; I'm more alive.
- Because I want to influence people; I have a mission.
- Because I want to find out the truth about myself.
- Because I want to be rich and famous.

But a letter I have never forgotten was from a writer who told me about hearing of the death of an old man who had always wanted to be an artist. His room was filled with pots of paint and empty canvases were in every closet. He always kept his brushes soft because someday he was going to use them. But when he died he left not a single completed painting. "That's the day," she said, "I put pen to paper with all those thoughts *I'd* been saving for someday when I would be a writer."

Families are beginning to discover that in our busy world of the 1990s, we are losing the opportunity to share not only the histories of our parents and grandparents but our own personal stories. How many times do the kids rush off to the computer game after dinner and you have to attend a meeting, so there's no lingering at the dinner table for sharing family experiences?

We make phone calls instead of writing letters.

If a person in front of us at the grocery express line lingers to tell something funny that happened to him, we get irritated at the delay.

WHO IS THIS BOOK FOR?

This book is *not* for people who only want to draw a family tree with names and dates.

This book *is* for people who want to give a lively view of themselves, the persons who were their family, and the period in which they lived.

This book *is* for genealogists who want to add writing skills to their professional research expertise.

This book *is* for teachers who would like to give students some purpose for writing other than to fulfill a grade assignment. Feel free to borrow some of the ideas in this book to help your students write their own chapter of a personal story that pinpoints their place in contemporary history. (It may be the first time they've talked to their own parents in weeks!)

Our history books tell us about wars and generals; the rise and fall of governments; the earthquakes, tornadoes and tidal waves; the innovators of science, medicine, the arts. Friedrich Engels reminds us, however, "Men make their own history, whatever its outcome may be, in that each person follows his own consciously desired end; and it is precisely the resultant of these many wills operating in different directions and of their manifold effects upon the outer world that constitutes history."

As a writer, you have a unique opportunity to change history from sterile dates and facts into a living chronicle of what you or your family left as a legacy for future generations. You are the only one who knows the communities you lived in, the history you were part of. Who, but you, knows the personal struggles you faced, the successes you achieved?

Whether your goal is to write a personal memoir, a family history or both, this book will give you specific helps on how to research, organize, write and produce the finished book.

We've included many examples of the techniques used by people just like you, to achieve memorable family histories and personal stories.

Along with the actual examples of excerpts from family histories and memoirs, you'll find throughout this book periodic Writing Reminders. They'll alert you to the kinds of writing objectives you'll want to accomplish with your own book and the techniques you can use to achieve them.

After you have finished reading this book — and writing your own — we hope you will share with us any advice you would give others based on your own experience. We'll incorporate your best suggestions into the next edition of this book. Send your letter to Kirk Polking, % Betterway Books, 1507 Dana Avenue, Cincinnati, OH 45207.

Chapter One

What Kind of Book Do You Want to Write?

T he book you write can take many forms and you will find numerous examples in this handbook to help you decide on your own focus. What are your options? Here are some possibilities:

✔ A family history that delves as deep into the past as available records permit. For this detailed genealogical record, you'll need several years to complete your research and writing. The book will be valued by your descendants.

✔ A family history that concentrates on just a few generations. This book will be enjoyed by family and friends who share the same memories of a certain time and place.

✔ A history of several families who carved a community out of a frontier America — whether it was New England, the Appalachian Mountains, the newly explored West.

✔ A story about an individual ancestor whose life experiences were adventurous, inspirational or both.

✔ A story of your own life because there is something you want to say about it for your family or others who could learn from it.

✔ A book about certain family relationships and how they affected the lives of those around them.

✔ A novel based on some real-life episodes.

✔ A personal journal for self-evaluation.

✔ A book for your local historical society on the county or region where you live.

✔ A fiftieth, seventy-fifth or one-hundredth anniversary history of your family's business.

✔ Plus any number of other interesting avenues.

Here are the experiences of some family history and personal story writers. Their stories will give you some additional book ideas to think about.

FAMILY HISTORIES

Billie Plumlee Cox, who subscribes to the Prodigy on-line computer service, says that just for a lark she tapped into the Genealogy Bulletin Board. She did not expect to find out anything about her ancestors, but before long she had found six published narratives about them. "I was hooked," she admits.

One of the family histories she found was *The Plumlee Family*, by Robert D. Plumlee. Here's a brief excerpt from page one:

> The first mention of Plumley this writer found was in Somerset — John of Plumley and William of Plumley in the early 1300s. John and William were allowed to cultivate a certain tract of land of the manor. They were required to work first for the lord of the manor and could use the remaining time to work their own plots.
>
> ... At least two Plumleys were transported from England to Barbados after supporting the unsuccessful Monmouth Rebellion in 1685. These Plumleys were Somerset men, as was Sir John Plumley who was lord of the manor and churchwarden at Locking. After the rebellion, Sir John, caught hiding in a well, was hanged. Many supporters of Monmouth were hanged, quartered, and left on bridges or fences to decompose. Lady Plumley's ghost is said to roam the area today.

Mr. Plumlee's weeks spent researching and walking the steps of earlier Plumleys in England was the climax of many years of study untangling various spellings of family branches and their probable origins in Somersetshire.

Writing Reminder: Plumlee gives us not only the names of his ancestors and the years in which they lived, but shows us the results of political alliances that shaped his family history.

Families who have listened to stories about the hardships of relatives who first settled the West, uncles who were on opposite sides of the Civil War, or the funny antics of a cousin who couldn't resist a practical joke, realize that if those stories aren't written down, they'll be lost to future generations.

PERSONAL STORIES

In contrast, writer Bernadine Clark says, "I see writing a *personal* history as a private, cathartic process that results in a 'product' that may or may not interest/help/amuse one's descendants. It's a tool for understanding people, eras, attitudes. It's also a gift to oneself and maybe to significant others."

The personal story you tell can come from any of the various aspects of your life. Have you reached a point in your life where you want to reevaluate your spiritual development?

In her *The Mystery of My Story*, writer/workshop leader Paula Farrell Sullivan says,

> All my adult life I had felt abandoned, unwanted, rejected. For the past twenty years there was little gratitude even for the gift of life. I had stored enough rage to start a war or ruin a marriage. Writing was an invitation to let go of the past. . . . In the hundreds of pages written before developing the My Story workshop, several themes wander throughout: the need for healing life's early wounds; an insatiable search for God; and accepting my life in this world.

Perhaps you have been part of an industry that has changed over the years. Do you want to record the part you played in its evolution?

Have you finished reading a book about a certain aspect of history or politics but have a totally different view of the same events because you were *there*?

Did you or someone in your family make a contribution to the sciences or education that you feel deserves wider recognition?

Do you have deceased parents you now wish you knew more about? Writer Alice Hornbaker says,

> How I wish I'd encouraged my mother to write a journal. Youngest of three daughters, I constantly fretted about Christmas and birthday gifts for her as she aged. Her answer was: "Buy beautiful lingerie." But she never wore it. Instead she wrapped the items in tissue paper and stashed them in dresser drawers.
>
> How much better it would have been had she written in a journal about growing up in Cincinnati in the early 1900s. How she felt about being one of ten children who, after the death of two older sisters and her mother, ran the household.
>
> What goals had she postponed or sacrificed to give those other younger children a home? How had she felt after her father denied her training for her operatic voice, saying only "bad" women went on stage?

Her journal would have become our legacy, a way to knot up loose family threads that could have given our family tapestry more texture and meaning.

A Journal Can Help You Develop Your Book

If you have kept a journal in the past, it may be a help in deciding the kind of book you want to write. If you haven't kept a journal in the past, you may discover it is an excellent way to get started putting down thoughts and ideas to consider for your book.

Mari Messer, who has conducted workshops on journaling for many groups, keeps seven simultaneous journals of her own on topics ranging from dreams, thoughts and feelings, to travel observations and spiritual notations. Some she may only write in once or twice a year; others, almost daily.

The joy of journaling is that you can start any place, with whatever you're thinking about or remembering that day.

"The voluntary seclusion that journal keeping requires," says Mari, "can be described as 'going into your egg'—into the soul's nurturant darkness to see what will hatch. Journal writing can be a dialogue with this unknown territory, a letter slipped through a chink in an ancient stone wall, that may prompt a response from the other side by return mail."

For example, a July 4th notation in Mari's journal about the boom-booming noise of fireworks recalls

> ... other July fourths watching Roman candles burst into fiery blossoms. I was just twelve or thirteen. We lit sparklers with a long stick of "punk," set off firecrackers in a tin can so they'd make a louder bang. But the noise also brings back the other memories: the sound of artillery fire during the Pakistan war in the sixties when we lived in Lahore. The anxiety of trying to sleep with explosions reverberating in my pillow; the children, only infants then, crying. After that, there was never again the same feeling of safety sitting on an old World War II army blanket watching fireworks, sipping an Orange Crush.

For Mari's widowed mother, the gift of a blank book in which to write her own happy memories of travels with her father gave the pleasure of writing both those memories and subsequent memories of her own childhood and family. "I have not minded the wrinkles and grey hair," she writes.

I feel as long as my mind remains clear, the physical impairments can be soothed by medications, so far. Even lack of social interests are not important. Going on alone was the most difficult for me, so many things one must learn, and unlearn. I look at pictures of when we were young and even pretty. When all of life seemed ahead of us, and planning and anticipation were more important than the realization of dreams fulfilled.

This journal entry was written by Hazel Thisell Friedrichs in her mid-eighties. Her formal education had stopped at the eighth grade. Are there some older relatives of yours whose diaries or journals of memories, stories and feelings could be resources for *your* family history?

Connecting With Family

Dot Darpel, a high school friend, says, "While I was raising eight children, writing a diary was not at the top of my priority list. But now that they are gone and have families of their own, I think they would be interested in knowing how things were when their parents were growing up. In fact, my daughter gave me a book for Christmas to write in entitled *Generations: My Grandparents' Reflections*. It is for her daughter. Since they live in North Carolina, we don't get to see her often." Dot is filling her book with recollections like this:

By today's standards, I suppose you could call my childhood days "The Dark Ages." We had no phone, no radio, no automatic washer and dryer, no car, no refrigerator and certainly no television.

The day our first radio arrived was an exciting event. It stood about two-feet tall and was rounded at the top. We listened to *Jack Armstrong* and *Little Orphan Annie*. Decoder rings that could be adjusted to any size finger were offered for sending in boxtops from Wheaties or labels from Ovaltine. I waited impatiently for each new episode so I could use my decoder ring to find out the secret message, a clue to the next episode.

Washers at that time were the wringer types, an "advanced" model from those that had to be turned by hand. The automatic dryer was a clothesline tied from tree to tree. There were no detergents, just soap. To keep white clothes and towels white, they had to be boiled in a special container called a wash boiler. These containers were usually brass, oval-shaped, about two-feet high by three-feet long and one-foot wide. A large wooden stick was used to stir the clothes while they were boiling.

Our "refrigerator" was an ice box that held a large block of ice in one section, and the food in another. A pan underneath the box was used to catch the water from the melted ice, and had to be emptied frequently.

Finally the day arrived when our new real refrigerator was to be delivered. Hooray and Hallaluya!!! No more water-filled pans to empty. As soon as the delivery truck left, Mother made ice cream and put it in the ice cube trays that came with the refrigerator. It seemed like it took forever to freeze. The ice cream was a little icy and didn't taste exactly like hand churned ice cream, but we didn't care. We enjoyed it as much as we enjoy Graeter's now.

Since the 1930s many new items have appeared on the market. Men are now orbiting the earth. There are more things to see and do and keep up with. Everyone is busy, busy, busy. Back in the "Dark Ages" people seemed more relaxed. It really wasn't "dark," but "light" and free of so many tensions.

Connecting With History

Frances Wise agrees that the most enjoyable benefit of writing a family history is that a memoir is a connection with grandchildren. She finds *current events are often a spur to memories* and combines interviewing relatives with readings in history that connect to the subject of the memoir. Here's a brief passage from a family memoir:

> My grandparents, Isaac and Mary Shapiro, came to America from Latvia in 1882 to escape the terror of the pogroms. They were bride and groom, nineteen years old. My grandfather had a clubfoot. He was considered a cripple, of no use to the Russian Army. He was a small, gentle, round-faced man with two passions: the Bible and a desire to accumulate real estate. My grandmother, small like her husband, was a frenetic woman who generated ambition in her children.
>
> The young couple's first home was in Massillon, Ohio, where their first child was born. My grandfather made a meager living peddling pots and pans, needles and threads from a horse-drawn wagon.
>
> Massillon was a small town, too small for my grandmother's ambition. The family moved to Cleveland. A second son was born,

my father. My grandfather opened a hardware store on Woodland Avenue, a busy neighborhood populated by immigrants. The store prospered when the oldest son came in to help his father and eventually took charge of the business. My grandfather had more time to study his Bible.

For a few years when I was a toddler, and an only child, my parents took me on Friday nights to the Sabbath dinner at my grandparents' house. They lived in a community of other immigrants with large families and small businesses.

We went on the streetcar, arriving before sundown. My grandfather, wearing a black felt hat and a black suit, sat at a small table in the dining room, hunched over his Bible, occasionally singing some of the words.

My grandmother, a small wispy woman with a stringy gray topknot over her sharp tight face, was running between the kitchen and dining room. My father's two sisters, of high school age, were her helpers. My father's youngest brother, jolly and convivial, arrived with greetings for each of us. Another of my father's brothers was a student at Harvard and rarely came home.

In my paternal grandparents' home I felt like a stranger. There was never any expression of affection. Were they in awe of an American grandchild?

"Reading memoirs by good writers," says Wise, "is the most helpful route to writing your own. The best memoir I ever read was by William Allan White, editor of the *Emporia Gazette*. It was about his sixteen-year-old daughter Mary. I read it first in high school and still remember it sixty-five years later."

Writing Reminder: What well-written memoir do *you* remember and why? Rereading it could prompt some ideas for your own book.

NOTES FOR YOUR MEMOIR

While you're considering the memoir you want to write, here are some resources and ideas to review:

- ✔ Do you still have your "baby book" that loving parents filled out about your birth and early childhood?
- ✔ When you cleaned out a desk drawer the other day, did you turn up some old paycheck stubs? What did a week's wages buy in those days in terms of food, clothing, entertainment?
- ✔ Is there a bill on your desk for a wedding present you bought for

the daughter of an old friend? Where did you meet that old friend; what nourished the friendship?

✔ Did you receive an angry phone call from a relative over some perceived insult from another relative that has upset you? Was the accusation fair? Have previous attempts at mediating only hardened both family members' positions and left you the sad and unsuccessful go-between?

✔ What personal crises have you gone through? A broken marriage? A teenage daughter dead of drugs or a car accident? A sudden dismissal from an employer you'd served faithfully for many years?

✔ What are the happiest times you ever had and why?

✔ Have you kept a diary beyond those teen years when only girlish sighs over special boys were kept under lock and key?

✔ Were you in military service with sometimes long, silent hours in which to record your personal war, the friends you made, and those whose deaths were so sharp in your memory at the time?

✔ Were you on hand when history was being made?

Bella Briansky Kalter visited Israel with her husband and son at the time Egypt's Anwar Sadat made his surprise journey to Jerusalem in 1977. "Each evening in Israel," she says, "I would jot down what we had seen, done and my feelings about the experience. It became a 400-page memoir." Here is an excerpt from December 18, 1977, the last full day of her visit:

> We turned to the right and found ourselves at the southeast corner of the Mount, atop Solomon's Stables. Beneath us were the huge vaulted ancient chambers where Solomon had kept his 4,000 horses and chariots. At our feet was a grove of huge, gnarled ancient olive trees. An elderly Arab man walked slowly past us, turned back, and stopped beside me.
>
> "Come," I heard him say in slow, careful English. "I will show you the tombs of Absalom and Zechariah. I am the watchman of the Mosque of El Aqsa. It will be my pleasure to take you to a height from where you can see Silwan village where I live and the Kidron monuments."
>
> Our eyes had met in mutual trust, but I couldn't contain my apprehension. He was holding his hand out to me, and I found myself walking beside him. We soon reached the top of the wall.
>
> "You see, there is Silwan," I heard him say, "and there are the tombs."

I looked at the primitive village on the slopes beneath us with the windows and doors of its squat little houses painted blue against the evil eye; then at the tombs of David's rebellious son Absalom and of the prophet Zechariah and I thought: Our time here goes centuries back and on the same slopes where our ancestors are buried are the dwellings of our Arab cousins. Our destinies are tied together. Whatever our fate in life, the outcome is the same. Why can't we help one another?

When we returned to the area over Solomon's Stables, our guide stood outlined against the El Aqsa Mosque, surrounded by the grove of ancient olive trees that bordered the flagstones on which we were all positioned, as if we were standing on different squares of a chessboard.

I had just lifted a frayed olive branch from the ground. As I raised my eyes I saw our Arab guide reach for a fresh green one from the tree nearest him and slowly move with it toward me as in a ritual dance celebrating peace between our peoples — a peace in a time not yet here, a peace which was mine for the viewing in cinematic slow motion. In the next instant he was holding the branch out to me, helping me put it between my fingers, next to the frayed branch that I had lifted from the ground. After I thanked him, he was about to turn and leave but, Harold took our pictures together — "Salom" and "Shalom" were exchanged between us. Then our Arab guide was gone.

Factual recollections are not your only options, of course. Are there some painful parts of your life that you would rather exorcise with a novel than put down in factual form? Or perhaps some pivotal events that your imagination has conceived as a series of short stories?

It doesn't matter. The earliest family histories were stories told around the campfire, and the most readable ones today incorporate not only the facts that no one could dispute but also the imaginative recall of writers who seek the truth beyond facts — the way people thought and felt about the things that happened to them.

What your book contains will depend on the audience for whom you intend it. Do you envision it as only a gift to your family? Is it a personal story only for your own eyes? Is it a contribution to your local historical society? Are parts of it potential articles of inspiration for an appropriate magazine? Might there be a commercial audience for your book?

We'll look at your motivations for writing your story in the next chapter, but you may not want to make up your mind right now about what you'll do with the end product. Your plans may change as you get into the writing. For now, you may just want to put down some thoughts and memories you have that you haven't taken the time to record before.

WRITING REMINDER: STYLE, TONE

As you can see from the examples in this chapter, Mr. Plumlee writes in a more formal third-person style, ("*this* writer found," "*they* were required"), while other writers choose to write more informal first-person memories, ("all *my* adult life *I* had felt abandoned"). But in all cases it is the specific details these writers give us that make us "see" them and the times in which they or their ancestors lived.

The style of writing *you* will use (formal or informal) depends on the kind of book you decide to write. The tone of your writing (serious, helpful, affectionate, etc.) will also depend on the subject matter and its intended audience.

As suggested earlier in this chapter, starting a notebook will not only provide you with a means of developing the kind of book you want to write, it can also serve as a writing handbook. Whenever you read a magazine article whose organization and clarity make the subject easy to understand, use a marker to highlight its main points to see how the author did it. If you find an author's tone extremely irritating (saccharine? preachy? arrogant?) write down the sentences that had effect on you.

The chapters that follow will help you come to some further conclusions about the focus and writing of your book.

Chapter Two

Why Do You Want to Write It?

T he motives for writing a family history or personal story are as numerous as the people writing them. As you'll see in some of the examples that follow, they include one or more of these elements:

- ✔ remembering an only son who died too young
- ✔ learning about a father's early life
- ✔ giving a gift to daughters
- ✔ letting children know that parents were kids once, too
- ✔ showing grandchildren who their grandfather was
- ✔ proving ancestors did arrive on the *Mayflower*
- ✔ writing it down before it's too late
- ✔ providing inspiration to others facing a challenge
- ✔ wanting to know a parent as a *person*
- ✔ searching for one's own identity
- ✔ writing for those who don't write

You'll see examples in later chapters in which writers concentrate on describing occupations and ways of life that are unknown to the present generation. You'll notice, too, in the following examples that writers can choose from a variety of formats to tell their stories.

In an attempt to work through his grief at the loss of his only son, twenty-eight-year-old Glenn, Bob Baxter decided to make a video biography of him. He had first recorded an audio cassette when Glenn was eight years old and Bob, the proud father, took him for his first golf lesson. Over the years Baxter had recorded other highlights of his son's education and career as a golf professional. Combining photographs from the family album with these audio histories of his son, says Baxter, helped his own healing process.

Writer and teacher Lois Daniel says, "Although my father had been

dead for nearly thirty years, I had . . . a great longing to know something
about him as a young man. I knew that in the late 1890s, before marrying
my mother, he had spent several years roaming around the western
U.S.A. I had occasionally heard him recount his youthful experiences —
hopping freight cars, doing menial work on ranches, and often winding
up penniless in drab, ugly, Western towns.

"I remember scolding him for telling his stories, because I didn't want
people to think my father had been a bum. I realize now that he was an
interesting and adventurous young man who had been part of the last
days of the Old West. And I had begged him not to talk about it! The
story of the youth of this man whom I loved wholeheartedly and who
showered me with love and made innumerable sacrifices for me is lost
to me forever because of my shortsightedness.

"I believe many people, especially in the United States, are beginning
to feel a sense of loss because of their lack of knowledge about the lives
of their forebears."

When Mary Elwell West received from *her* father a copy of his *Memoirs* written in longhand when he was eighty-one, she says, "I was surprised how little I knew about him — particularly his early years. Maybe
I'm like a lot of daughters who loved, but never really knew, their fathers.
I appreciate the time and thought he gave to them, since he did it
primarily, I would guess, as something to give his daughters. And maybe
for a feeling of accomplishment and purpose and respect — hard to come
by in later years."

Mr. Elwell got his A.B. degree in chemistry in 1915 and became a
teacher, a business executive, and a junior high school principal. But
he knew what hardship and grief were like in his younger days. He
remembers:

> . . . when we moved to the Athens school district, we moved
> into the very old original log house there. It was full of snakes and
> when it snowed, snow blew through the roof and covered the floor
> and beds upstairs, in particular. The yard was full of locust trees
> and we called it Locust Grove. I cannot forget when a neighbor
> called me at Bloomington and told me my mother had died sud-
> denly in 1914. I travelled all night by train to Crawfordsville, then
> to Indianapolis, then to Valley Junction. Trains to Brookville did
> not stop here regularly, but the kind conductor had arrangements
> for a train to stop and admit me for Brookville. I think he did this
> largely because I was crying all the way home. I got to Brookville

about eight o'clock and called Father and we got home by horse and buggy about eleven o'clock.

In a magazine article about family storytelling, writer Eileen Silva Kindig makes the point that since so much time in American families is spent in front of the TV, "most of the stories kids ingest come to them electronically, which means life's most valuable lessons are being taught by the Simpsons and the Teenage Mutant Ninja Turtles!" On the other hand, family storytelling

> . . . lets children in on the secret that their parents were once children too.
>
> Psychologists who understand the therapeutic effect of story-telling say that children take comfort in knowing their parents weren't always "perfect" and that they experienced doubts, fears and problems, too. A shared dilemma becomes a natural bridge between parent and child, which makes it easier to cross the infamous generation gap to build trust and intimacy. . . .
>
> Not long ago, a friend marveled that her eight-year-old son stood up to a class bully who was picking on a kindergartner.
>
> "How did you have the courage to do that?" she asked.
>
> "It was easy," he replied. "I just remembered what Grandpa would have done."

Florence Simmons wants to record her family history so *her* grandchildren will learn all they can about their grandfather, her husband, Joe, who died a few months ago.

Florence had a pretty dramatic opening to her own life story. Born at home during a blizzard, she weighed only a little over two pounds and her mother was not expected to live. "Forget about the baby," said the young doctor. "Let's try to save the mother."

But Florence's grandmother ignored the doctor's advice and instead, wrapped the baby in lamb's wool, placed her in a cigar box, then a warming oven, and fed her with an eyedropper. Both mother and baby lived.

Florence's eighty years are filled with happy memories of a husband whose devotion was confirmed even after death by the loving notes she found in his home office desk. Their sixty-year marriage and its values is what she wants to impart to her own grandchildren who live in a world so different from the one she and Joe grew up in.

WILL YOUR BOOK ANSWER QUESTIONS LIKE THESE?

Are there some things you would like to put down on paper because if you don't they will be lost forever? How much do you or your children know about your own parents and grandparents? Do your children know what it was like to live through a war, the threat of a nuclear bomb, the days before television and VCRs?

Did you discover an interesting ancestor in your family tree and decide to fill out the rest of the branches not with just dates and names but stories about the role they played in the development of your community?

Were Your Ancestors Important?

In a *Bostonia* magazine article several years ago about New England genealogical resources, writer Kathleen Cahill asked Joseph O'Connor about his search for ancestors.

> "What made me start? Snobbery," he says. "When I was a kid, Thanksgiving would come around and everyone would say, 'My ancestors came over on the *Mayflower.*'" O'Connor's mother piqued his interest with a family tale that one of her ancestors had, indeed, arrived in Plymouth on the *Mayflower*, a story he substantiated as an adult.
>
> During twenty-seven years of research, O'Connor has compiled thousands of pages of family lore and produced a hefty summary of his findings, which he distributed to family members. He described himself as an Irish Catholic Protestant Jew, reflecting centuries of marriage and migration made familiar through diligent research.

In his book, *Family Names, How Our Surnames Came to America*, J.N. Hook points out that we know the names of all the *Mayflower* voyagers and twenty-eight of them (starred in the list below) are each the name of ten thousand or more Americans today! *Are you one of them?* There were 101 passengers on the Mayflower, says Mr. Hook; this list includes only the surnames of the men on the ship:

Alden	Browne*	Dotey	Gardiner*
Allerton (2)	Carter*	Eaton*	Goodman*
Billington	Carver*	Ellis*	Hopkins*
Bradford*	Clarke*	English*	Howland
Brewster*	Cooke*	Fletcher*	Langemore
Britteridge	Crackston	Fuller* (2)	Leister

Margeson	Rigdale	Thompson*	Warren*
Martin*	Rogers*	Tilley*	White*
Moore*	Soule	Tinker	Wilder*
Mullins*	Standish	Trevore	Winslow*
Priest*	Story*	Turner*	

Their female descendants who married will, of course, each have different names.

Did You Work With or Know Someone Famous?

Not very many of us are celebrities, but some of us have known them and people are fascinated by stories about them.

A *New York Times* "Relationships" column about an Intergenerational Life History Project in which fifty-three teenagers in Brooklyn and Manhattan interviewed elderly community members and collected oral histories of their lives described this encounter:

> Diamond Jim Brady's dishes. That's what Giulio Corsani told the teenagers about when they began asking him question after question about his ninety-four years on earth. When he came to New York from Florence in 1914, Mr. Corsani started working as a busboy at Delmonico's and he cleared the table for Diamond Jim many a time. By the 1940s, Mr. Corsani had worked his way up to headwaiter at the Stork Club. Of course, the teenagers had no idea who Sherman Billingsley was. So Mr. Corsani quickly enlightened them.

Robert Disch, the project's director, pointed out:

> This is the first generation of kids who have been so cut off from the elderly due to the age segregation and mobility in our society. Now kids have to be formally trained in relating to the elderly—something that those in previous generations learned naturally.

Will Your Experience Comfort/Inspire Another?

A person who has faced a daunting life challenge and come through it with courage sometimes finds that writing the experience will not only provide a release for the author, but inspiration and comfort to others facing the same exigency. For example, Catherine Maurice (a pseudonym) in her book *Let Me Hear Your Voice* describes her family's triumph over the autism of their two children, documenting the diagnosis, therapy and recovery using behavioral modification techniques.

Similarly, Margaret Moorman's *My Sister's Keeper* describes her sudden responsibility on the death of her mother to be the caretaker of her mentally ill sister, Sally. Moorman explores the relationships between her mother, her older schizophrenic sister and herself, and describes the ongoing turmoil of mental illness and the prospects for the future every caregiver hopes for. Here is part of her closing page:

> I think this was the moment when I realized that resolution was possible, after all. It was true that Sally and I had grown up amid family conflict, secrecy and sadness, but here we were to tell the tale—both of us strong, both of us going forward in our lives, both of us more whole than we had ever been. We had come through a lot, together and separately, and we were no longer controlled by the past. I've always felt that the relationships that are most difficult to resolve are those in which we continue to long for something—approval, respect, recognition—that will never be ours, at least not just the way we want it. When Sally spoke of Mother with sympathy, she was, in effect, forgiving her for all the disappointment she'd felt at not being able to elicit the kind of love she wanted. And I had at least begun to accept Sally as she was, without so much of the resentment that marked my years of denial.

Can a Family History Project Help Someone in a Nursing Home?

Ellen Cook, executive director of Senior Services of Northern Kentucky says, "I remember watching a nursing home resident in her eighties, who usually sat with little to say, come alive and begin to sparkle when I asked her about her wedding day. Her story was far from boring, and I felt privileged to be able to share this experience through her vivid memories. I got to know her better and received a history lesson as well, as she explained how shortages resulting from the war affected the arrangements for her reception and honeymoon.

"Sharing a memory is one way that an older adult can help you to know them, to help you understand that there is more there than what you see."

Older relatives—especially those who recently have been ill—may be alarmed when you start asking about their family history. *Does he think I'm going to die? Why is she asking all these questions?* One writer who convinced her mother that she really just wanted to know her better discovered a new intimacy in their hours together as the daughter recorded their conversations and transcribed them for her mother to read. Even some painful memories were resolved — things the mother had never revealed before, and could not put aside.

"In fact," says Dr. David Sobel, coauthor of *Healthy Pleasures*, "taking ten to fifteen minutes to write continuously about one's deepest thoughts and feelings, especially about stressful experiences, can clear our minds. Studies show that writing and confiding also reduce physical complaints and doctor visits and may boost immune function."

David Greenberger who worked as activities director at The Duplex nursing home in Boston would engage the residents in conversation by asking both ordinary and outrageous questions to stimulate their imaginations. That experience resulted in the book: *Duplex Planet, Everybody's Asking Who I Was*. Greenberger says:

> I'm fascinated by the fact that you can grow older and feel like the same person you were when you were younger. There's something that carries forward, no matter what. That's an amazing thing.
>
> Old people get viewed as repositories of oral history. But if that's the only way in which you view them, you're cutting short your own ability to age in a healthy way. You get to know a person through his or her sense of humor, pathos, outrage and surprise; those qualities, not historical facts, establish an emotional range.

What were some of Greenberger's questions? Here's just one, and a couple of answers:

Q. *What can you tell me about the behavior of fish?*

A. I eat fish. I don't want to know about their behavior. — Frank Wisnewski.

A. They're always spawnin', always makin' whoopee. That's why there's so many of them. That's all they do. It's a good sport, fishin'. — Andy Legrice.

A. All I can say is fish must be very observant, because they must notice the way you bait your hook. If one little bit of hook is showin', they don't bite it. — Walter McGeorge.

Who Am I?

What do people know about the interior you, as opposed to your exterior as a family member or co-worker?

What do you know about yourself? A memoir can tell you.

A writer who decided to write her personal story said, "I've always told stories to my children about what life was like when they were growing up but I never told them how I *felt* about life or the things that happened. They don't know the real me, and I'm not sure I do either. But I want to find out."

Perhaps you've kept a journal over the years, but really never tried to organize it into a readable family history or personal statement.

If the generation that came to maturity during World War I was deemed the Lost Generation, those of us who came later seem to fulfill one book jacket blurb that "the twentieth century is the century of the Identity Crisis."

There are adopted children seeking birth mothers and families seeking long lost brothers and sisters, separated by wars or poverty or divorce. The search for personal identity is especially poignant in cases like that of Margaret Brown. In a March 7, 1994, *Newsweek* "My Turn" personal essay, she pointed out,

> I only recently found out my father was not really my father. My parents divorced when I was seven, and . . . . at sixteen, when I expressed interest in seeing him again, my mother decided to tell me that my "dad" wasn't really my father and that my father's half of me came from a test tube. With no records available, half of my heritage is erased . . . . "Who am I?" is a hard question to answer when I don't know where I came from.

A similar dilemma faces an older generation of today's memoir writers whose ancestors were part of the Orphan Train movement, in which the Children's Aid Society of New York sent more than 100,000 orphaned or abandoned children from New York City to foster homes in the West between 1854 and 1929. Today's descendants of these orphans are helped in the search for their ancestors who lived during those specific years by The Orphan Train Heritage Society of America, Inc., 4912 Trout Farm Road, Springdale, Arizona 72764.

THE NEED TO WRITE THE BOOK NOW

Why is it that as we get older time seems to go so much faster? University of Cincinnati psychology professor Joel Warm says, "There are a couple of theories about time perception. For example, U.C.'s Dr. Lemlich's fraction hypothesis points out that time at an older age is a smaller fraction of a person's total life than time to a ten-year-old and time seems to go faster. Other studies have shown that time perception changes as one gets closer to a danger point. As they get older, people see their life as coming to a close, so time seems to rush by. Or, as you get older, the things you have to attend to and want to accomplish become more and more numerous. As a result, you never seem to get it done as you would like, and time seems to go quickly."

That sense of urgency to accomplish something affects not only older people. In 1986, when thirty-two-year-old artist Sandi Gold was told by doctors that it would be a couple of years before they knew whether the new form of neurosurgery for her brain tumor would work, she told a *New York Times* interviewer, "I had two years where it felt like I was walking around with a time bomb in my head. I would think, 'What are my last thoughts?' I started seeing things in a far different way—the best way to describe it would be falling in love with life."

She received an invitation to paint a mural in the Westerly Rhode Island Public Library's art gallery. She agreed to do it "only if it can be erased, because life is temporary." She spent twelve-hour days and six-day weeks producing a sixty-foot mural that was on display for a month. Then she washed it all away. She was especially pleased by the praise her work received from terminally ill visitors. "They never asked me not to destroy it," she said. "It's not the end of life that's frightening. It's what we don't do that's frightening."

GETTING CHILDREN INVOLVED IN MEMOIR WRITING

One way schools interest children in writing their own stories is through guest appearances by authors of children's books and other works. On a 1993 visit to an Ohio school, the Russian poet Yevgeny Yevtushenko read some of his poetry and answered questions from the students. One wanted to know how he became a poet. In a newspaper account of the visit, Yevtushenko said that as a hungry child living in Siberia with two grannies during World War II, he had smoked a hibernating bear out of its den and shot it with his one cartridge. The poet said he still remembers "the human eyes, full of fear, surprise" before the bear died.

"All poetry begins with guilt," he said, and that killing inspired his first serious poem. He dedicated it to the bear that fed his family. "I asked for forgiveness. Writing has to be your confession, but that isn't enough. You have to be the writer for those who don't write. Only art discovers the secret of immortality."

FAMILIES COMMUNICATING

Today's parents are beginning to discover that unless they interest their children in writing at an early age, these children won't be as likely as they grow older to communicate to *their* children the legacy that binds the generations together. Some families encourage their children to share their own experiences as part of a family history project. Others discover that ancestor research holds fascination for some younger "detectives" in the family.

Writing Reminder: Any form of writing that appeals to young children can nurture the skills they'll need as adults to write their own family histories and memoirs.

Some excellent advice to parents of young children for involving children, in a non-threatening way, in writing more is given in Peter Stillman's *Families Writing.* For example, he suggests that the kitchen bulletin board should not just have pedestrian messages such as, "Harry, set oven at 350" but encourage the posting of:

> Any short forms of prose or verse, especially home-grown and meant to amuse. This would include limericks, epitaphs, T-shirt slogans, riddles, knock-knock jokes (the last two with answers folded under, as in)
> "Knock-knock."
> "Who's there?"
> "Arch."
> "Arch who?"
> _____
> "Gesundheit."

Stillman describes another constructive use of family writing this way:

> A young parent I recently spoke with told me that she and her twelve-year-old agreed years back to reduce family tensions by writing out their side of any thorny issue that crops up, and then dialoguing on paper until the matter is resolved. "It doesn't always work," she said, "but it usually does cut back on misunderstandings. We don't just write about the particulars of a disagreement; we also deal with how we feel. I confess I have a hard time saying out loud, 'I hurt,' but I don't have any trouble writing about it. Neither does she." (This dialogue journal entry by another young mother writing to her ten-year-old daughter after a misunder-

standing offers perfect proof of how we can write what we often cannot say: "I wish it was as possible to yell 'love' as it is possible to yell 'anger'.")

WHY DO YOU WRITE?

In a letter to a writer who asked: "Why does one write?", Anais Nin said,

> Why one writes is a question I can answer easily, having so often asked it of myself. I believe one writes because one has to create a world in which one can live. When you make a world tolerable for yourself you make a world tolerable for others.
>
> We also write to heighten our own awareness of life, we write to lure and enchant and console others, we write to serenade our lovers. We write to taste life twice, in the moment, and in retrospection. . . .
>
> . . . We write to be able to transcend our life, to reach beyond it. We write to teach ourselves to speak with others, to record the journey into the labyrinth, we write to expand our world, when we feel strangled, constricted, lonely. . . . When I don't write I feel my world shrinking; I feel I am in a prison. I feel I lose my fire, my color. It should be a necessity, as the sea needs to heave. I call it breathing.

Your own reasons for writing your family story may be less vital to your self-preservation than Nin's. You may, in fact, never pinpoint why you want to invest time and effort in your story. But it's helpful to fix in your mind a reason for why you're writing this, a vision of what you hope your readers (or simply you) will gain from the project.

From a practical standpoint, knowing why you're writing this book will help you determine what belongs in it. You can more easily decide which topics and events you should write about and which you should leave out. Less practical, but perhaps more important overall, is this benefit: Your vision of the book will sustain you through the research and writing processes. It will keep you going during those times when you might otherwise grow discouraged or lose interest.

WRITING REMINDER: EMOTION

In the *Writer's Digest Guide to Good Writing*, writer Mildred Reid says "there is only one 'must' in creative writing—or any other writing for that matter. You must transfer an emotional experience to the reader."

We know from experience that reader identification is a way to do this. "Suppose we analyze this business of transferring an emotional experience to the reader," says Reid. "Since we quite obviously do not habitually go around overcome by the deeper emotions — the more dramatic emotions such as fear, anger, hatred, sorrow — what are the other emotions we might be feeling?

"Certainly frustration may be one — and a popular one with writers! And how about anticipation, amusement, pleasure, hopelessness, pity, envy, agitation, helplessness, humility, timidity, boredom, gratitude, jealousy, avarice, antagonism, greed, pride?"

Take a look at the part emotion plays in some of the examples in this chapter. And for further guidance on how to use emotion for reader identification, analyze your own emotional reactions both to life situations and to the things you read. Write down how you felt about something that happened this week. How did the author of something you read recently make you *feel* a certain emotion? Write down how he or she achieved it.

Chapter Three

What Will Be Its Scope?

T he biographer's problem," says writer Russell Baker, "is that he never knows enough. The autobiographer's problem is that he knows too much. . . . the whole iceberg, not just the tip . . . ."

Russell Baker's memoir *Growing Up* was 450 pages of manuscript before he realized he had spent most of them talking about his relatives and not about the tension between his mother and himself, which was the real story. It was only after writing that first draft that he discovered the importance of what he had left out. So the lesson here is to get a first draft written. You can always alter its scope later—either putting in or leaving out.

Your purpose may change as you get into the memory recall or research, but it's a good idea in the beginning to decide on a focus for your book.

As William Brohaugh points out in his book *Write Tight*, "Many writers err by trying to cover too much territory. . . . Focus is also known in the world of freelance writing as angle or slant. . . . Identify exactly what you're trying to say. Then, identify who you're trying to say it to. The combination of these elements (which feeds back to the whole matter of value in a manuscript) dictates your focus."

Throughout this chapter we'll look at questions to consider when deciding on the focus of your book.

What Time Frame Will It Cover?

Only as far back as your grandparents? The arrival in America of your ancestors? Just your own lifetime? Or even just a piece of that life?

Before making social work her career and raising a family, Sue Ransohoff had worked in a Royal Canadian Air Force control tower in Gander, Newfoundland, in World War II. "My favorite times," says Sue, "were those when large numbers of aircraft were coming in on their way over-seas, or taking off on the last lap. We were really busy on those days, or nights, and I loved it. Usually departures were scheduled to begin around midnight. Aircraft would be lined up by the hangars, sometimes as many as eighty at a time, ready to go. One after the other would warm up, wheel out of line, taxi to the starting point and take off. One after the other sped down the runway, roared past our window with a terrific crescendo of sound, and vanished into the night. I loved watching them, but I was usually too busy at the phones. I managed to get to the window for a few seconds, and then would dash back to the table to note the time of take-off and aircraft number from the tower, relay the information to the American Air Force or to the RAF, and then dash back to the window to watch the next take-off. For the whole fifteen months I was at Gander I never tired of that sight — the great expanse of runways spread out before me, often covered with packed-down snow and lined with huge walls of snow pushed aside by the blowers. The dim yellow lights of the barracks and hangars, the stars frosty and far away, the lines of aircraft with engines glowing through whirling propellers, two or three planes still circling the field before they headed out over the Atlantic — it was a thrilling sight."

Sue Ransohoff echoes other writers' motives when she reports that she just sat down and wrote her memoir spontaneously. "I wanted my children to know me as a person, not just a Mom, so I wrote about this earlier part of my life."

Sue's father, Milton F. Westheimer, also wrote a memoir about his earlier life. (His was written for his 50th wedding anniversary in 1956.) In it he described, among other things, his earlier life as a traveling salesman at the end of the last century up to 1906:

> I didn't take the road to seek — or even to expect — adventure. I went to sell goods, and to take over Leo's (an older brother) territory, his customers, and to show my partners that I could make good. I found before long that I hated the job, the constantly recurring pressure and tension of getting a profitable order; this was so different from my college work that I even would have welcomed an accident or illness as an excuse for a vacation; but it was four trips a year, of three months each, with a hiatus of three or four days between getting home — and getting off again, except ten days at the year's end. Seven years of this. The very aversion to the job spurred me on to get relief in success.

II

FIRST THREE GENERATIONS

Johann Muller   Georg Muller   Paul Muller

Seven of the nine brothers and sisters, Friederice, Caroline, Johanna, Detlef, Peter Henry, Marie, and Therese, children of Gustav and Wiebke Franzen Muller born in Dellstedt, Dithmarschen, Holstein, Germany, emigrated to the San Francisco Bay area from 1878-1892. Willy, Therese, and Hanna, children of the eighth child Wilhelmina, arrived in the early 1920's. Wilhelmina and Diedrich, the first-born son, remained in Germany.

One hundred and ten years and four generations later, the descendants of the immigrants have remained in contact with each other through an annual family picnic. It was at one of these in the mid-1950's that a genealogical chart of the Muller family first appeared in this country. It was made by Louis Smaus, son of Marie Muller Smaus, from information given by the immigrants themselves. It names Paul Christian Muller as the first known ancestor. The only other known record was the Muller-Franzen chart by Heinrich Peters, son of Wilhelmina Muller Peters who also remained in Germany. It names Paul Christian Muller as the first known ancestor and Magdalene Christine Kadsen as his wife. This is all that was known about them.

It has always been assumed that the Mullers, as well as the maternal Franzen line, had been inhabitants of Dithmarschen for many generations. Continuing research discovered as recently as February, 1988, in the archives of the Evangelical Lutheran church in Bredstedt, two more Muller ancestors, neither of whom had been born in Holstein.

FIRST GENERATION

1   **Johann Muller**[1], b. (circa 1690 ?) m. ? Rusch
Johann was a Magister legis. in Jena. Majister legis. means he had earned an academic degree in law. A Majister in those times was entitled to teach in a university. So, it could well be that Johann Muller was a professor teaching law at the famous university of Jena. Jena is a city in East Germany. Their son:
2   i. Georg Theodor Muller; b. 6 Dec., 1719

SECOND GENERATION

-2   **Georg**[2] (Johann[1]) **Theodor Muller**;
b. 6 Dec., 1719; d. 7 June, 1788
Georg was a Pastor in Bredstedt who came from Jena. He was married four times.
1) ? Petersen; their child:
3   i. Paul Christian Muller
2) Margaritha Dorothea Schmidt; their son:
ii. Johann Peter Muller
3) Dorothea Sophia Claushen; their children:
iii. Christian Detlef Muller
iv. Margaretha Dorothea Muller
4) Margaretha Anna Elizabeth Laurop; no children

THIRD GENERATION

-3   **Paul**[3] (Georg[2], Johann[1],) **Christian Muller**;
b. ? m. 18
Oct., 1780 Magdalene Christine Kadsen in Heide.
Paul's birthdate and place are not given on the Bredstedt church record. It is quite possible that he came from Jena with his father Pastor Georg Muller. He was a merchant. Their son:
4   i. Johann Diedrich Muller

Will It Be a Formal Genealogy?

Will you almost solely be concerned with the historical record of the descendants of a particular family ancestor? (For a sample, see the text above, taken from the book *Gustav Muller of Dellstedt: An Account of His Descendants through the Fifth Generation*, by Luciel Muller Harriman).

Do You Plan an Anecdotal Account?

A history of your family that will make a "story" whose characters will be as interesting to read about as those in a novel? For example, Elizabeth Stone, in a *New York Times Magazine* article titled "Stories Make a Family," tells us about her ancestor this way:

In the beginning, as far back in my family as anyone could go, was my great-grandmother, and her name was Annunziata.

. . . I never met her, but my mother often told me a family story about her that I knew as well as I knew the story of Cinderella.

. . . Annunziata was the daughter of a rich landowner in Messina, Sicily, so the story went, and she fell in love with the town postman, a poor man but talented, able to play any musical instrument he laid eyes on. Her father heard about this romance and forbade them to see each other. So one night in the middle of the night — and then came the line I always waited for with a thrill of pleasure — she ran off with him in her shift.

I didn't know what a shift was and didn't want my version of the story disrupted by any new information. I loved the scene as I saw it: In the background was the house with the tell-tale ladder leaning against the second-story window. In the foreground was my great-grandmother, like some Pre-Raphaelite maiden, dressed in a flowing white garment, holding the hand of her beloved as she ran through a field at dawn, toward her future and toward me.

Family histories tell stories of lost ancestors as well as founding families, as does this excerpt from *Book of the Hulls*, by Oliver Hull, who recounts:

An old nurse, Mrs. Brown, once lived in my family, with whom I had frequent conversations of her early recollections. Of one of these pleasant gossips, as it was in reference to my relatives, I took notes. It gives a graphic account of a passage in the life of a bashful Quaker uncle, and so seems worth recording. It is nearly in her own words.

"I was present at your father's wedding. I was acquainted with Miss Avery before she was married. I knew her very well. Your father married out of Meeting, but after a while your mother joined the Quakers. I knew your uncle Joseph too. He was a very pretty-behaved, bashful young man, and very handsome. He was called "the handsome Quaker." We young folks all thought he died of love. He was very fond of a Miss Wilmot, ye see, Jenny Wilmot, and she married a Doctor Johnson, of Newark, New Jersey. Her parents were against her marrying your uncle, ye see, because they were strong Episcopalians, and he was a Quaker. Your uncle found out that they did not like him, for Mr. Wilmot made some disparaging remarks before him; and then he did not go so much to see Miss Wilmot; and somehow, Dr. Johnson stepped in between them — and her parents liked him, for he was an Episcopalian like themselves. But la! She would have had your uncle Joseph, for she was very fond of *him*, if he had only been bold and persuaded her—but your uncle was very bashful. She was engaged to Johnson some time before your uncle's death, which your uncle knew. So he kind of fell away, and died in the fall of the year; and we all thought he died of love. Miss Wilmot was married to Johnson the winter after your uncle's death."

How Much History Will Your Story Include?

One of the things authors of memoirs and family histories remark on is how much more meaningful history is when they're researching it for themselves rather than learning it in school. They see how history affected their ancestors. Annie Dillard, writing about her book *An American Childhood* in a collection of essays called *Inventing the Truth: The Art and Craft of Memoir*, says:

> I learned a lot by writing this book, not only about writing but about American history. Eastern Woodland Indians killed many more settlers than Plains Indians did. By the time settlers made it to Sioux and Apache country, those Indians had been so weakened by disease and by battles that they didn't have much fight left in them. It was the settlers in the Pennsylvania forests and in Maryland and Virginia who kept getting massacred and burned out and taken captive and tortured. During the four years the French held Pittsburgh at Fort Duquesne they armed the Indians and sent them out from there, raiding and killing English-speaking settlers. These were mostly Scotch-Irish because the Penn family let them settle in Pennsylvania only if they would serve as a "buffer sect" between Quakers and Indians. When the English held Pittsburgh at Fort Pitt, they gave the Indians unwashed blankets from the smallpox hospital.

Will You Focus on Your Professional Life?

Warren Bennis described his intentions in his book, *An Invented Life: Reflections on Leadership and Change*, this way:

> Not long after I sat down to write this brief, intellectual autobiography, I had a small epiphany: I realized that what I was doing was actually *biography*, imagining a narrative about someone named myself. The result is a selection of stories, some called

memories, that I—and to some extent others—have created to give coherence and meaning to my life.

What I'm talking about is self-invention. Imagination. That's basically how we get to know ourselves. People who cannot invent and reinvent themselves must be content with borrowed postures, secondhand ideas, fitting in instead of standing out. Inventing oneself is the opposite of accepting the roles we were brought up to play.

Do You Have a Diary That Is a Book?

To paraphrase Dickens, diaries are the chronicle of "the best of times, the worst of times." A very young writer (she was about eleven when she started), Zlata Filipovic, is the author of *Zlata's Diary: A Child's Life in Sarajevo*. Her diary tells us what it was like to grow up in war-torn Bosnia.

Thomas Mallon's *A Book of One's Own: People and Their Diaries* divides diarists into seven groups: Chroniclers, Travelers, Pilgrims, Creators, Apologists, Confessors and Prisoners. He reminds us that there are as many motives for writing a personal memoir as there are for compiling a family history.

Many memoirs focus on the writer's personal story about a turbulent time through which he lived and can describe with feeling.

For example, Infantry Captain Dominic Caraccilo kept a journal of his 227 days in the Middle East during the Gulf War. In the April, 1994, *Writer's Digest*, Caraccilo described how, after reading about a Vietnam veteran who sold his memoirs to a scholarly book publisher, he was encouraged to submit (and sell) his *The Ready Brigade of the 82nd Airborne in Desert Storm: A Combat Memoir*. "I didn't picture myself as a scholar, but I did consider myself an expert in my field. . . . Because the acquisitions editor couldn't know that my information was accurate. . . . I included newspaper articles acknowledging the events I wrote about, photographs of significant individuals who factor into my memoir, and official documents justifying chronology. This extra attention to detail certainly helped sell my work."

What personal story do you have buried in a diary or journal or in a box of documents, clippings, photographs? Do you have any letters from relatives in the Civil War that can add vivid detail to your family history? Were you part of the anti-Vietnam War movement, the civil rights marches, a pro bono lawyer for an indigent plaintiff? What notes from your diary can be expanded into a personal story?

Writing Reminder: Your own diary is yours to use in any way you wish, of course. But keep in mind that diaries of others cannot be used without consent of the authors or their heirs. (See similar cautions in chapter six about *letters addressed to you.*)

You may have second thoughts about how much to use of your own diary, depending on how long ago it was written. Writer Nick Clooney, commenting in his newspaper column on some diary entries discussed at a 1994 Congressional hearing, said, "I don't know about you, but I occasionally tried to keep a diary when I was younger. When I now look at those entries, I am amused and embarrassed. The language is florid, the characterizations of other people are thoughtless and incorrect, the conclusions are sweeping, rumors are put down as if they were gospel. The material is entertaining, but to call it accurate is to turn the truth on its head."

Will You Focus on Your Avocations?

The passion for certain life experiences impels some authors of personal stories. One is Robert Leonard Reid, who writes of mountain climbing in his book *Mountains of the Great Blue Dream*:

> One cannot climb for long without meeting someone who is marked. I have a friend who three times has lost a companion on a climb. Late one chill March afternoon, as the wind howled and a vanilla-colored sun slunk down behind a nameless peak in California's High Sierra, I watched in fascination as a ripple in the snow high on the east face of the mountain grew gently and beautifully into the wild rush of an avalanche. Starry-eyed at my side, safely out of the range of fire, stood a wonderful climber named Vera Watson. I didn't know her well and it wasn't an avalanche that eventually ended her life, but I have never forgotten the comment she had as we watched the snow pouring down that peak: "There will be lots bigger ones than that where I'm heading."

My own passion for flying was nurtured by reading about Amelia Earhart and the mystery of what happened to her on that 1937 flight around the world that ended in disappearance in the Pacific Ocean. But it wasn't until the mid-1960s that I took a *Life Magazine* coupon and five dollars to a Cessna dealer for a flying lesson. My first solo flight nine instruction hours later was a thrill rarely matched since.

A columnist in *Flying Magazine* points out:

Flying is satisfying because it's one of the few times in our lives that we have both the responsibility and the authority to make decisions that directly affect the outcome of what we're doing. Only rarely are accidents caused by mechanical failures; typically they're the result of pilots making decisions that force them to fly in conditions beyond their capability. It's not far from the truth to say that flying is as safe as we make it.

Can You Describe Yourself in One Word?

In the fall of 1993, a *New York Times*/CBS News poll asked 1,136 adults if they could describe themselves in only one word, what would it be? Could you define yourself in one word? Ambitious? Candid? Liberal? Conservative? Curious? Confused? Idealistic? Or do you agree with Suzanne Keller, a sociologist at Princeton University who was quoted in the *New York Times*: "You cannot reduce yourself to one, it's too complicated. People really feel multiple. . . . If they're forced to choose between family and work and leisure roles, which are not even roles but personas, they can't really, because they live a multifaceted, multitudinous life, not single track."

Still it's a good question to ask yourself as a way to investigate the many facets of your personality and how they have assumed varying levels of importance as you grow. Your answer may help you bring a focus to your personal story.

HOW MUCH SHOULD YOU TELL?

How much should be told in a family history? Sue Ransohoff, a clinical social worker describes the dilemma this way: "Telling everything— 'warts and all'—is a great opportunity to clear the air, but many things would cause a great deal of hurt. Perhaps writing as much of the whole truth as possible is the answer. For the most part, people who will read it, such as adult offspring, already have inklings of family secrets, and learning the truth can only help. When one doesn't know the truth, one is apt to envision the worst. For example, if a family history says every sibling and every in-law got along wonderfully, you know it can't possibly be true. It's perhaps the memoirist's reality to *believe* that it was true."

WRITING REMINDER: AUDIENCE

You might want to tack up over your desk the question: "Who is this book for?" It will help you keep on track with what you want to put in, how you want to say it, and what you want to leave out.

In this chapter when Sue Ransohoff says, "I wanted my children to know me as a person, not just a Mom," she set the parameters for her memoir in the earlier part of her pre-mom life. When Luciel Muller Harriman wanted to write her history, she chose the scope of more than 150 years and a readership of many branches of the family tree. When this chapter asks you what your book's scope will be, it is asking you to consider your intended readers and what they will want to know.

Chapter Four

How to Start Your Research

I n his revision of William Strunk, Jr.'s, perennially useful little
book, *The Elements of Style*, E.B. White offers a perspective on the
sometimes laborious task of writing telling us,

The mind travels faster than the pen; consequently writing
becomes a question of learning to make occasional wing shots,
bringing down the bird of thought as it flashes by. A writer is a
gunner, sometimes waiting in his blind for something to come in,
sometimes roaming the countryside hoping to scare something up.

I recommend his first suggestion of bringing down the bird of thought
as it flashes by. If you haven't already been in the habit of journal writing,
start right now, with a notebook and a quiet place to reflect. Just put
down whatever memories occur concerning any experiences in your life
that you can recall.

What in your life are you proudest of? Which person or event do
you think had the greatest impact on you at what stage of your life?
Which memories still make you cringe with pain or laugh out loud?
What stories did your family tell you as you were growing up?

Some writers find it easiest to start with whatever is freshest in their
memory. Others feel an intense need to learn the roots of their family
tree and find that this unearthing opens doors to history they wouldn't
have knocked on otherwise.

Bill Valentine, a telephone repairman who spent fourteen years tracing his ancestors back to the 1600s, said he felt a great sense of accomplishment in creating his book *My American History Notes*. But in a
feature story about his family history in the Western Electric company
house organ, he admitted there were drawbacks, too. "I uncovered some
skeletons in the closet — like my grandfather's being an illegal alien —
and exploded some sacred family myths — like discovering that two of

my forebears were privates in the Union army instead of colonels as my relatives had told me. One of my uncles also told me that one of my ancestors was killed in action in the Civil War. My research showed that he was killed by a falling tree while deserting the army."

Bill's ancestral research included a challenge faced by family historians — discovering family name changes, especially among immigrants who bore (to the customs officials of the day) strange names. Bill's grandmother told him that his Lithuanian grandfather came to America on a cattle boat. "To check her story," he says, "I wrote to the Lithuanian Church in Elizabeth, Pennsylvania, where my grandparents were married. Their marriage license showed that his name was Stanislaus Valantiejus.

"I then wrote to the National Archives for ship lists of passengers and found his name listed on that of a ship which arrived in the U.S. in 1904. And it *was* a cattle boat."

RECALLING MEMORIES AS A START

Sheila McKenna, a writing teacher who compiled oral histories of older African-American women who had been field workers in North Carolina and "only got to school when it rained," found them eager to come to a community center to tell their personal stories.

"All of my life," said one, "I never had school, but this interests me. It makes me want to get up in the morning."

Sheila would ask them questions like:

What was the most important thing you ever faced?

What was the most difficult part about growing up?

What about you would people be surprised to know?

She didn't pop those heavy questions right away, of course, but led into them gradually by asking the women to remember things like their mother's kitchen, the smells, and what it looked like.

You can do the same thing when exploring your own memory. Give yourself some short writing assignments, like the questions above, to help you get started in memory recall.

Some families find it easier to assemble an oral history with a tape recorder. Later, they can take comments from the tape when they *write* their family history. (More details about the interviewing and oral history process are coming up in chapter six.)

One family that compiled an oral history offers an example of the kinds of detailed recollections that can help the family history writer. Before the rush of modern life, they recall, there was much visiting between children and grandparents, aunts, "double first cousins" and even more remote relatives. They know, for example, that they are descended from Huguenots who fled persecution in France to settle in England and they migrated to Barbados and the southeastern U.S. They remember not only details like the door with a hole in it left by a Yankee cannonball and the fact that great-grandmother died in childbirth because Union troops were camped across the drive and the doctor couldn't get through, but also the story published in a book about Shakespeare that one of their forebears was the Dark Lady in the sonnet.

They know the relatives who were active in business and government and Democratic politics, and that in some families it was all right to change your religion but never your politics.

They remember their grandfather's short temper and put it down to the fact that "Poppa was so busy being polite to people downtown, he didn't have any left over by the time he got home to his family."

But they also remember the quiet life, the Southern courtesies and the way when milk was delivered to the doorstep in glass bottles, the cream would separate and freeze on cold mornings and rise to the top, pushing the cardboard cap up half an inch.

GET IN THE HABIT OF WRITING

Because good writing only comes with practice, many writers discover that keeping a personal journal is one way to get in the *habit* of writing. Freelance writers always carry a notebook for ideas, observations, snatches of overheard dialogue, but a journal is a place for private reflections, assessments of our lives; it is a ready-made source for your personal story when you're ready to write that.

In his book, *At a Journal Workshop*, psychotherapist Ira Progoff refers to the "Steppingstones" of our lives, "those events that come to our mind when we spontaneously reflect on the course that our life has taken from its beginning to the present moment." He compares steppingstones to the term Dag Hammarskjold used for the title of his autobiography, *Markings*. Hammarskjold's metaphor referred to the markings a mountain climber leaves behind him—not only going upward but also downward into a valley or ravine—as a record of the route followed.

Kathleen McNamara, a clinical social worker who has used journaling with her clients, says,

> It is one of the most useful ways to get in touch with your feelings. You can spend as much time with it as you wish. You

can say whatever you want and your journal won't talk back, won't judge you.

It's been successful with each client I've tried it with. The few times there has been an emotional block against this kind of written expression, it's been for one of these reasons: (a) the person had been criticized in school for penmanship or punctuation or just the way they expressed themselves and somehow they have transferred that to their adult life. (b) Others listen too much to that internal critic we all have which says "these are things I should or should not feel; it's bad to feel rageful; if I put this down, it's who I am forever."

But that's *not* how we are forever, it's the way we felt at that moment and expressing it is therapeutic, McNamara reminds us. Others who have used journals to work their way through experiences for their own self-development confirm what she says.

THE STAGES OF MEMORY

A *Psychology Encyclopedia* article tells us that "an experimental demonstration of memory involves three stages: encoding, storage and retrieval." Most people seem to lose detailed visual information within seconds of experiencing it. How far back can *you* remember?

Donna Remmert says she was four . . .

on a December evening when my brother Jimmy and I put on our pajamas and snowsuits and lugged pillows and Grandma Schwister quilts up to our bran' new house, not even moved into yet. We spread the quilts onto the fluffy living room carpet because that's where we would sleep that night. All alone, without Mama or Daddy or anyone. Jimmy was eight, I was four and for a reason I can't remember we were honored with being the first members of the family to sleep in our bran' new house.

"Writing stories in my child's voice, using the words I used then, has been an aid in remembering," says Remmert. "I purposely don't analyze my stories with my adult mind. That would spoil everything; it would take me out of my trance.

"When you write childhood stories for the purpose of psychological completion, it's a real adventure that goes beyond writing them for family members to enjoy. I wrote mine with both purposes in mind."

USING YOUR DREAMS AS A RESEARCH SOURCE

One member of a memoir writing course revealed that she had kept a dream diary for years. It provided a starting point for self-development.

We have been wondering what our dreams mean for a long time. One of the earliest specimens of writing is an Egyptian papyrus from about 2,000 B.C. – a record of dream interpretations. Contemporary sleep researchers tell us that most of us spend one-fourth to one-fifth of our sleep in dreams. And if we are deprived of that dream time, it affects our minds and bodies.

Some of us dream in color, some in black and white, and some never seem to remember dreams at all. If you do dream, writing them down may help you trigger aspects of your memory you might otherwise have forgotten.

Can you *program* your dreams to help you remember things about your childhood? In her book, *Living Your Dreams: Using Sleep to Solve Problems and Enrich Your Life*, Gayle Delaney suggests that from her study with clients you can target specific problems to solve in dreams if you follow this procedure:

- ✔ Choose a night when you are not overly tired and have not had any alcohol or drugs or sleeping pills.
- ✔ Record a few lines about what you did/felt during the day.
- ✔ Discuss with yourself what problem you want to address in your dream and write down questions related to it.
- ✔ Narrow discussion down to one question that you want to concentrate on in the dream.
- ✔ Turn out the light and concentrate on the one question, repeating it over and over in your mind.
- ✔ Sleep.
- ✔ When you wake up, record all you remember dreaming.

"Part of the beauty of dreams," says Allan Gurganus, whose 718-page first novel, *The Oldest Living Confederate Widow Tells All* was a best seller and the basis for a TV mini-series, "is that they're eternally mysterious. And that's part of their meaning and power for us. They seem to have a kind of wisdom that we don't have in our waking lives."

LASTING MEMORIES

Many writers have made connections between their dreams and their creative writing. Twenty-six writers talked to dream researcher Naomi Epel about them in her book, *Writers Dreaming*.

Joe Murray, senior writer for Cox Newspapers says some of his earliest memories are of childhood's embarrassing moments. But a friend of his confided an indiscretion that happened thirty years ago and still keeps him awake at night. He said he would give anything if it had never happened.

"The mind," says Murray, "reminds me so very much of a computer. I wish there was a procedure where you could selectively erase stuff from the mind the way you can from a computer. To have no memory of humiliation, rejection or cowardice: Think what that would do for your self-confidence.

"I told my friend that idea. He said it would solve part of the problem. But what you would really need, he said, is a procedure that erased that same stuff from other people's memories, too."

Judy White Edelson echoed that thought in her "Not All Bridges Can Be Burned," the "My Turn" essay in *Newsweek*'s December 13, 1993, issue. In it she says, "I used to laugh about my mother telling me 'That will go on your permanent record.' I thought I had no permanent record. I was young and had a long, full lifetime in which to make mistakes and explore endless possibilities. . . .

"There *is* a permanent record. It lives on in the memories of all the people you have come in contact with. It lives on in your own perception of yourself, coloring and flavoring who you become, what you expect to be able to accomplish and how you live your life."

This need to confront an earlier life is what propels some writers to consider writing a personal memoir—of putting the "record" on paper. In many cases it's only for themselves, not a national magazine audience.

IS LOCALE AN IMPORTANT MEMORY RESOURCE?

A sense of place has been the touchstone for many writers, and creators of family histories are no exception. Included in a *Snyder Family History*, by Frank Rickman Snyder, is this description by family member Jane Fonville Snyder of a small village, now a part of the Great Smoky Mountains National Park.

TO CADES COVE WITH LOVE
from
Jane Fonville Snyder

I have always been fascinated by little-traveled roads. They wander out of sight on unpredictable courses and I invariably wish there were time to turn off and see where they go. One of my favorite leads to Cades Cove.

The time was, not so long ago, when the only access by car was this magnificent old twister that toils to Rich Gap, then eases down in smoother cadence to the lower end of the valley. On the county side, outside the Park, maintenance of such a road was an almost insurmountable problem. Its tight-wound turns were gullied, its few straight stretches deep-rutted except just after the vernal run of the scraper. Both the ride and the views were spectacular then. Neither has changed with the passage of time. Going up, anyone who dares to look down can still see about six laps of the road below and almost the whole of Tuckaleechee at a glance through any gap in the trees. Once across the Park boundary, no other road anywhere in East Tennessee intrudes so little on the forest interior. In any season, driving it was the next best thing to hiking. Only the "natives" and a few hardy devotees ever pass that way anymore. What wonders are lost to the rest.

Down on the level past the Missionary Baptist Church, suddenly there lies the cove, a pocket of tranquility surrounded by its protecting mountains. Viewed from any lower-end vantage point they range around in full majestic sweep — the long strong spine of Rich, Thunderhead brooding in the distance, and the curving string of inexplicable balds. Serenity envelopes the beholder like a warm cloak and the cares of our ever more hurried present evaporate unnoticed into the air.

With relatively little relocation, the paved one-way road that skirts the cove was once the main thoroughfare of an isolated community. It meandered then, as now, around the edge, taking as little space as possible from cultivation and grazing of the land. The people who lived there snuggled their cabins against the ridges for it behooved them to beware of the considerable changes in weather. In winter, even in this latitude, snows are frequent and the north wind doth howl. The lush hush of summer is broken almost daily by sudden crackling thunderstorms which flood the streams and obscure the sight.

Most of the cabins and outbuildings along the way are gone now. A few linger on in sad state of decay but some are preserved by the Park Service as historic mementos of the past. The restored, water-powered grist mill operates most of the year for the edification of tourists and the profit of the Great Smoky Mountains Natural History Association. Land that reverted to nature when people moved out or died off is once again cultivated or grazed and cattle are back in sizable herds.

The intermittent donkle-donkle of a cowbell here and there is but a faint reminder of the almost forgotten large-scale cattle drives to the fine pastures atop the balds, yet those drives were once as much a part of the business of the cove as were the crops, the forge and the mill.

No more does the road pass through a barnyard or two on its way around the cove. I regret that and other omissions. Before modernization set in, circling the cove was an exciting adventure. One could expect with certainty to get stuck in a mudhole, hang the oil pan on a rock or drown the engine fording a stream. In dry weather suffocation by dust might have been a hazard had there been any traffic to speak of. It was always a trip to remember.

The slower progress of other days did, for all its drawbacks, allow the traveler more time to succumb to the timeless mesmerism of this place. In all my years of going there I have never been able to decide in which month, which hour, which fleeting moment the cove is most beautiful to me. In any light, it is changeless, yet ever-changing. Its spell is indescribable. I only know that each time I look out across its lovely fields to the haze-hung mountains I silently breathe, "I will lift up mine eyes unto the hills from whence cometh my help . . ."

Entirely within the park, the new road is a fine one. Anyone can get there now and thousands do each year. Why do they go? The cove's simple yet awesome offerings: Peace and beauty and the hovering ghost of its past.

Just think. Had it not been for the foresight and determination of early conservationists to preserve Cades Cove as part of the Great Smoky Mountains National Park, this unique and irreplaceable cranny of world natural history would have been lost long years ago to unfettered commercialism's blight.

How big a part will locale play in your book? Not just geographical location, but the values and attitudes that go with the places. If you're unsure about the social as well as the physical landscape of your ancestors, you'll want to do some research. Be wary, however, of generalizations. Zero-in on the particular.

MYTH VS. REALITY

A search for the real person behind stereotyped images of her ancestors provoked Shirley Abbott to write *Womenfolks: Growing Up Down South*. "I grew up believing," she says, "though I could never have voiced it, that a woman might pose as garrulous and talky and silly and dotty, but at heart she was a steely, silent creature, with secrets no man could ever know and she was always, *always* stronger than any man. ('Now you don't have to let on about it,' my mother would advise.)"

Prodded by an eighty-year-old aunt who wrote to ask, "Who are we? What is this special thing we know? Who were these women we remember?" Abbott writes,

> Hoping to make short work of it, I replied that as far as I knew, we came from a line of scrawny old dirt-dobbers, Scotch-Irish with more than one or two Indians thrown in, and that there was no way I could go to the library and read up on southern country women, let alone our own family, because they didn't make it into the history books.
>
> But that was not enough. She wanted particulars, real things to hold in her hand, real women. She wanted the names and stories. She wanted me to raise the dead. "Who was the first of us?" she asked. "You can track her down." When I protested that I had other things to do and nothing to go on, Laura answered, "Never mind, I'll send you some papers I have. I'll tell you everything I know." And so I began work as an archaeologist might, trying to imagine what a whole village was like by looking at a few pottery pieces in the kitchen midden.

Along the way Abbott gives a clear eyed picture of "the invisible Old South, without azaleas or King Cotton or any of the usual props, the vast sector of the antebellum population that had no stake in slavery."

FICTION AND REALITY

Arline Chase, who has conducted workshops in family history as a springboard to fiction, says, "I wrote my first short story about my great-grandmother and her life on a remote Chesapeake Bay Island. It was serialized later in *Chesapeake Bay Magazine*. Historical short fiction is very difficult to place, but I kept trying, because I believed in the story." Here are the opening paragraphs from that work, *The Drowned Land*, which received sixty-seven rejections from literary journals before it won the Maryland's Governor's Award for Fiction and was serialized:

CHAPTER ONE

James Brannock's bulk seemed to fill the slanted space of the dormer bedroom. He slid strong arms under the paralyzed body of his mother-in-law, Monnye Bolden and carried her dead weight down the back stairs to the kitchen of the farmhouse.

"Good morning, Mama. You're looking pert this morning." Brown-haired, blue-eyed Lottie Brannock held the high, caned back of the invalid chair to steady it as James settled the old lady gently onto the seat and covered her bone-thin legs with a knitted afghan.

A watery sun shone through the eastern window of the room, where wainscoting reached halfway up the walls. A claw-foot oak table, covered with cheerful red-checked oilcloth and set with time-crazed ironstone, stood in the middle of the room.

"I thank you, James." Monnye pulled a shawl around her shoulders and checked to see if her bag of 'hand work' was in easy reach.

"A pleasure, Ma." James laughed. "You ain't nothing but breath and britches, anyway. Lighter than a bird."

"Get along with you, James. A bird, indeed! Old crow, likely! But I got to admit that you carry me with no more trouble than a tune."

In a letter, Arline Chase commented on the sometimes thin line between fiction and reality:

One thing that amazes me is how often, when using family history, bits of reality creep in that you are not aware of. In writing a short story, "A Man's Share," I incorporated some of my brother-in-law's experiences, with like ones that happened to my great-uncle Henry. It's a coming of age story about a young boy being hazed by the older crew members. For weeks I puzzled about what kind of climax I could use as a plot device whereby the protagonist could prove his courage. I toyed with the idea of a huge storm, decided against a man-overboard, and finally settled on a fire in the hold. Henry dove headfirst into the fire, duly saved his crew-mate and burned his hands in the process. Once I had chosen the venue, the scene almost wrote itself.

A few weeks later, when my mother read the story, she looked up and frowned, "You got that one all wrong, Arline." My mouth went dry as I wondered where I had failed. Did my characters not ring true? Did the dialogue not reflect the correct Chesapeake Bay twang? Was my fire too unbelievable?

"It wasn't Uncle Henry who burned his hands. It was Uncle Lou!" The scorn in her tone told me she couldn't believe I had actually mixed up such an important piece of family history. Uncle Lou had burned his hands — not Uncle Henry. But the fire in the hold of a dredger and the resultant burned hands were facts I had not *consciously* remembered at all. I thought I had made them up. No wonder the scene wrote so smoothly. Sometimes you incorporate details from a reality you choose to weave into fiction. Sometimes, I'm convinced, the reality chooses you. Now, whenever a scene or story practically writes itself, I stop and wonder.

RESEARCHING THE TIME OF YOUR BIRTH

For those who want to simply start their stories at the beginning, T.S. Matthews, who later became an editor at both the *New Republic* and *Time* magazines, started his autobiography *Name and Address* this way:

> I was born in the city of Cincinnati, in the year 1901. Queen Victoria was still alive. Much later, I discovered that Cincinnati was not the whole world nor 1901 its beginning. Last of all I learned that this old lady (who, though a Queen-Empress, apparently resembled a small, bad-tempered turtle) had presided over an age that shaped my youth.
>
> My father was a parson. I never quite learned to think of him as a priest, which was a name he preferred. My mother was an heiress: poor dear, she would never admit it; it embarrassed her too much. From my father we learned to despise; from my mother, to be ashamed. As I have never learned to tell "the whole truth," whatever that may be, I cannot truthfully say more than this about what we learned from them. We also learned to be afraid — not only afraid of outsiders and of the outside world but most of all afraid of being judged and found wanting — although many things and people, perhaps our ancestors included, must have had a hand in that.
>
> I was the second of six children and my parents' only son. Until my father grew old and began to weaken, I was a constant disappointment to him; until my mother lay dying, she would have sworn I was her dearest hope.

Writing Reminder: As you can see, we not only have the facts of his birthplace and his parents, but some conclusions about their effect on his life that we want to know more about.

GETTING THE FAMILY INVOLVED

When you have an older family member at the dinner table, you might want to spark some bits of family history by playing the Memory Game. I might start such a game by saying: "I remember that silver-gray, cast-iron, dog nutcracker we used as a doorstop. At Thanksgiving and Christmas time, we'd be given walnuts. When you lifted the dog's tail, his mouth would open and the trick was to bring the tail down hard enough to crack the shell in the dog's mouth but still be able to get the whole, sweet meat of the walnut out without it crumbling into pieces."

That might make Grandma remember where she got the doorstop/nutcracker and how it wound up in your mother's house.

That will make someone else remember the old-fashioned hardware store and the "rich" family who owned it. "I remember I saw a man running across the street to catch the streetcar and he must have had a hole in his pocket because a coin fell out and rolled into the streetcar tracks. Mr. Hardware Store (what *was* his name?) wasn't too rich to pick up the coin when he came along behind him."

And one story leads to another.

In fact, a game manufacturer has produced something that might be helpful in providing stimulating conversations between generations. Called "Life Stories — a fun game of telling tales and sharing smiles with family and friends," it uses prompting cards such as "the most courageous thing I ever did" or "what I liked best about my third grade teacher." It's available in game stores, or call 1-800-232-1873.

SHOULD YOU COLLABORATE?

You might choose to work with another family member on a family history. Working together offers the benefits of more minds to the task and support in sharing the experiences within the family. Two Ohio friends, Mary Jean Johnson Lehman and Nancy Felson Brant, who discovered they were second cousins through their husbands' families, collaborated on two family histories.

"When my mother was ill in the 1970s," says Nancy Brant, "and I realized that when she died, the history of the family for our children, and theirs, would be lost if I didn't put down a record of them, I started research on our ancestors. I gathered a lot of documents, verified sources, and then got busy raising my family and put it all away. Twenty years later, in 1992, Jean and I decided to combine our resources and produce two family histories of our earliest ancestors to come to America."

Their research — and the kinds of cross references it requires — is brought home in this passage by Jean:

> After discovering through the census records that Aaron and Rachel De Groot Pareira had come to Albany, New York, Nancy Brant and I decided to see if we could identify the ship they took to come to this country. In looking through *Germans to America* ship records, by Ira Glazier and P. William Filby, we found not Aaron and Rachel, but Aaron's parents, Abraham and Meintje! They had sailed on the *Koophandel* from the Netherlands to New York, and arrived August 28, 1854. Abraham, age 58, was listed as a peddler, and Meintje as age 57. It is probable that Abraham was 68 at the time of his arrival rather than 58, as Malcolm Stern (author of *The First American Jewish Families*) lists his birth in 1785. Many birthdates do not tally with the official census and ship records. In some cases dates have been deliberately changed. An example often noticed is in the census which is taken every ten years. A man who is 28 in 1870 may become 44 or more in 1880! We know it is the same person as his wife and children will be listed in each census although some of their ages may also vary.

GETTING HELP FROM OTHERS

Local genealogical societies can provide a convenient support for persons seeking their family histories. Writers of personal stories may find a stimulus for their efforts in a workshop or correspondence course.

For example, the writing of autobiography is a recurring theme in the workshops conducted by the International Women's Writing Guild, including their annual week-long summer conference at Skidmore College in Saratoga Springs, New York. Other workshops are offered at local public libraries, historical societies, community colleges and senior centers.

WRITING REMINDER: DESCRIPTION AND DIALOGUE

Description, says *Writing A to Z*, is "the art of showing the reader how a person, place, or thing looks, tastes, feels, sounds, smells, or acts . . . it is bringing something to life by carefully choosing and arranging words and phrases to produce the desired effect." When Jane Fonville Snyder writes in this chapter about Cades Cove, we can imagine the size of the mountain as she dares us to look down at the six laps of the road below. And she captures perfectly the "donkle-donkle" sound of a cowbell in a distant pasture.

As you research, remember to note more than just the names and dates. Seek out details, information that will make your people and events and locales come alive for the modern reader.

Listen for the words, too. How did people speak? What words did they use? Notice how family history writers use dialogue when they quote relatives in the family stories excerpted throughout this book.

Chapter Five

Ideas for Topics to Include

I n that very famous monologue in Shakespeare's *As You Like It*, Jaques tell us,

All the world's a stage,
And all the men and women merely players;
They have their exits and their entrances,
And one man in his time plays many parts,
His acts being seven ages. . . .

In just twenty-three lines, Shakespeare takes us in those seven ages from "mewling infant," "whining schoolboy," and lover "sighing like a furnace," to maturity, "second childishness and oblivion."

Even though you may not write your book in strict chronology, it's still a good idea to get a three-ring notebook or set up a series of manila folders labeled Childhood, The Teens, Career, Relationships, Marriage, Family, etc., into which you can put the notes of your memories *as they relate to the book you want to write.*

You'll have your own other special categories but, depending on your book's focus, the questions that follow will give you a way to start remembering.

FOR YOUR NOTEBOOK: REMEMBERING CHILDHOOD

What early childhood experience sticks out in your memory?

Arnold Gingrich in his book *Toys of a Lifetime* remembers this:

I was walking along the curbstone, kicking the first falling leaves ahead of me, one early autumn day before the re-opening of school in the year I was six, when I saw coming toward me one of the idols of my life, a "big boy" whose name was Roger Verseput. In my eyes, he was a lordly creature, a sort of super-adult, and much more glamorous to me than any of the mere grown men I had watched coming and going on their way to and from work. . . .

I wondered whether I dared address him individually. . . .

I finally decided to risk it, when he had drawn even with me . . . and . . . ventured a very diffident and tentative, "Hello, Squeech."

He appeared to be passing on without deigning to answer but then, much worse, he turned back and down to regard me, with the air of a robin reconsidering a worm that he had first thought too insignificant to be worth the bother of digging up, and said,

"Hullo, you darn ol' Arnie — with yer girl's coat on!"

I ran home howling, to tell my mother what he had said.

My coat, which she had made, was a double-breasted, bright red jacket, of the type known to sailors as a pea jacket, and she had deemed it not only very natty but manly too, an opinion in which up to that awful moment, I had fully concurred. But of course she had made it to button, like anything of her own, from right over left, instead of left over right, as any male garment should.

A memory trigger for many writers is simply to draw a floor plan of the earliest house they lived in, branching out from that with as much detail as they can remember about various rooms, the kinds of furniture in them — a favorite chair, perhaps, in which they curled up to read.

Some writers find drawing a map of a neighborhood where they grew up with names of the neighbors on the houses around theirs revives memories they wouldn't have thought of otherwise.

Do you remember the street games you played as a child? Did anybody in your neighborhood have a tree house? A playhouse in the backyard?

In her book *Love and Laughter*, Marjorie Holmes's essay "Packed Suitcases" traces those we carried from childhood visits to Grandma to summer camp exiles, wedding trips, hospital visits and new grandchildren celebrations.

Childhood and Education Memory Triggers

What is your very earliest memory? How old were you? Did you believe in the tooth fairy? The Easter Bunny? Santa Claus? Do you remember your first trip to the dentist? Braces? Your first visit to a beauty shop? Barber? Did you have any childhood diseases? Are you adopted? If so, when and how did you find out? What games did you play as a child? Where did you live? Did you go to summer camp? Do you remember some of your playmates? Where did you go to elementary school? High school? College? Graduate school? Do you remember any of your teachers? Do you still see any of your school friends? Do you go to reunions? What details do you remember of your childhood or growing up that were particularly joyful or painful or embarrassing?

Marie Van Campen remembers a missed opportunity: "I was given the opportunity in an American history class as a grade option to write 'A Family History and How Events Affected our Lives.' I regret now I didn't do it."

But that topic is one that can still be addressed. We've all lived through the dynamic decades of the twentieth century (some of us more than others) and we may find ourselves more interested in that contemporary period than in ancestors we've had little access to.

For some reminders of what was happening in the U.S. as it might relate to your own life, see the decade-by-decade Memory Trigger Calendar at the end of this chapter.

FOR YOUR NOTEBOOK: FAMILY RELATIONSHIPS

How family members feel about one another and their images of each other are a never ending source of diaries/journals/memoirs.

Harry Golden, the Lower-East-Side New Yorker who moved to the South to edit *The Carolina Israelite*, collected his essays in a 1958 book called *Only in America*. In observing the relationship between "Fathers and Sons," Golden wrote that the one thing a son could never forgive a father for was infidelity. He commented:

> The son cannot help himself, of course. It goes back thousands of years. It is deeply grounded in our theologies and in our histories. That is the real reason a second marriage must always come as a shock to the children. This is not wholly a matter of being "selfish," as so many people suppose, or that the "children do not understand that a father (or a mother) has a life of his own." Children look upon their mothers as "virgins" no matter how many children fill the household, and they look upon their fathers not as someone who has had sexual intercourse with the mother but purely as the instrumentality of their own being. Centuries of taboo have conditioned us. We cannot possibly think of them and ourselves otherwise. Thus the introduction of a "stranger" smashes these concepts ... whether the introduction of this "stranger" is "legal" or "illegal."

I wonder how Harry Golden would describe today's father-son relationships, complicated as they are by high divorce rates and multiple marriages. How would you?

Significant Relationships Memory Triggers

Do you know where your parents were married and when? Are any of their witnesses still alive? How did you meet your own spouse? Describe him/her. What attracted you most? Describe his/her personality. How many children do you have? Where are they? What are their occupations? How are your relations with your in-laws? Do you have grandchildren? Are they nearby? What is their image of you? What is your children's image of you? What is your image of yourself? Are there any significant others in your life now? Were there in the past? What were the circumstances? Are you divorced? What were the circumstances? What is your relationship with your ex-spouse? How did the divorce affect your children? Have you remarried?

FOR YOUR NOTEBOOK: OCCUPATIONS

Most of us spend the greater part of our lives working for a living, so the jobs we've held and the people we've met in them have impacted our personal and family histories. Our parents may have lived through the Great Depression, but we have faced the specters of layoffs, "downsizing," "rightsizing" and the quick dance on a hot griddle required to keep up with technologies before they can replace us altogether.

A series of short pieces in *Reader's Digest* called "My First Job," compiled by Daniel R. Levine, developed the theme that it's not what you earn — it's what you learn.

In one of those articles, here's how Gary Franks, a Republican Congressman from Connecticut, described his first job:

THE FLOOR MOPPER

"Be proud of what you do," my father always told me, "whether you're boss or mopping floors."

When I was seventeen, I got a summer job at Waterbury Hospital Health Center in Waterbury, Connecticut, where I was told my duties would include — mopping floors. I smiled and remembered Dad's advice.

Even though my job was the lowest, I was thrilled to have any work at all. Each morning, I imagined all the sick people not being able to eat if I wasn't there to scrub the pots coated with oatmeal.

Once breakfast was done, I cleaned toilets and in the late after-noon, mopped floors. Though I was dead tired, I knew that if the floors didn't shine, it would reflect badly on me. I wanted people to say, "That young man sure does a nice job."

Working at the hospital taught me that it takes people on every level, from pot scrubber to CEO, working as one, for an organiza-tion to function effectively. I understood this and never had a problem being motivated.

Through every job I've ever held, my father's wise words have stayed with me. I've mopped floors and I've been the boss. I think Dad would be proud.

Memoirs can be not only a record of a working life, but also a chance to comment on the vagaries of people we have come in contact with there. Here is how Horace Dutton Taft, headmaster of a private boys school, set the scene in his *Memories and Opinions*:

A man is amazed to find how very little thought a parent has put upon a given problem. A college graduate, a man of ability, was visiting the school to see his boy and walked in on me. He said, "I do not think much of the way you teach English these days."

"Neither do I."

"When I was a boy I used to browse in my father's library."

"So did I."

"I read Cooper and Scott and Dickens and Thackeray with no prodding or compulsion."

"So did I."

Then we two foolish men proceeded to match the books we had read, whereupon he said, "I would rather have done that reading on my own than have the compulsory reading which is involved in your English course."

"So would I."

He then looked at me as though he thought it was my move.

"You realize, or course," I said, "that browsing is a voluntary thing and depends on the boy, himself, on his whole environment, but especially on his home influence. You have had that boy of yours fifteen years all to yourself, with the influence of the entire family brought to bear on the single boy. I have it from his own lips that he never read a single book except what he was compelled to read by school authorities. Fifteen years! And yet you send him to me, one of two hundred and fifty boys, and expect me to teach him to browse! Could anything be more absurd?" I added, "We have a goodly number of boys here who have read more than you and I together, and they go on browsing whenever they have time for it."

I am only pointing out how amazing it is that an intelligent man could miss a point as plain as this.

Some present-day teachers and principals can empathize with Mr. Taft, even though this was written in 1942 about an earlier time.

Occupation Memory Triggers

What part-time jobs did you have during high school/college? What was your first "real" job? What was the nation's economy at the time? Good? High employment? How many times have you changed careers? Why? Which jobs were the most satisfying? What's the worst job you ever had? Are you still friends with any of your former co-workers? Which bosses did you admire/hate the most? Why? Are there any occupations you wish you had trained for?

FOR YOUR NOTEBOOK: ENTERTAINMENT MEMORIES

Today's entertainments are high tech glitz and glamour, but Dale Hearn, whose business card lists him as a member of the Circus Fans Association of America, includes this remembrance of another time in his book *The Family Record*:

> In popular days of a large tented American Circus, another show tent was pitched beside the Big Top: thus the term "sideshow." The sideshow was owned by, or leased to, the circus that had booked the route to travel in a given season. The sideshow has been known by showfolk, past and present, as "kid show," "freak show" and "exhibits show."
>
> In front of the sideshow was a "ballyhoo" stage where stood a talker—be he called "bally man," "speiler," "barker" or "lecturer." Here I take such role standing on a bally. I am pointing with my cane to banner line paintings strung out in front and above an exhibits tent. Each banner hanging there depicts an exhibit to be seen "on the inside"—just beyond this spiel.
>
> Take a look at a living blue baby ... Don't miss magicians in conclave. Hey! ... Notice the rare self-made man that might put Horatio Alger to shame. Don't miss Great Aunt Alice as she dab-

bled with astrology and other occult arts. Learn how she used these to advise and comfort relatives.

Entertainment Memory Triggers

What do you remember best about the entertainments in your childhood? Did anyone in your family play a musical instrument? Did you study piano or ballet? What do you remember about your first introduction to "the arts?" Was it a not-so-leading part in a school play? A school trip to a children's concert? What is your favorite entertainment today? Movies? Theater? Opera? Concerts? Line Dancing? Comedy Clubs?

FOR YOUR NOTEBOOK: MISCELLANEOUS

Travel: When you travel, do you send postcards back home to friends to comment on what you've seen, things that surprised you, funny or frightening things that happened? You may discover postcard collector hobbyists among your relatives, neighbors and friends, who saved these cards. They could trigger more detailed memories of your travel experiences.

Are you a collector? What were your feelings at the time you bought a beautiful piece of native art or craft that would remind you of a culture you had never been closely in touch with before?

For example, Dr. Martin Macht, retired internist/professor, and his wife Carol, retired art museum curator/professor, have a collection of Chinese glass and ceramics they have assembled over forty years of traveling. Each piece has a special memory and some new learning connected with it. "We started collecting on our honeymoon," says Carol, "at which time we resolved we would never spend more than $2." Obviously that changed over the years, since Cincinnati's Taft Museum recently displayed "The Art of the Vessel: Decorative Arts from the Macht Collection."

"Finding a beautiful piece of glass was great fun," says Dr. Macht, "but part of the fun is that you don't just collect objects, you collect the memory of finding the pieces and you collect the knowledge that you gain from them." What memory triggers line your bookshelves, or end tables or other nooks and crannies in the house that represent happy memories of gifts from friends or souvenirs from travels?

Of course if you are a photographer, snapshots are a wonderful way to recapture the details of a travel experience. The editors of *Travel*

Holiday magazine once asked readers, "What's the best souvenir you have brought home from your travels?" That's a question you might ask yourself to spark ideas for your memoir.

Are there some other special moments in travel that have fulfilled their promise or disappointed the seeker—such as that "green flash," the optical illusion that is supposed to appear on the horizon just after the sun drops out of sight? I read about that phenomenon in a travel magazine article about Key West, whose author reminisced about the "sunset celebration" in the early seventies in Mallory Square when "all eyes strained to see the elusive 'green flash'."

The few times since reading the article that I've been at a spot on a lake or an ocean where I could watch the sun go down, I've never seen that optical illusion. Perhaps you need a margarita to sip while looking!

Avocations/Hobbies/Sports: How did you happen to get interested in your present hobby or avocation? What do you like about it? Are you a sports spectator or active participant? Are you good at it? Do you like it mainly for the exercise? The friends you've met through it? Some other reason? Does your hobby or favorite sport take up a disproportionate amount of your disposable income?

Money: The number of books available on money—how to get it, use it wisely or multiply it—never seem to diminish, and in an era of unemployment for the young, layoffs for the middle aged and high medical costs for the elderly, money is much on our minds. In their *Sky Magazine* article "Money for Something," Joe Dominguez and Vicki Robin remind us that:

> We come to see how our own attitudes about money were shaped by the psychological environment we grew up in. Did your family consider itself rich, poor or average? Did you grow up in a family where money was discussed openly? Did you have an allowance? Did you have to earn it by doing chores? Did you grow up believing your family had enough money to buy you anything you really wanted and needed? If your parents said no to one of your desires, was it because of money? In your family, did you associate money with rewards? With arguments? With never seeing your father? What were the messages your parents gave you about money?

Copies of old bills and receipts you can find can provide a valuable insight and perspective for considering the role of money in your family history.

When my father died and I cleaned out his desk, among the copies of deeds, business agreements and other papers, I found a copy of the bill for my own birth at St. Elizabeth Hospital in Covington, Kentucky. The cost was:

One week hospital stay	$20
Delivery	10
Medicine and supplies	5
Total	$35

That receipt reminded me of a friend who ran across the receipt for her wedding night in the (then) Netherland Hotel in Cincinnati: Cost: $6 in 1945. She was having lunch in the 1980s at the same hotel and showed it to the hotel manager. He said, "That's terrific, may I have it?" She said, "I'll trade it to you for a night's lodging on our anniversary."

"It's a deal."

She reminded me that, "of course it will cost us a fortune, since we're inviting all our bridesmaids and their husbands for a cocktail party that night."

Military Service: Military memoirs can be not only a legacy for children and grandchildren, but a potential for publication as well. If you are related to a famous person, as Robert H. Patton was to World War II General George S. Patton, Jr., and have sole access to the private letters and diaries of successive family generations, you can produce a book similar to *The Pattons: A Personal History of an American Family.* But others, not so famous, have had their contact with interesting aspects of that war, too. Here's an excerpt from a World War II memoir by Edwin J. Kirschner published in a 1991 *Defense Transportation Journal:*

All eyes now turned to Mountbatten's new command in Burma, which was randomly referred to as the forgotten front. Everything appeared to be going wrong. Soldiers trained for desert fighting found themselves groping in the thick Burmese jungle, amidst five months of uninterrupted monsoon downpour, being attacked by leeches and malaria-carrying mosquitoes, where sickness was always present and food and medical provisions in short supply.

At this juncture, the Allied forces in Southeast Asia were not winning. Mountbatten's first offensive was to instill a winning frame of mind into his men by putting some fresh morale-building activities to use, such as films, theatrical shows, news bulletins, periodical publications . . . and a mobile brewery.

The "traveling brewery" fitted neatly on a 1,500-weight Army truck. The brewery set-up included a boiler for water; a mash-tub where malted barley and water were mixed, changing them to malt sugar before the mash was sprayed with boiling water; and a copper boiler to simmer the extract with hops, which in time was thickened and sterilized. In the next sequence, the mixture was placed in a cooler to reduce the temperature; yeast was added for fermentation; and lastly, the brew was placed in a fermentation vat under controlled temperature to complete the brewing process.

The one-of-a-kind process took only three days. The wholesome beer had to be drunk within twelve hours after preparation. The cloudy brew appearance from suspended yeast cells didn't affect the taste.

Brewing the grain and yeast produced healthful vitamins and protein-rich by-products. Notably, the yeast added Vitamin B and protein to the draught, essential to the troops' regimen in a tropical environment, and a likely morale-booster as well.

An occasional beer became a soldier's sustenance and pleasure as he moved from one crisis to another. Francis Hutcheson's (1694-1746) perception gives meaning to: "That action is best which procures the greatest happiness for the greatest number."

Military Service Memory Triggers: Which branch of the service were you in? Why? Did you or Uncle Sam select the particular branch? Where were you stationed? What were your responsibilities? Did you make any lasting friendships? Have any of these service-related experiences left you with especially good or bad memories? On leave, did you visit any foreign countries? Have you been back to visit since leaving the service? How long were you in service? Are you in the Reserves? The National Guard? Are you a member of any military veterans organizations?

Social Activities: In addition to our families, most of us at one time or another have been part of an alumni group, professional association, bridge club, athletic team, fraternal organization, military veterans group, or just a group of workers who had an informal beer and bull session for no special reason. What did your membership in these groups mean to you? Did any lasting friendships result? What are your memories of those times and those people?

OTHER SOURCES FOR TRIGGERING MEMORIES

Some writers don't keep diaries, but they save correspondence with friends because that's where they've written down not just things that happened in their lives, but thoughts they've expressed about current events, books they've read, the civil and moral issues of the day.

You may already have the skeleton of a personal story in those old folders of correspondence.

Maybe you have pieces of creative writing stashed away that will remind you of the times surrounding their writing. Have you been moved to write a poem when something you have seen or heard or felt affected you deeply? On the other hand you may find a spot of humor in an experience.

Brownie Morgan, a gift shop owner and metalsmith, retired to a rural area where he had more time to observe nature and write what he called his "throwaway verse." This observation was submitted by his wife to suburban newspaper columnist Regina Villiers:

> When the water in the cistern's low
> We can only choose one path,
> We can either water the flowers,
> Or waste it on a bath.

Whether you write throwaway verse or serious poetry, they both require time away from the hustle-bustle of life. Pollyanna Sedziol, a poet friend who is a patient representative at a large hospital, says she needs the relaxation of vacation to have the time and solitude to observe, reflect and think about the ideas that become poems and her own personal story. Here is a copy of her most recent poem:

PROPS
Last week it was a hummingbird
God sent to dry my tears;
today a soaring goldfinch
left grace notes in my ears.

Faith, 'tis said, is only faith
when standing by itself,
but God is gracious to support
my faith with nature's wealth.
                    —Pollyanna Sedziol

Things you read in a newspaper, magazine or book can spark related memories of your own. I read in *Rotarian* magazine an article by writer Lois Daniel about . . .

... a woman whose family emigrated from Scotland when she was a child [who] said her family's great adjustment to the U.S.A. was living in a house built of wood. In Scotland, all buildings were built of stone. "We were terrified of going to sleep at night and being burned up if the wood caught fire. For the first few nights we took turns sitting up all night so we could awaken the rest of the family if the house should catch fire."

That reminded me of a visit from my older sister who had been living in the south, and who relished her visits back home to the north where there were so many "solid brick houses."

SPEAKING FOR A MISUNDERSTOOD GENERATION

Market researchers have analyzed the buying habits of baby boomers (those born between 1946 and 1964) and baby busters (those born between 1965 and 1976), but what do they really know about the individuals who make up those statistics? If you're in those age groups, you know.

A *New Yorker* movie review by Terrence Rafferty commented that:

Ben Stiller's *Reality Bites* is a romantic comedy about what has come to be called Generation X (after Douglas Coupland's 1991 novel). The label is meant to designate a large subculture of white middle-class kids born after the baby boom, who now, as they enter adulthood, feel cheated by history: The boomers had all the fun, in the sixties, and then they took all the good jobs and basked in their media-fed sense of cultural superiority. The characters in *Reality Bites* are just out of college, and they're not thrilled about their prospects: They're overeducated and underemployed, and worse, their disillusionment isn't winning them any sympathy (much less practical help) from their elders—no one appears to know or care what they're going through.

Do you care? Do you have some statement to make in a personal story about the real people in Generation X? Or are all generations misunderstood to some extent? Can you speak for your own generation in a memoir?

THE HARDEST PART

Writing family histories and personal stories also means recalling the toughest memories, facing the deepest questions about who we are.

Do you remember the first death in your family? How old were you? Was it mother? Father? Sibling? What were the circumstances?

Did your religion come with your parents? Or was it searched for individually? Do you believe in God? In the hereafter?

What have been the real crises in your life and how did you cope with them?

You may not want to deal with these issues right away or in any forum other than a private journal. But save a place in your workbook to consider how you may wish to address the tragedies and triumphs that have made you who you are.

In a little booklet called "Writing From Your Memory, An Aid to Creativity," Jean Rosenbaum, M.D., and Veryl Rosenbaum, Psa, say, "Whenever we repress memories and their associated emotions, they assume exaggerated proportions. . . . Children often respond to loss, anger, or rejection as if the pains were a miniature death. Some adults think that if they allow themselves to relive repressed feelings they'll feel as if they were dying again. However, you have obviously survived your past and will not be damaged if you penetrate the walls of recall. Retrieving and writing down the contents of your psychological history will present you with an endless source of rich material. . . . The release of memories and descriptions of your past should not be used to pinpoint personality flaws or neurosis, but rather as a springboard for totally unique creative material."

WRITING REMINDER: FOCUS

Are you keeping in mind the focus of your book? Only some of the questions and memory triggers in this chapter may apply to the book you want to write. As you file away notes in the notebook or folders you have set up for your family history or personal memoir, keep your intended readers in mind. Make sure those notes support your book's purpose.

In her book, *Twelve Keys to Writing Books That Sell*, Kathleen Krull uses this analogy: " 'Focus,' a term usually encountered in photography, is indeed the right metaphor for evaluating your book. . . . Does the picture make a strong statement? Or are the edges blurry, the outlines ill-defined—does one theme or message tend to merge into another? Is the whole picture balanced? Is attention centered on the picture's real subject?"

While Krull is talking about writing books to sell to editors, her advice can also help us who are writing memoirs for specific readers.

MEMORY TRIGGERS BY THE DECADES OF THE TWENTIETH CENTURY

1900-1909

- Steerage rate for immigrants to the U.S. on foreign ships: ten dollars
- New York policeman arrests woman for smoking cigarette on the street.
- San Francisco earthquake kills 500.
- The first Model T Ford produced.
- "Casey" Jones dies at the throttle as he tries to slow down the Cannon Ball express train from a crash.
- The U.S. buys the Virgin Islands from Denmark for twenty-five million dollars.
- Orville Wright makes the first powered flight at Kitty Hawk, North Carolina.
- Presidents this decade: Theodore Roosevelt, William Howard Taft.
- "Tinker to Evers to Chance" celebrates one of baseball's best known double-play stars.
- Robert Edwin Peary reaches the North Pole.

1910-1919

- S.S. *Titanic* hits iceberg on maiden voyage, sinks; 1,513 drowned.
- The "dime store" — F.W. Woolworth's — founded.
- Panama Canal opens.
- Millions of immigrants arrive from southern and eastern Europe.
- U.S. enters World War I.
- First 1040 Tax Form in use: Minimum tax: 1% on income up to $20,000; top rate: 6% on $500,000 plus.
- Presidents this decade: William Howard Taft and Woodrow Wilson.
- Ray Harroun wins the first Indianapolis 500 in six hours, forty-two minutes, averaging 74.59 miles per hour.
- Congress passes resolution to make second Sunday in May Mother's Day.
- First transcontinental telephone call by Bell and Watson.
- Sugar ration reduced to two pounds per person per month.
- Treaty of Versailles ends World War I.

1920-1929

- First radio station in U.S.: KDKA in Pittsburgh.
- Ku Klux Klan violence in southern U.S.
- "Flapper" era: no-waistline dresses worn above the knee, cloche hats, the Charleston.
- Prohibition is the law, but bootleggers get rich.
- Average life expectancy: fifty-four years.
- Supreme Court says Nineteenth Amendment (voting rights for women) is constitutional.
- First radio play-by-play coverage of a World Series by Grantland Rice.
- Presidents this decade: Warren Harding, Calvin Coolidge, Herbert Hoover.
- First American cellophane produced.
- Colonel Jacob Schick gets patent for first electric shaver.
- First Academy Awards. Best Picture 1927-28: *Wings*. Best Actor: Emil Jannings. Best Actress: Janet Gaynor.
- Stock market crash.

1930-1939

- Lindbergh baby kidnapped.
- A new Chevrolet costs $530.
- Harvard annual tuition is four hundred dollars.
- U.S. establishes forty-hour work week.
- First televised U.S. baseball game.
- Hitler's Germany invades Poland.
- Al Capone convicted of income tax evasion.
- World's tallest building, Empire State, opens in New York.
- Presidents this decade: Herbert Hoover and Franklin D. Roosevelt.
- Banks reopen after a panic run, and then a week long "bank holiday" mandated by Congress.
- First night baseball game in major leagues at Cincinnati.
- Social Security Act signed.
- Dirigible Hindenburg bursts into flames as it approaches its mooring mast in Lakehurst, New Jersey.
- First transatlantic regular air passenger service by Pan American Airways: Long Island to Lisbon, twenty-three hours, fifty-two minutes.

1940-1949

- Japan bombs Pearl Harbor; U.S. enters World War II.
- First class postage three cents; special delivery ten cents.
- Roosevelt re-elected to a third term.
- Gasoline curfew in 1941 closes gas stations from 7 P.M. to 7 A.M.
- Tire rationing became the first rationing regulation.
- New car and truck sales banned in 1942.
- Joe Louis defends his world heavyweight championship for the twentieth time and defeats Max Baer.
- Cocoanut Grove nightclub fire in Boston kills 487.
- Meat, fat, cheese rationing starts in 1943.
- Roosevelt dies eighty-three days into fourth term. Harry Truman becomes president.
- U.S. drops atom bombs on Japan; World War II ends.
- United Nations established in San Francisco conference.

1950-1959

- Color TV introduced.
- Racial segregation in public schools declared unconstitutional.
- Hurricane Audrey and tidal wave kill five hundred in Texas and Louisiana.
- U.S. enters Korean War.
- In 1950 a minimum wage of seventy-five cents per hour established.
- General MacArthur, removed from command by Truman, gives his "Old soldiers never die, they just fade away" speech to Congress.
- Eisenhower elected President.
- U.S. and Canada agree on construction of St. Lawrence Seaway linking the Great Lakes to the Atlantic Ocean.
- Senator McCarthy censured by U.S. Senate for his conduct in Senate committees.
- Vice President Nixon visits Russia. Khrushchev visits U.S.
- The "TV dinner" is invented.

1960-1969

- The Beatles' first big song hit.
- Civil Rights March on Washington.
- Bay of Pigs invasion flops; Cuban missile blockade works.
- President Kennedy assassinated.

- TV viewers see Jack Ruby kill Lee Harvey Oswald in Dallas.
- Lyndon Johnson becomes President.
- U.S. says its embassy in Moscow had been bugged.
- First U.S. "space walk."
- Riots in Watts, Los Angeles, Detroit and other cities.
- New York World's Fair closes after fifty-one million visitors in two years.
- Nixon beats Humphrey for Presidency.
- Dr. Martin Luther King assassinated.
- U.S. lands man on the moon.
- 400,000 young people at the Woodstock, New York "love-in."
- 250,000 anti-Vietnam war protestors demonstrate in Washington.

1970-1979

- Four Kent State students killed by National Guard at anti-war demonstration.
- Nixon visits China.
- Watergate break-in conspirators indicted.
- Nixon first U.S. President to resign.
- U.S. pulls out of Vietnam.
- Gasoline shortage resulting from oil cartel fuel embargo.
- Amtrak begins operation.
- Trans-Alaska oil pipeline approved by Congress.
- Freedom of Information act passed over President Ford's veto.
- The Concorde initiates supersonic jet service, Europe to U.S.
- Jimmy Carter defeats Gerald Ford for Presidency.
- Congress ratifies treaty giving Canal control to Panama in the year 2000.
- Mass suicide of Jim Jones's religious sect members in Guyana.
- Near disaster averted at Pennsylvania's Three Mile Island nuclear power plant.

1980-1989

- Ronald Reagan is fortieth U.S. President.
- John Lennon shot by a fan.
- Reagan wounded outside Washington Hilton.
- Pope John Paul II wounded at St. Peter's Square.
- Sally Ride first woman astronaut in space.
- Geraldine Ferraro first woman vice presidential candidate.

- First reusable space shuttle, *Columbia*, lands in California.
- U.S. captives released in Iranian hostage crisis.
- Space shuttle *Challenger* explodes killing all seven on board.
- Chernobyl nuclear accident in Ukraine.
- Sandra Day O'Connor, first woman member of Supreme Court.
- Stock Market falls 508 points on October 19, 1987.
- Shuttle *Discovery* marks U.S. space program comeback.
- San Francisco earthquake halts World Series game.
- George Bush is forty-first President.

Chapter Six

You the Author as Private Eye

I n earlier times, when we lived in small villages and never traveled beyond their boundaries, a first name was all we ever needed. But with wars and invasions and merchant trade, things changed.

After the Norman conquest of England, for example, William the Conqueror's "census" of England became the eleventh century Domesday Book. As family historian Otis Marble Botsford pointed out in *Origins of the Botsford Family*:

> When surnames were gradually coming into existence in England and France, the aristocracy, who were the landowners, were designated by the names of the places where their chief estates were located. After the Conquest, most of the large landholders were Norman-French followers of the Conqueror, who had been rewarded with the lands of the dispossessed English. Speaking French instead of English, they employed the French "de," meaning "of." Thus, William de Bottlesford or Bottesford was simply William of Bottesford—the place where he had owned estates.

> After surnames had become more firmly fixed, in England the "de" was gradually dropped, although in France as a rule it was retained. Thus even today many French families employ the "de" in the same way German families of the aristocracy use "von" and Dutch families use "van" [to indicate where they came from]. In more democratic England, the "de" was eventually lost, so that a later William de Bottesford would be plain William Botsford. Even if landed estates were sold or forfeited, the surname derived from their location continued to be used, and younger, unlanded branches retained the parental surname unless a youth were so fortunate as to marry an heiress. In that case, he usually assumed the name of his bride. . . .

Not many of us can trace our ancestors that far back, but for those interested in going beyond the grandparents we know about, there are rich resources to mine.

ANCESTOR RESEARCH BEGINS AT HOME
Historian and video producer Dan Hurley believes that the responsibility for the passing on of family stories "lies not with the older generation to tell, but with the younger generation to ask. Questioners should try to discover the conditions and beliefs that surrounded a particular family."

As you begin your exploration of your family's history, the best place to start is right at home:

✔ Are any of your grandparents still living? What do you know about your own parents?
✔ Is there a family Bible in the house?
✔ Have any older brothers or sisters saved important family documents?
✔ What about deeds to the old homeplace?

Has a distant cousin hosted a recent family reunion and is the address list still available? (If there has never been a reunion of your relatives, you might consider planning one as a way of collecting stories and information. One resource is *Reunions Magazine*, which offers suggestions on all kinds of reunions—alumni, family, military—but also lists forthcoming reunions by family name and carries articles related to family history research. The address is P.O. Box 11727, Milwaukee, WI 53211-0727.)

Are some kin buried in a nearby cemetery? The cemetery caretaker may have records of who bought which lots and where they lived at the time.

What about old letters? Diaries?

Do you have a photo album with some information on the back of the photos?

Another Perspective on Your Family
Newhouse News Service writer Jann Mitchell suggests that the role aunts and uncles can play in families offers special advantages to both parents and their children. These same benefits apply to the person writing a family history. You may find out things about your family and yourself that are better seen through their more objective eyes.

Mitchell says, "nieces and nephews, aunts and uncles can:

Offer perspective about a parent. My relationship with my father has always been complicated, but I understand him — and his upbringing and subsequent life better — when I talk with his sister, my Aunt Cherry. I get a sense of parental connection.

Act as a role model. We can show our nieces and nephews options they might not otherwise see regarding careers, parenting, education, travel, relationships. Knowing my Great-Aunt Esther, nearly 102 and bright as a button, helps me see that turning fifty this year doesn't mean the party's over.

Offer help that our nieces and nephews can't get or won't take from parents. Children can't always accept advice from parents, or parents may not be close enough emotionally or physically to provide support. Aunts and uncles are the closest thing to parents — and may feel less threatening.

Provide respite when the parent-child relationship is difficult. When a brother was getting a second divorce and my former sister-in-law was having a tough time, their two children bused up from California for a visit with me. It provided the parents respite, the kids relief and fun and me the opportunity to know these young people better."

And don't forget your in-laws. Sometimes a member of your spouse's family did some genealogy work and your own family can benefit by work they've already done.

ONE FAMILY HISTORIAN'S RESEARCH

Two young grandsons doing class projects sparked a family history by Harriet Lazarus. "That was twelve years ago," she says, "and their specific questions sent me to old Bibles, family records, and recalling family stories and memories. I had always heard, for example, that my father's parents came over from Germany on a sailing ship in 1844 and that they came down the Ohio River from Pittsburgh to Cincinnati on a steamboat. But how they got from the seaport to Pittsburgh sent me to books like Charles Lyell's *Travels in North America*, published in 1842, who had travelled the National Road across the Allegheny Mountains, route of many immigrants to new settlements in the West."

Lyell's description of early Cincinnati was supplemented by other travelers' accounts such as Charles Dickens's *American Notes* and Mrs. Frances Trollope's *Domestic Manners of the Americans*.

Harriet Lazarus's memoir of her family contains this episode with its unexpected contemporary conclusion:

> Many years ago I received from my mother a pearl and diamond stick pin that had belonged to my father. I could remember my father wearing the stickpin with his dress-up cravats and wing collars, his black cutaway coat and pin-striped trousers, when he called on friends on Sunday afternoons. The pearl was an unusual one, a freshwater pearl which I thought quite striking. Accented by a small diamond, it made a handsome piece of jewelry, too nice to be kept in a drawer. I took it to my favorite jewelry store, Newstedt-Loring Andrews, where my friend, Mr. George Warren, designed a modern gold setting for it, into a ring.
>
> I have always treasured the ring because there is a romantic and poignant story attached to it. When my father was a young man, in his early twenties, he became very attracted to a French woman living in Cincinnati. She apparently returned his affection. They were quite serious about one another and wanted to marry. Social conventions were very powerful in those days and one conformed to very strict rules. My father's family was no exception. Madame X — as I think of her, and indeed in my mind she resembles the Sargent portrait — was a divorced woman, and a Christian as well. These two facts made her an unsuitable wife for my father, out of bounds as far as his parents were concerned. Their disapproval was a hurdle even the great love my father felt could not surmount. One can only imagine with what torture and grief the two young people agreed to part, and Madame X returned to Paris. Her name was Marguerite Felice.
>
> My father wore his stick-pin, a gift from his French lady love, for many years. He did not marry until he was forty-four years old. He loved my mother, eighteen years his junior, very, very much, and she did him.
>
> He did make two trips alone to Europe when we were growing up. I remember asking my mother why she didn't go with him. She replied in her straightforward way, "I think it is best for him to go alone."
>
> It is hard to understand today how the pressures of society and family control can interfere with strong, indeed passionate, love between two people. But it all comes home to us in the masterful

movie production of Edith Wharton's Pulitzer Prize-winning book, *The Age of Innocence.*

I have a small picture of my father, taken when he was a handsome young man, dressed in quite formal clothes. It is in an old velvet frame and has been in my bookcase for at least forty years. I was curious that there might be a date on the back and also the name of the photographer. So I decided to remove the picture from the frame. There was no date, but something far more explosive—the picture was made in Paris.

Because of the age of the photograph and its subsequent faintness, one cannot see if the cravat holds a stickpin.

Recently, I found in my mail an announcement of an interesting-sounding company called Photo Revival. What could be more fortuitous than the service this flyer offered for restoring my father's picture—faded by the years since it was made, long ago in Paris! (Probably in the 1890s.)

In short order, I visited the company where I was utterly bewitched by the skills and techniques of these experts in computer imagery. What they have been able to do with this treasured picture seems little short of miraculous. Watching the computers bring out hidden details from the background, and enhance those already visible, was an exciting experience. It was made even more enjoyable by the enthusiasm of the young computer operators—for this picture and its story.

Now we know the pearl stick-pin was there—in the picture—just as it is still here today in my ring. Somehow I feel that my father would be elated, as we remember him one hundred years after he first wore his stick-pin. He would be fascinated, as is his daughter, by the magic of the computer—something neither one of us ever dreamed or could understand, although our children and grandchildren do with ease.

But we do have a new appreciation of the computer, as the search for the past is helped by the technology of the present and the future.

Your Own Camera Can Help

Harriet Lazarus's experiences point out the value of old photographs to the family historian. But some of the most interesting family photographs or historical records you want for your book may be in the hands of relatives who are leery of your request because photos they lent to other relatives were either never returned or lost in the mail.

Photocopying may be one solution, but "it is at times like these," says Wilma Sadler Shull, "that cameras have saved my day." In her book, *Photographing Your Heritage*, she reminds us how useful cameras are, too, when you're in a library and the copy machine is out of toner; or the book you want to copy was recently rebound and "is more difficult to open than a warped door after a four-inch rain." Shull's book gives some practical advice on camera equipment and techniques for the genealogist/photographer.

PLANTING YOUR FAMILY TREE

If your local library's history department doesn't have a sample chart on which you can start listing yourself and your family, you can easily make up one for yourself.

A word of caution: Genealogists use a particular date writing system to avoid confusion about transposed dates or which century is involved. Your ancestor's birthdate is written day/month/year, such as 14 July 1895, not 7/14/95.

Researchers in eighteenth century and earlier records may also experience "double-dating." The root of the confusion is the 1582 switch from the Julian Calendar (established by Julius Caesar) to the Gregorian Calendar (established by Pope Gregory XIII) to make the calendar coincide more accurately with the solar year. England and her colonies didn't get around to changing to the Gregorian until 1752, however, so when they moved back New Year's Day from March 25th to January 1, it required "double-dating." For example, an event might be listed as having taken place 21 March 1680/81 or 21 March 1680 O.S. (Old Style) or 21 March 1681 N.S. (New Style).

In her book, *How to Climb Your Family Tree: Genealogy for Beginners*, Harriet Stryker-Rodda points up a couple of other problems for family history researchers:

> Another pitfall is the change that has occurred in the meanings of words signifying relationships. Found in wills or deeds is the word "nephew," which sometimes meant grandson, (since it originally came from the Latin word "nepos" meaning "grandson"). "Cousin" very often meant any blood relative. The term "in-law" included adopted or step relatives while "sister" or "brother" meant not only blood relatives of the same parents (siblings), but

were also ecclesiastical terms that included brothers or sisters in a religious denomination.

The pitfall of generation designation can cause great confusion. "Junior" was a term applied to the younger of two persons of the same name in the same location but not necessarily closely related.

TRACKING ANCESTORS THROUGH THE CENSUS

One of the best immediate sources we have available to find our ancestors and *their* origins is the U.S. Census. Although created for other reasons, it is an invaluable resource for genealogists.

Why do we have a U.S. census? The founding fathers couldn't decide how representation of the citizenry to the legislature should be decided. Should each state have the same number of representatives? Or should population of the state influence the number? We know now that they decided on both methods — the Senate would have two representatives from each state and the House would have representatives based on population. To get the population figures, the Constitution mandated a census every ten years.

Under federal privacy laws, no census records are available to the public for the most recent seventy-two years. For example, the details of the 1920 census were opened to the public in 1992. The 1930 census won't be available until the year 2002.

But most of the others are there, back to 1790 when the first U.S. census was compiled. Although I now live in Ohio, I was born in Kentucky and so were my parents, so Kentucky census records might show where my parents and grandparents lived each time the census was taken. Census records not only show where a family lived at a given census year, but recent ones (beginning in 1850) also list the members of the household, the age, marital status, occupation and place of birth (state or country) of each individual, as well as his/her parents.

Since census records are not listed alphabetically but rather by the order in which they were visited by the census taker (by state, county, city ward, township), indexes have been published to help the family history seeker locate the last name of the head of household. The index will then tell the researcher the page number of the census to refer to.

As we all know, a family name can be spelled a number of different ways. With that in mind, beginning with the census of 1880, the federal government began preparing a surname indexing system called Soundex, which lists names by sound rather than spelling. By using the Soundex code, you can search the index state-wide by name code. The Soundex lists the head of the household, family members, their ages, and state or country of birth. Since Soundex lists all members of the household, you can quickly determine whether or not you have found the right family. Then, by noting the census enumeration district on the Soundex listing, you can obtain the actual census report.

Many people think the census questionnaires now ask for more personal information than we should have to provide, but the earliest census records don't tell enough for some genealogists.

For example, from 1790 to 1840 only the head of the household was named. Other household members were simply grouped by gender and age, such as "two males, age 9 and 5, and twin females, age 7," but no names were given. While slave schedules in 1850 listed names of slave*holders*, the names of the slaves were not given. It wasn't until 1870 that all African-Americans were listed by name.

In her memoir *Black Seeds in the Blue Grass*, writer Jacqueline Annette Sue describes her search for her black ancestors. On the positive side, she had a large family Bible and a network of relatives to whom she could write for copies of personal birth records. Family reunions she attended provided additional contacts. On the negative side, she discovered that Kentucky records contained little or no information on individual Negroes before early 1900. Her salvation? A helpful archivist at the Oakland, California, Latter Day Saints Family History Center, with whom she made an appointment to go over her assembled information.

It took two hours, but he looked at every piece of my collection. He furnished me with resources and a bibliography. He provided a Mormon format with guides to tracing my ancestors further than I had anticipated. When he finished he sat me in front of a microfilm reader with a film of the North Middletown, Kentucky, 1870 census and walked away.

I was tired. It was a long day. My session with Mr. Henderson was exhausting. My mind was exploding with the task to which he had challenged me. I certainly did not feel like looking at more census records. Slowly, I started to roll the microfilm on the reader. Towards the end of the spool, a couple of familiar names caught my attention. Then, I saw it! I held my breath.

I could not believe my eyes. I must have gone over this census a dozen times at the Federal Archives and I had never seen the information I was looking at now. I was so emotional over my find that I felt as if I were fainting. I jumped up, knocking over my chair, and ran to find Mr. Henderson. I wanted him to read what I had found. More than that, I wanted to share my excitement with him. The 1870 listed my great-great grandfather, born in 1791.

Mrs. Sue's experiences remind us of two things: first, after so many hours in front of a microfilm reader, you sometimes lose concentration and you might want to come back later when you feel fresher to tackle that detailed work; and second, how to let readers share in the excitement of discovery. She shows us not just what she found, but how she felt. (For more leads on African-American ancestors, see chapter seven.)

Here are a few more facts about the census pertinent to genealogy researchers:

Beginning in 1880, the census tells the parents' country or state of birth as well as that of each person tallied.

The 1890 census was destroyed in a fire.

The 1900 census began listing the year of immigration for those born outside the U.S.—a helpful addition for those of us whose ancestors didn't come over on the *Mayflower*!

For those native Americans whose ancestors were already here when the Mayflower landed, a separate census of the Indian population didn't occur until 1900.

If you want a copy of a census record from 1930 to 1990 that has not yet been released to the public, can meet the requirements for releasing this confidential information, and know the specific census year for which you want a copy of a specific person's census record, the Census Bureau will provide a transcript for a search service fee of forty dollars. This fee pays for a search of one census year for an applicant and the preparation of a transcript showing the results of the search, if found. The transcript will reflect the applicant's name, relationship to head of household, age at the time of the census, place of birth, citizenship, and the name of the head of household for the years searched. No other family members will be listed on the transcript. The address to write for an "Application for Search of Census Records" is: Bureau of the Census, Age Search, P.O. Box 1545, Jeffersonville, IN 47131.

Most people using this service are seeking a confirmation of age or place of birth for proof of age or a passport, but genealogy is also listed as one of the purposes for which the record is to be used. All transactions are handled by mail. There is no walk-in customer service, nor is the Age Search Service available through any commercial online service or the Internet. Office hours are 7:00 A.M. to 4:30 P.M., Monday through Friday (EDT) and the phone number is (812)285-5314. After office hours an answering machine is activated.

Why Can't Some Ancestors Be Found?

Keep in mind that early census takers accepted information on a household from any available source—a neighbor, a landlord, a child. Language barriers and foreign names added other discrepancies in names, ages, places of birth. And some households were just missed.

RESEARCHING BEYOND THE CENSUS

Census records, of course, are only one source of research. There are city directories, county histories, recorded deeds and wills, marriage licenses and cemetery records. Some local genealogical societies might know more about your family than you do yourself!

The Public Library of Cincinnati and Hamilton County claims it has the fifth largest genealogical collection of any public library in the U.S. and they give the beginner some excellent advice, which I've adapted here:

- ✔ To begin tracing your own ancestry, begin with yourself and go backward generation by generation to your grandparents, great-grandparents, etc. (Everyone has 1,024 direct ancestors in the tenth generation back, so most people do not try to learn about every ancestor.)
- ✔ Start with a five-generation ancestor chart (many libraries have samples you can use). You may be able to fill it in using resources you have at home.
- ✔ Be sure to search such things as family Bibles, family journals, letters, clippings, diaries, school reports, religious records (confirmation, marriage, baptism, etc.), photographs, passports, citizenship papers, etc.
- ✔ Be sure you contact older members of your family. Ask questions about names, places, church membership, dates, property ownership, military service.
- ✔ Oral history is especially important for African-Americans and Native Americans. But all facts drawn from memory should eventually be verified by another source before they can be accepted as true family history.
- ✔ Be sure any initial how-to-do-it books you read on genealogy con-

centrate on American research. You can worry about your German, English and French ancestors later.

✔ The local history department of your public library may have a printed list of genealogical resources available in your area, which may help you in your searches. Depending on the size of the library, it may also have collections of different types of records, such as graveyards, wills, marriages, passenger lists, tax lists, etc.

✔ Few public libraries in the country have *all* available U.S. Census Records from 1790, but your local library may have census information for just your state. For example, the Greene County Library in Xenia, Ohio, has the census data from 1820-1920 for the state of Ohio.

✔ Always be sure that you note accurately the sources of your information. Do not remember a book as "the green book on Kentucky marriages." Note the source by exact author and title (if it is a book) or by its file number in the institution where you found it.

✔ Keep a research record on which you list the sources you contact—whether that contact is a personal visit, a telephone call or a letter, or through a library or other institution. Also record what you were looking for, what you found and the date. This keeps you from repeating searches. Some genealogists set up this record by dates, others by the source or family name. You can buy research calendars and research logs or make up your own variation to suit your purposes. (A sample appears on page 85.)

Historical research calendars are also useful in helping to relate ancestors with the times in which they lived. Here is an excerpt of how family history writer Mary Russell traced in chronological order some of the events that were significant to the Gillpatrick family, or that affected them as settlers in the Saco Valley in Maine:

1750. The everyday clothing for boys and men was a pair of buckskin breeches costing £1. They were worn to the knee and had five buttons for the closure. They seldom wore out. The rest of the clothes were homespun. Men of means had tailor-made clothes from Boston. There were sometimes colorful breeches and waistcoats with ruffles and embroidery rivaling women's clothes.

At this time, it became popular to use a double name in addition to the last name. In our family the mother's maiden name was a son's middle name, e.g., Robert Bond Gilpatrick son of Abigail

Bond. Bible names were not used as much. Esquire after one's name indicated a judicial position.

Marriage ceremonies were not lengthy in preparation and did not require a special dress. Generally there was a cake, drinks and a place for the couple to spend the night. In 1738 girls were required to love their husbands sincerely, obey and submit in the fear of the Lord.

Funerals among the well-to-do required much more expense. Gloves were needed for the bearers, the women and the men, which often required delaying things until supplies could be ordered from Boston. Ribbons and cyprus cloth were also requirements, one pound of allspice, and liquor and food for the guests. People were called to funerals as well as town meetings by the drum.

Mary Russell has been researching her Irish family roots for twelve years, but says her initial interest was sparked by her son's school assignment:

> After many phone calls to local relatives for information, my son had enough clues to concoct a story, but I was left dissatisfied that we knew so little about our grandparents and beyond. I was a member of the American Association of University Women at the time and I joined one of the interest groups that begàn the next year called "Family Tree."
>
> I subsequently took genealogy classes at the Mormon Family History Center here in San Diego and became the Irish Interest Chairman for a new British Isles group formed after our classes.
>
> My suggestion to anyone interested in writing a family history is to interview the eldest relatives by bringing up a topic and just letting the person ramble. Talk about simple topics like describing how they shopped, obtained food, went to church, moved to a new home, took care of a sick child. Once, while my mother was comfortably "put" while she was soaking her feet, I succeeded in getting her to talk about her vivid memories of women's marches for suffrage in Boston and her family's trials and tribulations after her father died. During her years in a nursing home I would spend long afternoons talking about her past. When I returned home I would write the stories down right away and file them in a notebook for that story I plan to write someday.

As a freelance writer on nonfiction subjects, I frequently use the public library's children's section as a starter to get simply worded explanations of things before I move on to more academic or scholarly approaches. By the same token, beginners in genealogy may appreciate a look at the Boy Scouts of America Merit Badge booklet on *Genealogy*. In a section called "Is All That Information True?" for example, the author reminds readers of the difference between primary sources (those created at the time of the event by someone who knew) and secondary sources (those created any time after the event happened). The author also cautions readers to distinguish between facts, evidence and opinions.

Because today's Boy Scouts are often members of "blended families" — the results of multiple marriages producing half, step and adopted siblings — the booklet offers advice on how to chart these family groups.

Combining Vacation Travel and Research

If you now live in a state other than the one your ancestors called home, the lure of records in a distant courthouse or archival library may be your incentive to stop in that town on your next vacation. Every genealogy researcher tells stories of visits to small towns, looking up addresses, and finding ancestors' neighbors who helped them fill in missing details about a relative.

There aren't always happy endings to the treasure hunt, of course, and you'll also meet uncooperative courthouse personnel, offices closed on weekday afternoons, missing (or misplaced) records and other hurdles for the less-than-persistent researcher. As more than one family history writer comments, "Genealogy is not for the fainthearted. It's a never-ending process."

Sometimes we need information about ourselves — not an ancestor. A friend who was applying for a passport was unable to provide a copy of her birth certificate (the courthouse records were burned and the state had no records for that time). She had to get an affidavit from someone who had known her since birth or had witnessed the birth to testify to the date and place of birth. Two other proofs were required and for this she obtained a baptismal record and a first communion record from the church where these events took place. These three notarized statements were sent to the state vital records office which then provided an acceptable birth record for the passport office.

SOME HELPFUL TIPS ON INTERVIEWING

As we've said, relatives can be a rich source of information for your family history. While simply swapping stories over the kitchen table will be useful, you'll collect more and better information by "interviewing" your source. Here are some helpful techniques:

- ✔ Prepare in advance a list of questions to ask during the interview. When you sit down to talk, it's easy to get involved in the stories your relative is telling and then forget to bring up key points you wanted to explore. A list will help you get all the information you can.

- ✔ You can either take written notes or use a tape recorder. There are pros and cons for each. Few of us can write as fast as people can talk. A tape recorder, on the other hand, allows us to not only get a full record of what was said, but also observe the details of the surroundings and to watch the expressions or gestures as the speaker recalls memories. These notes help us add personality and color to our subsequent writing. Some people might be inhibited by a tape recorder and not reveal some things they think they'd later regret. (You may want to reassure these subjects they could see a copy of what you write before you print it, and get their signed permission.)

- ✔ Make sure your interview is in a quiet place without distractions and the recorder is picking up both your questions and the subject's answers. If your recorder doesn't have an audio signal that the tape is at the end, check the tape frequently or watch the clock to see how much time the tape has to run.

- ✔ Try to avoid interviewing more than one person at a time. People will interrupt the conversation, offer conflicting opinions and cause confusion in the recording.

- ✔ Don't be afraid of silence. A subject may pause while recalling some past event. If you don't rush to fill the gap, they will likely go on to tell you more.

- ✔ Be sure to get the correct spelling of any names or towns or other important things mentioned. Either ask for these while the tape is running, or include them in your handwritten notes to accompany the tape.

- ✔ Be sure to ask questions that can be answered with more than a yes or no. Ask open-ended questions, such as "What do you remember most about Grandfather Hobson's coming to America?"

✔ If a relative has difficulty remembering an exact date, help them
narrow down the approximate time by referring to other events —
either within the family ("it was about five years after your cousins
arrived in 1898") or in world affairs ("he was born after World
War I but before the Depression").

✔ Even though an elderly person may not remember an exact date,
and their short-term memory is lost, it's important to record their
past (which is often still very clear to them).

✔ Use these oral interviews as a springboard to search for factual
records to document the memories of those you interview.

More Interview Techniques

Some professional interviewers find role-playing useful. In his book
The Craft of Interviewing, John Brady quotes reporter Sally Quinn on
this point:

> I majored in theatre in college. I studied the Stanislavski
> method, and then I quickly forgot it, because I thought it was
> ridiculous. But I recently starting thinking about how, in a sense,
> you can almost use that method when you're interviewing some-
> body. You can put yourself into that person's place and try to feel
> what he's feeling, what she's feeling; try to think what the things
> are that really get to them. They can sense that empathy, and
> they'll open up to you. And this just never fails.

If you can't interview a relative in person, you may want to make an
initial contact by mail and then follow up with a phone call.

Your initial letter would explain who you are and what you are trying
to find out, and the reason why. Depending on the circumstances, you
may want to include a list of questions the relative can answer in a
letter to you, or a more formal questionnaire with each question followed
by a blank space where the person can write in the answers.

Your letter, on the other hand, may simply inquire as to the best time
when you could call and talk to them about your questions. If you
include the questions in the letter, your source will have time to think
about them before you call.

Electronics stores like Radio Shack sell devices you can attach to
your phone jack that allow you to tape record your phone interviews.
You would mention to the subject both in your letter and when you
make the follow-up call that you are "recording the conversation for

accuracy if that's okay with them." His or her answer on the tape is your protection related to federal and state laws.

Another variation on this idea (and cheaper than long-distance phone rates) is to mail a cassette tape with your questions. Your relative records her answers and returns the tape to you. (This will be even easier if you include a stamped, addressed padded envelope.) For example, for a book I'm working on about *Modern Pioneer Women in Aviation* I found it difficult to catch airline pilots or commercial helicopter pilots home long enough to interview. But I could send them a list of questions and a blank audiocassette to record at their convenience and return.

Robert Coles and Jane Hallowell Coles, who used tape recorders extensively in researching their books on *Children of Crisis* and *Women of Crisis*, admit that in later years they used the tape recorder less and took more notes.

"I used to think it was 'overkill,'" says Jane, "too much taped, not enough 'extracted' by us as we listened: the heart of things. That's what listening should be, close and careful attention paid on the spot. With the tape recorder present you tend to sit back and be a piggy eater, indiscriminate, the machine slurping everything in. Without the machine, it's your ears and your eyes and your brain, and then your fingers holding the pen: it's *you*, working and noticing and keeping what you think is important, . . . providing a context (as a writer) for what you've heard as a person called researcher, who is . . . an eager, interested listener."

LEGAL QUESTIONS

What are some of the legal problems you need to avoid when gathering interviews and writing the information for your family history or personal story? Here's a quick overview of some things to remember. You may never run into situations such as these, but they are yet another reminder of the need for accuracy and awareness of others' rights. Keep these potential pitfalls in mind as you write.

Libel: Only a living person can bring a suit for libel—that is, an accusation that a published statement is untrue. Even in those states that recognize defamation of the dead as a crime, courts have said such statutes do not give relatives the right to sue. Nevertheless, as a writer who wants to be accurate, a family historian would not accept as fact statements about a person without proof. Truth is the best defense against a libel suit, and the burden is on writers to defend their versions of the truth.

Another reminder for writers is mentioned in the introduction to Art Buchwald's *Leaving Home: A Memoir.* He writes, "At one point I called my friend Russell Baker and asked, 'What do you do if you're discussing someone who was mean to you in your childhood and that person is still alive?' He replied, 'Change his name.'"

That's good advice. You'll achieve an extra measure of caution by also changing the locale and circumstances so that no third party could still recognize your antagonist. In certain circumstances, writers have been sued for libel when a third party recognized the person even though his or her name was changed.

Invasion of privacy: Truth is not a defense against invasion of privacy. While you may be interested in your family's history, some relatives may not wish to be part of a published history — even one only produced for family members. Whatever their reasons, you must respect their desire not to be interviewed. But what about including information about them given or found by you in other places?

Some family members may not want you to mention uncomfortable topics, such as an ex-husband or a child of a previous relationship. You may, through public records or other research, already know who this person was. Once your relative realizes the information is available, he or she may relent. On the other hand, the relative may feel few people would ordinarily be aware, compared to the many who might read your family history, and ask you to not include the information. To save your relation from distress, and yourself legal worries, it's safer to forget that twig on the tree. Sometimes years later, a descendant of the objector gives permission.

Copyright: One of the legal points that many writers overlook is the rights to letters. While a recipient of a letter may own the physical property, the written contents of a letter are still the "intellectual property" of the letter writer. That means, you must receive permission from the writer of a letter to quote anything from the letter in a manuscript of your own. If the letter writer is dead, then you'd need permission of his or her descendants.

ADDITIONAL RESEARCH REMINDERS

Experienced genealogy researchers who have learned the hard way pass along these tips to beginners:

- ✔ Make notes when you *don't* find something, too, to avoid duplication of efforts in that same research area.

✔ Each county is different in the way it lists and records kinds of information.

✔ The same person's name may be spelled differently in different records, so it's important to verify by cross-checking sources. In the past, names were often spelled phonetically by the person recording the information.

✔ Be persistent. If a courthouse employee is uncooperative, try a different person on a different day.

✔ Census records are not always accurate — people lied about their age for a variety of reasons — for example, to get into the military or to avoid the military — or they simply gave incorrect information.

✔ When writing anyone for information, always enclose a self-addressed, stamped envelope.

✔ Cemetery lot records may show the names of people for whom there is no tombstone.

✔ Photographs of tombstones are important records since pollution and vandalism can destroy them.

✔ Death records sometimes list the birthplace of the person who died.

✔ Search just one generation at a time.

✔ Be broadminded about your research. (As one researcher pointed out, "My grandfather always said his father left him. I discovered he had been ill and was in the next town.")

✔ Check with neighbors — some children may have been living in neighboring homes; others were "in service" on neighboring farms. Neighbors may be related to your ancestor.

✔ Copy everything on important records. (Baptismal sponsors may be related and their names a clue to other information.)

✔ Christening records may be another check against census dates.

✔ Obituaries only started appearing in most newspapers in 1900.

✔ Funerals are a good place to meet relatives you'd never see or know about otherwise.

WRITING REMINDER: FAMILY NEWSLETTER

Let everyone even remotely related to you know that you're starting a family history. They may start out by sneering, "All you ever do is talk about dead people" but once they get interested themselves, they'll find the search fascinating. You may find it useful to publish a periodic family newsletter containing some interesting historical items and soliciting contributions about the family from others. For an example of one family's newsletter, see the sample on page 86.

Jane Bracht, editor of the *Dvorak News Network* has a few suggestions for people who want to start a family newsletter:

- ✔ Have each family contribute a little money towards engraved binders in which to keep them. I have found that they can be misplaced or damaged unless they are immediately protected.
- ✔ If you don't own expensive desktop publishing software and hardware like I do, utilize the various types of laser papers available. Companies like Paper Direct sell colorful newsletter templates that can be laser printed or run through a photocopier.
- ✔ Solicit information from "distant relatives." I'm finding that when people receive a copy of the newsletter and are asked to contribute to the next one, they usually will.
- ✔ Give yourself and others permission to be honest when writing an article for a family newsletter. Writing may be difficult for some, but the process of telling your story is a wonderful way to explore your roles and your feelings. There is much self and "other" discovery in creating family newsletters.
- ✔ Don't be surprised if family members are reluctant at first or if some of them consistently "forget" deadlines. Be firm about cut off dates just as you would on your job. Your obligation as family "editor" is to be true to the people who care about the newsletter.

RESEARCH RECORD

FAMILY SURNAME BEING RESEARCHED	SOURCE CONTACTED & HOW (MAIL/PHONE/IN-PERSON)	IF LIBRARY CALL NUMBER	PURPOSE	RESULT	DATE

dvořák news network

Reunion Reminder

As you all know, the **Dvorak Family Reunion** begins on Saturday, June 27 (Jim's birthday! Someone bring a cake!) and ends on Saturday, July 4 (the Nation's birthday). You each received a brochure from Pat, who is coordinating this grand event, outlining the overall features of *KarLee's Silver Shores Resort.*

In addition to the numerous activities available at the resort, we've come up with a list of possible family activities for the week, such as: fishing and boating (Mom and Dad have rented both a pontoon and a ski boat), sunning and swimming, shopping in Traverse City (serious shoppers only), volleyball, croquet, softball, horseshoes, family video night, family trivia night, adult dinner out at Bower's Harbor Inn (Lisa, will you babysit?), kid's bananna split and activities night, family talent show (Lisa can show off her Tae-Kwon-Do moves, Mary can fill us in on the latest horse-back riding tips, Rick and Joe can play their guitars... you get the idea).

If you have other ideas for family activities, jot them down, send them to me or bring them along!

As far as what to bring to the reunion, you "out-of-state folks" obviously don't have to worry about bringing linens, towels or food products. You *can* bring games, an alarm clock, binoculars, camera, sun tan products, and bug repellent. Also, bring any recent photos and/or videos.

We "in-state folks" will bring linens, towels, cleaning supplies, paper products, fishing equipment, food stuff, charcoal, portable radios, flashlights, a TV and VCR and anything else we can think of!

N-u-r-s-e Spells Love!

It seems we now have two nurses in the family! Congratulations to Marge on her graduation from Macomb Community College and her new job at Pontiac General, in Pontiac, Michigan. Jean has a new job too at St. Mary's Regional Medical Center in Lewiston, Maine. We're proud of both of you and we love you!

The only "rule" we have for the week is that each family will cook one meal for the whole family. Uh, oh, I think I better brush up on my cooking skills. How do you like your frozen dinners, medium or well done? And gee, I thought I heard Mary volunteer to do all the dishes for the week ... (Just kiddin' Mary!) Seriously though, we'll probably do most of our grocery shopping when we get there, but you might want to think of possible menu ideas.

By the way, we're having t-shirts made, based on the unique artistic ideas of Steve and Joe. They will be available when you arrive.

Well, see you all in June!

Future Issues of DNN

In future issues of this newsletter, I hope to be more creative with art and photos. The next issue will probably have a photo spread and lengthy article about the reunion.

I have some ideas for regular columns such as: KidTalk (news for, about and by the kids), Looking Back (stories about past family experiences, complete with old photos), Travel Log (information about your travels), and of course, I'll be soliciting information from you about what you're doing and topics of interest to you.

Kitty Comments
by Jack-the-cat

I would like to thank the Lorenz family for letting me visit with them for a month. I had a great time, and I especially miss my Aunt Beth.

Chapter Seven

Where to Find What

Outside the family Bible and other home resources, the best place to begin your search will be the libraries and public records' offices in your parents' hometowns.

If you, like I, have no living family members who know anything about your grandparents, but you do know where your parents were born, then that's a place to start. Even that can be tricky, however. For example, my father was born in 1878 in Sanfordtown, Kentucky, a town that doesn't even exist anymore. But it was part of Kenton County, which was created out of Campbell County, which was part of Virginia before Kentucky became a state.

LIBRARY RESOURCES

The Handy Book for Genealogists (see the bibliography) is an especially helpful tool for persons unsure of the evolution of counties in their state. The book gives a brief history overview of each state, lists which printed census records and census mortality schedules are available, and shows you county by county the territory from which the state was formed.

Another research tool to keep in mind is this: In Kentucky, as in some other states, where census records for certain periods are missing (destroyed by fire, etc.), reconstructed lists have been made from taxpayer records and published in certain books that are listed and available in some public or historical libraries.

Even if you don't know where your parents were born, you probably know where and when they died. Using that information, you can search backward through census records to find when they first appeared as children of your grandparents, and so on.

Many local libraries have indexes to census information for the state in which they are located, and nearby counties. These published indexes as well as older city directories, lists of births and deaths registered in your state, and atlases of maps and place names, may help you in your searches.

You may find some helpful information about place and date of birth on a tombstone. You may also find this information in copies of cemetery records that are on file in many local libraries. Some libraries also keep copies of courthouse, civil marriage, church and military records regarding people who lived in their communities.

Another place to look is the *International Genealogical Index* in your local library. The 1993 edition of the *IGI* contains the names of more than 200 million deceased persons throughout the world. These include the names of members of the (Mormon) Church of Jesus Christ of the Latter Day Saints, which publishes the index, as well as names compiled from other vital records.

Some relative of yours may have already done some research on your family. That information also may be accessible through the *International Genealogical Index*.

Gathering as much information in one place — the library — is a good idea before expanding your search in the community.

COURTHOUSE RECORDS

Your next stop might be the county courthouse where these kinds of records may be available:

Common Pleas Court: divorce records, petitions for partitions of estates

County Health Department: birth and death records for the twentieth century

County Recorder's Office: copies of deeds, some military discharge records, locations of veterans graves

Probate Court: copies of wills, marriage indexes, some pre-twentieth century birth, death and naturalization records.

Remember, each county is different in the way it lists and records various types of information.

Vital Records by State

If your relatives moved around — meaning their births, marriages, divorces and deaths are recorded in different states — you might want to get a copy of *Where to Write for Vital Records* from the Superintendent of Documents (U.S. Government Printing Office, Washington, D.C. 20402; a 1993 copy carried the Stock Number 017-022-01196-4 and cost $2.25). It tells you where to write in each of the fifty states, plus American Samoa, the Canal Zone, District of Columbia, Guam, Northern Mariana Islands, Puerto Rico and the Virgin Islands, for birth, marriage, divorce and death records. It also tells you the price for a copy of the record, who to make out the check or money order to, and for what years these records are available.

Finding Land Records

Land records for the original thirteen states plus Maine, Vermont, West Virginia, Kentucky, Tennessee, Texas and Hawaii are maintained by the states, usually in the state capital. Federal land records for the other states from 1800 to 1974 are in the National Archives in Washington. These include bounty-land-warrant files, donation land entry files, homestead application files, and private land claim files relating to the entry of individual settlers on land in the public land states.

A history of how Congress granted certain public domain lands to war veterans and other citizens is detailed in *The Researcher's Guide to American Genealogy*, by Val D. Greenwood (see Bibliography).

FAMILY HISTORY CENTERS

If there is a Mormon Family History Library near you (see your telephone book under Church of Jesus Christ of Latter Day Saints — there are two thousand centers or branches throughout the U.S. and in sixty-two countries around the world), you may be able to find some other data in its catalog — such as copies of land deeds, wills, marriage licenses, cemetery records filed by country or state then county. The Latter Day Saints Church's Family History Library in Salt Lake City, Utah, is the largest collection of genealogical data in the world. (Its holdings cover not just Mormons; many non-church members have contributed their family history information to the library's records.) All the libraries are open to the public to use without charge other than duplication and postage costs. For a list of centers in your region, write to: Family History Library, 35 N. West Temple St., Salt Lake City, UT 84150. Telephone: (801) 240-2331.

Before visiting a nearby Mormon Family History Library branch, you may want to view their video: *How to Use the U.S. Census and Using a Family History Center*. To order, write for a copy of the library's Family History Publications List, which includes many other publications and forms useful to genealogists. Address: Salt Lake Distribution Center, 1999 West 1700 South, Salt Lake City, UT 84104-4233.

IMMIGRATION RESOURCES

Do you have a relative whose entrance to this country was by ship from abroad? Lists of ships that arrived in the U.S. between 1820 and 1957, and the names of passengers on them, are on file at the National Archives in Washington. The largest waves of immigrants arrived in the U.S. between 1880 and 1914. Many published lists have been indexed in books like *Passenger and Immigration Lists Index* in your local library. This is an index by name to 2,500,000 arrivals to the U.S. and Canada in the seventeenth, eighteenth and nineteenth centuries. Another helpful book is the *Passenger and Immigration Lists Bibliography*. While it is set up alphabetically by the name of the author who compiled the list, a cross-reference index in the back will show you what kinds of lists are involved, such as "Germans to America since 1790."

The pamphlet "Tracing Immigrant Origins" offers a helpful research outline including search strategies for country-of-arrival records and country-of-origin records. It's available from the Family History Library at Salt Lake City.

We think primarily of Ellis Island in New York as the entry point for immigrants, but it was just one of many ports of arrival. A publication on ports of entry, *Immigration and Passenger Arrivals: A Select Catalog of National Archives Microfilm Publications*, may be available in your public library.

The *News of the Family History Library* in Salt Lake City says that:

> Since 1985 many newspapers and genealogical periodicals have reported the possibility or actual existence of an Ellis Island database with fifteen to sixty million names. Currently no such database exists. Ellis Island has the Kodak Family Album (digitized photographs) and the Immigrant Wall of Honor (names of financial donors and their immigrant relatives).
>
> [In 1994,] we will begin to create a FamilySearch resource file containing information from the Ellis Island passenger lists, 1892 to 1924. The resource file will contain the following information about each passenger: name, age, marital status, last residence, nationality, birthplace, names of relatives, name of vessel, and date and port of arrival.

To consult passenger lists, of course, you need to know the year in which your ancestor arrived in the U.S. If this information is not available in family records, you'll have to uncover it by tracing backwards from yourself to ancestors through census records and other sources.

An example of such a search is this one by Billie Plumlee Cox:

> One of the family branches that several of my relatives think we may come from starts with an English ancestor who, during Oliver Cromwell's time, was transported to Barbados to work on plantations there. I have a reference showing a John Plumly on a Parish register in and about the Towne of St. Michaels . . . Barbados in the year 1680. He is listed as a planter and landowner, but I haven't yet found how he got to the United States.

The National Archives does not have passenger lists for every place an immigrant might have arrived. Records of arrivals during colonial times especially would have to be searched through other sources at ports of entry.

GENEALOGICAL RESEARCHERS

Americans who want to trace foreign ancestors and have done all their preliminary homework through research sources available in the U.S. can contact genealogical researchers in foreign countries. Before hiring a researcher, ask for details of his or her experience, background, expertise and rates based on what you want them to do. Periodicals like *The Genealogical Helper*, available in most libraries, and recommendations from local historical or genealogical societies would be a way to start.

Here's an example of how one American, Skip Churchill, after networking with family and pursuing her own in-depth research, engaged a British researcher to solve a particular puzzle in her family's history:

SKINNER HUDSON – STOWAWAY

It was through a distant relative that I learned that Skinner Hudson, my fifth great grandfather, had been a stowaway from England. An intriguing tale, but no proof could be found nor sources cited.

But there the story lay until one extraordinary day, while thumbing through one of the volumes of Filby's *Passenger and Immigration Lists Index* I found: "Hudson, Skinner, na (no age), America (destination) 1767," followed by a code which identified the source. This led me to Peter Coldham's *English Convicts in Colonial America, Vol. II*, p. 76, listing Skinner as "S" (sentenced) April, "T" (transported) May 1767, *Thornton* (ship).

Many months later I received a verbatim account of Skinner's jury trial in Old Bailey. Skinner's crime was stealing a till (cash drawer) from an engraver's shop, for which he was imprisoned, tried, sentenced to transportation to the colonies, and seven years indenture.

Desperately needing to know which colony, my English researcher located a local newspaper, *Lloyd's List for 1767*, which documented the sailing and return of ships across the European continent and British Isles. One of these noted the departure on 18 May 1767 and return on 23 November 1767 of the *Thornton* from Maryland — the unknown colony.

The 16 July 1767 issue of the *Maryland Gazette* documents the arrival of the *Thornton* in Annapolis with "152 of his Majesty's seven year passengers" — the then-current euphemism for indentures. So Skinner and the others were sold.

In 1778, nine years later, Skinner enlisted in the Revolutionary War to fight against his countrymen, the first of two enlistments. Records in Pennsylvania, Kentucky and Ohio, and networking with other researchers, have fleshed out this ongoing saga — including the 1785 marriage bond in Kentucky when Skinner's bondsman was one of Daniel Boone's brothers.

Skinner died about eighty-two years of age, well regarded by his community and a man of fair substance. He is buried near London, Ohio, the headstone replaced by the National Society Daughters of the American Revolution with a metal plaque attesting to his military service.

Many families' folklore says an ancestor arrived in America on the *Mayflower*. But how do you go about verifying it? You'd have to start with yourself, of course, working your way back to the seventeenth century using all the resources previously mentioned. Some resources to contact after you've completed all your other findings would be:

✔ General Society of Mayflower Descendants, P.O. Box 3297, Plymouth, MA 02361, which has twenty-two thousand members and publishes research on descendants through the fifth generation

✔ New England Historical Genealogic Society, 101 Newbury St., Boston, MA 02116-3087, charges thirty-five dollars per hour for help with research problems for non-members, twenty-five dollars per hour for members

Midwesterner Marjorie Neely described to me one successful search for *Mayflower* ancestors using a variety of resources. Neely's family history was researched by an aunt, who traced ancestors back to John Alden and Priscilla Mullins who were among those who landed at Plymouth in 1620. The aunt, Marjorie Edson Armstrong, used not only information from relatives, but also pension roles from Connecticut Men in the War of the Revolution; historical societies in Connecticut, Vermont and Massachusetts; probate files; birth and death registrations; and other genealogical resources. Her documentation of ancestry was approved by the Connecticut Society of the Colonial Dames of America.

ORAL HISTORIES

Oral history is gathered today not just for historical societies, but also for families who want an oral history to complement the written one they'll compile. They like hearing about the times of their parents and grandparents in their ancestors' own voices.

Cynthia Stokes Brown, author of *Like It Was: A Complete Guide to Writing Oral History*, points out that until tape recorders became widely accessible in the late 1960s, people who lacked the skill or confidence to write detailed accounts of their experience could not give their personal version of history. These people may have been natural storytellers, but they still needed writers to transcribe their stories into literary forms. One response to this need came in 1967, when students at Rabun Gap High School in the Appalachian Mountains of Northern Georgia began publishing their oral history interviews with elders in a little magazine called *Foxfire* (named after a local organism that glows in the dark). "The Foxfire project," says Brown, "stands for the idea that high school students, not just adults and outsiders, should take part in documenting the cultural life of their community."

Sometimes oral history videos were recorded as a free service at public libraries or other local community centers in programs sponsored by insurance companies. For example, Dr. Robert C. Atchley, Director of Scripps Gerontology Center at Miami University in Oxford, Ohio, was approached by the Aetna Life and Casualty Insurance Company a number of years ago to visit ten different cities with Aetna technicians to videotape half-hour interviews with seniors. The half-hour videotapings were preceded by a fifteen-minute pre-taping interview to select the highlights, and the senior, or married couple, was given the videotape to take home at the end of the session.

If you think some relative may have participated in an oral history project, you might want to contact your local library, or historical society to see if it has a copy. If your relative lived in another part of the country,

you could contact the Oral History Association, P.O. Box 3968, Albu-
querque, NM 87190-3968. The Executive Secretary could put you in
touch with whichever of its twelve hundred members is familiar with
the oral historians in that part of the country.

MILITARY RECORDS

Genealogical researchers can find helpful information on documents
issued to military veterans at their time of discharge (or to next of kin,
if the individual died in service). Records for service in World War I,
World War II and subsequent wars are housed at the National Personnel
Records Center (Military Personnel Records) at 9700 Page Ave., St.
Louis, MO 63132-5100.

Earlier records from the Revolutionary War, War of 1812, Indian
Wars, Mexican War, Civil War, Spanish-American War, along with
Pension Records, Bounty Land Warrant Records, and other records
related to army, navy and marine military service are in the National
Archives, Washington, D.C. 20408 or its field branches.

Genealogical researchers may also find helpful resources in these two
organizations' libraries: National Society, Daughters of the American
Revolution, 1776 D St., N.W., Washington, D.C. 20006-5392, and National Society, Sons of the American Revolution, 1000 S. 4th St., Louis-
ville, KY 40203.

Records in the National Archives relating to burials of veterans in
national cemeteries are incomplete. Requests for additional information
should be addressed to the Director, Cemetery Service (41A), National
Cemetery System, Veterans Administration, Washington, D.C. 20420.

DO YOU HAVE NATIVE AMERICAN ANCESTORS?

If so, your genealogical research would begin as any other with yourself,
your parents, your grandparents, etc. Some early records or censuses of
Indian bands, tribes or groups are on file at the National Archives and
Records Service, Natural Resources Branch, Civil Archives Division,
8th and Pennsylvania Ave., N.W., Washington, D.C. 20408. These
records, identified by tribes, are dated chiefly 1830 to 1940. The Bureau
of Indian Affairs does not maintain comprehensive lists of persons pos-
sessing Indian blood. Copies of census and membership rolls, however,
are often on file in the Bureau of Indian Affairs field offices throughout
the country.

Your local library may have current copies of the publication, *Journal
of American Indian Family Research*, which could provide some helpful

information and leads. If none are readily available, ask your librarian to recommend alternate sources.

TRACING YOUR JEWISH ROOTS

In a booklet of that title by Dr. Malcolm H. Stern, Vera Weizmann, wife of the first president of Israel is quoted as saying, "We Jews are a strange people: We remember Moses, the Kings David and Solomon, but we know next to nothing about our own forefathers besides our parents and occasionally our grandparents."

The first Jewish immigrants to the United States arrived in New Amsterdam in 1654. Those who settled here before 1840 primarily came from Germany and Eastern Europe and are listed in Dr. Stern's *Americans of Jewish Descent.*

One of the fortunate few able to escape Germany in 1937 before the horrors of World War II and the Holocaust, Hannelore Hahn, describes in her memoir, *On the Way to Feed the Swans,* her experiences as a young schoolgirl on the day she left:

> I remember the day in November, 1937, when I saw Stitterich outside of the school building standing at the side of the car.
>
> What was he doing here, I wondered.
>
> I had never been chauffeured home from school but always took the tram. When I asked him why he had come, he said, "Get in!" He slammed the doors, stepped on the accelerator and drove much faster than was his usual habit.
>
> We are driving home, he said. I was to get my things and then he would drive me across the border. Nothing unusual about that part of it, I thought. It was Friday. But there was one thing that was exceedingly unusual. My parents had already left.
>
> The feeling that something was odd, even ominous, was substantiated when we arrived at Bergstrasse Number 16. Gertrud, our maid at the time, was in a highly nervous state. She, too, was standing waiting for me. And now all she was doing was telling me to hurry. "Quickly, quickly!" "Mach schnell, mach schnell!"
>
> I ran into my room. There, everything was packed. Why? I obviously didn't need all these things for a weekend trip. And then I knew.
>
> "You think I'm never coming back?" I screamed. "Well, I will! You wait and see! I will! I'll be back before you know it!"
>
> I opened my suitcase and threw everything on the floor.

"I'm not taking all this junk!" I yelled. "I don't need it. I'll take my toothbrush and that's all!"

Then I got into the car and drove off, with Gertrud standing at the door, tears in her eyes, trying not to show that she knew too.

Of course, I never came back. Never. And even if I did now, Bergstrasse Number 16 would be no more. It was destroyed by firebombs in 1945. So was Dresden. Stitterich and Gertrud have since died. And Hertha? Yes, I could still see her. But it would not be the same. Nothing was the same again from that moment.

Forty years later, Hahn returned to Germany for a nostalgic meeting with Hertha Baumann, a woman who had been a cook and nanny in her parent's home and had "maintained a loving contact with my family, particularly with me whom she had loved as her child." This is how she described their planned meeting:

At the Kurhaus C., the young woman behind the desk requested to see my American passport. Had Frl. Baumann already arrived, I inquired between these formalities.

"No," the registration clerk said. "She will not be coming."

"Not be coming?" I repeated in disbelief. "You mean not at all?"

"The Kurhaus received a card from Fraulein Baumann only yesterday," the woman explained, "canceling her arrival." Sensing my distress, she went to get the card. It was dated August 23, 1979, and was written in German.

"I must regretfully cancel my reservation at your hotel. Our East German authorities require, besides name of hotel, city and country, the exact street address, and since this was not indicated in your brochure, nor on your letterhead, permission for me to leave Dresden was not granted by the police.

"P.S. Unfortunately, it is now too late to rectify this situation for even if you were to supply the street name and number, it would be to no avail, since the process for obtaining permission to travel takes six weeks. I am very sad."

H. Baumann

In addition to the usual genealogical resources, people with Jewish American ancestors may find help at the American Jewish Archives, 3101 Clifton Ave., Cincinnati, OH 45220-2488. Another source is the

American Jewish Historical Society, 2 Thornton Rd., Waltham, MA 02154.

If your Jewish ancestors lived in Germany, you may find some data at Leo Baeck Institute, 129 E. 73rd St., New York, NY 10021.

If your ancestors came from Eastern Europe, you may want to consult YIVO Institute for Jewish Research, Inc., 1048 5th Ave., New York, NY 10028.

The Central Archive for the History of the Jewish People is at P.O. Box 1149, Jerusalem 91090 Israel. These records, of course, could be in either Hebrew, Yiddish or German Gothic script.

OTHER CHURCH RECORDS AND ARCHIVES

While both Catholic and Protestant denominations maintain local parish and diocesan records, if you're searching for a grandparent who migrated from another state, some other sources might prove helpful. *The Official Catholic Directory*, for example, has been published since 1820 and lists which parishes were part of which diocese or archdiocese during which years.

The *Yearbook of American and Canadian Churches* published annually by the National Council of Churches, gives a brief history of all major and minor denominations in the U.S. and Canada. Also listed are addresses for each one's national headquarters and depositories of church history material.

Your local library may also have a copy of E. Kay Kirkham's book, *A Survey of American Church Records*, listing denominations before 1880 to 1890 and the migrations of some of the major denominations. The state-by-state list of records by counties could prove helpful in locating church members.

RESEARCHING "THE OLD COUNTRY"

Angus Baxter points out in his book *In Search of Your German Roots* that "Because you have a German surname and a family story that 'great-grandfather came from Germany', do not assume that he came from that area of Europe marked 'Germany' on today's map. He could have come from Austria, Belgium, Czechoslovakia, Denmark, France, Italy, Yugoslavia, Liechtenstein, Poland, Romania, Switzerland or countries of the former Soviet Union. . . . All these countries are either German-speaking or have large German minorities."

But don't be discouraged. Baxter points out that Germans are great record keepers and you can do all your searching by correspondence and using available resources in the U.S. before you hop on that plane to visit discovered relatives.

One way to research foreign-born ancestors without leaving the U.S. is to advertise in genealogy magazines of the country of origin. Here's one example:

Russell Bloss, a retired insurance administrator whose meticulous restoration of pianos and organs is a hobby, carries over the same dedication to his family searching. Bloss says, "My original interest stemmed from the fact that my father and mother didn't discuss their families much and I was as interested as most twenty- to thirty-year-olds are. I was especially intrigued about my Grandfather Bloss, who came to this country in 1850. I have traced members of my mother's Swiss and Amish ancestors to the 1200s, but my Grandfather Bloss, where my interest is concentrated, has been a real challenge. The most severe stumbling block was erroneous information on my grandfather's death certificate."

After pursuing this unsuccessful search for information, Bloss says that his advertisement in a German genealogical magazine brought him helpful correspondence about his family — especially since the unification of Germany. "Before," says Bloss, "many times if an East German citizen got more than one letter from the U.S., he could be put under surveillance by the government."

The archivist at the Castle in Rudolstadt, Germany, was also the source of correspondence that included a copy of Bloss's grandfather's birth record, which showed the name of the grandfather's mother. That name wasn't the same as the name on Bloss's grandfather's death certificate. The archivist also disclosed that the baby's father's name was not recorded on his birth record. (See the letter on the next page.)

A letter to a church office resulted in letters from a German lady whose maiden name was Bloss and whose husband was a prisoner of war during World War II (and who saw more of the U.S. as a POW than has Mr. Bloss!).

Russell Bloss confirms the importance of looking at tombstones. He learned from his grandfather's burial site near Goshen, Indiana, that his grandfather came from Rudolstadt, Germany.

Your local genealogical society may have special interest groups that concentrate on German or Irish or English or other European ancestors. They can suggest foreign publications in which to place your advertisement, and where necessary, find someone to write it in the foreign language.

Translation of the letter from Jens Beger, Rudolstadt, to Mr. Russell E. Bloss:

Rudolstadt,
February 2, 1993

Dear Mr. Bloss,

   The Johann Theodor Bloss sought by you (Family Notices, Volume 8, Number 7) (Jan/Feb 1991), Advertisement Seeking Information . . .) was born on 29 June 1830 in Thalendorf in the principality of Schwarzburg-Rudolstadt. His father is not mentioned in the baptismal entry; the name of the mother is Johanna Dorothea Blos(s). Apparently, Johann Theodor Bloss was born out of wedlock.

   Concerning his emigration to America, we find two newspaper notices from the years 1849 and 1853, copies of which are enclosed. It is not possible to establish from these exactly when the emigration occurred.

   With warmest greetings,

   Jens Berger

ARE YOU AN ADOPTED CHILD?

Social agencies and state laws in the U.S. have upheld the birth parent's right of privacy over an adoptee's right to know, so adopted children who reach adulthood and are searching for their natural parents (or vice versa) face real difficulties. One group that offers aid in this area is the Adoptees' Liberty Movement Association (ALMA), P.O. Box 727, Radio City Station, New York, NY 10101-0727.

   ALMA maintains a registry databank on adoptees, natural parents, and people separated by adoption, for possible matching. In most cases adoptees do not know their original names and natural parents do not know adoptive names of children they gave up for adoption. But they do know the sex of the child, and the date and place of birth. If, for example, a mother gave up a son born May 20, 1930, in St. Luke's Hospital in New York City, and an adopted male with matching information is registered with ALMA, "we put them in touch without delay."

ALMA's membership includes adoptees over eighteen years of age, natural parents whose adopted children have reached age eighteen, foster children over eighteen, unwed mothers, adoptive parents, and persons separated through adoption.

Additional registries, support groups and advice can be found in *Search: A Handbook for Adoptees and Birth Parents*, by Jayne Askin, and *Adoption Searchbook*, by Mary Jo Rillera (see the Bibliography).

One birth parent who successfully found her adopted daughter is Mary Ann Kroger. Using some of the search techniques mentioned in Mary Jo Rillera's book, *Adoption Searchbook*, Kroger learned that her daughter had listed her own desire at age eighteen to find her birth mother. They met recently for the first time. Mary Ann Kroger recommends adoptees and birth parents seek out whatever support groups they can find to help in the search.

A number of these, with their addresses, are listed in the *Encyclopedia of Associations* in your nearest library. They include the Adoptees' Birth Mother Support Network, American Adoption Congress, Concerned United Birth Parents, and the National Adoption Information Clearing House.

ILLEGITIMATE CHILDREN AND OTHER LOST RELATIVES

The May, 1994, issue of *Money* magazine describes the search by World War II veteran and successful farmer/businessman Jim Davis for the son he believes he conceived in 1942. The article also includes some guidelines for others seeking living relatives.

There are alternatives to hiring a private investigator to conduct a search (at a cost that runs $400 to $2,000). Among *Money's* suggestions is Seekers of the Lost (800)669-8016, a non-profit group that will research its 160 million-name database for two candidates and supply you with addresses of the likeliest possibilities in the U.S. The cost is $59.

You'll recall the 1993 news story about the young woman, Kimberly Mays, whose natural parents sought custody of Mays after a genetic test determined that the child they brought home from the hospital, and who subsequently died, was not their biological daughter. *Money* reports that Genetic Design, a laboratory based in Greensboro, North Carolina, with three thousand affiliates nationwide, performs a million DNA tests annually, with roughly a third of them related to family searches.

In terms of earlier historical records, Doane and Bell, in their book *Searching for Your Ancestors*, point out that "... in the New England colonies, an illegitimate birth was frequently recorded under the mother's name and the child given its father's surname; in some instances the birth may be recorded under both names, paternal and maternal."

SOME OTHER RESEARCH CONCERNS

Medical history is the goal of some researchers who want to know about the possibility of inherited diseases such as hemophilia or a past family history of cancer, diabetes, high blood pressure or heart disease. Such knowledge benefits not only the present family members, but those to come. For example, Catherine Berenson says,

> When we first married twenty years ago, I researched my husband's family tree. He had always been told that his grandmother had died at age twenty-six of a heart attack when his father was a little boy. Her dying at a young age caused considerable damage to his insurance rates.
>
> During my research, I found that no, his grandmother had not died of a heart attack but of "toxemia-complications of a pregnancy." Until this time, no one had known she was pregnant and that there had been a baby who had died in utero with her. It had been kept a secret for over fifty years.
>
> The good news is that this information removed my husband from the high risk rates. The bad news is that it put me in the toilet with my in-laws. But with documentation in hand, I have set the record straight for the coming generations.

Death certificates, hospital records, military pension records, family letters and diaries would aid in medical history research.

The census reports for 1850 to 1880 included mortality schedules that reported names of those persons who had died in the previous twelve months to the date of the census. In some cases, entries give the cause of death.

AFRICAN-AMERICAN RESEARCH

While the same techniques used to research any American ancestor apply to African-Americans as well after 1870, African-Americans who seek information on their ancestors immediately preceding or following the Civil War may find help in the *Ante-Bellum Plantation Records* and *The Freedman's Bureau Records*. Both of these are available in microfilm at the National Archives and selected public libraries and historical societies.

The plantation records include slave lists, slave owners' letters and diaries, and occasional letters written by slaves. Freedmen's Bureau records can provide names, residences, occupations, and physical descriptions of former slaves. The records also include lists of abandoned and confiscated land, names of former plantation owners and relatives' names.

Some references in this area include *Afro-American Genealogy Sourcebook*, by Tommie M. Young, *Generations Past: A Selected List of Sources for Afro-American Genealogical Research*, by Sandra M. Lawson, and *Slave Genealogy: A Research Guide with Case Studies*, by David H. Streets. (See the Bibliography.)

Researchers may find additional help from the *Journal of the Afro-American Historical and Genealogical Society*, P.O. Box 73086, Washington, D.C. 20056-3086, available in some libraries.

ELECTRONIC RESEARCH SOURCES

If you have a computer and a modem, you may already be subscribing to one of the online companies with access to their genealogy bulletin boards. Here you can make specific requests for information on ancestors (as Billie Cox described in chapter one) and get hints in doing research from more experienced enthusiasts. If you're not now online, you might want to call each of these services to get their current rates and more detailed information on what genealogical research services they can offer you:

America Online: (800)827-6364

Compuserve: (800)848-8199

Prodigy: (800)776-3449

America Online, for example, according to information received from them in February, 1994, indicated that their Genealogy Forum was set up with three basic sections: an Ancestral Digs conference room, Software area, and a Message area.

Compuserve offers a Genealogy Forum.

Prodigy offers an online genealogy advice column and also lists these Bulletin Board topics under Genealogy: Adoption, African-American, British Isles, Canadian, Census Information, Genealogy Software, German, Italian, Jewish, Missing, Native American, Other Countries, Other Europeans, Other Records, Other Resources, Scandinavian, U.S. State Resources and Vital Records.

A genealogical software program for home computers called Personal Ancestral File, developed and sold by the Mormon Church, can help you manage the data you collect. For price and order numbers, call (801)240-2504.

A quarterly journal, *Genealogical Computing*, can help you keep up to date on other software programs, computer research techniques and sources. Subscriptions: (800)531-1790. (Be sure to investigate just what each software program does and how complicated it is or how useful it may be for your particular purpose. You might ask for a demonstration disk before you buy.)

Most colleges offer access by their faculty and students to the world-wide Internet, the computerized information database. Internet access is also offered by Delphi Internet Services Corp. For information call (800)695-4005.

The Census Bureau's Internet site can be accessed via three types of Internet applications: Gopher, World Wide Web (html) browser, and anonymous File Transfer Protocol (ftp). If you have questions about accessing the Census Bureau's Internet site, call the Internet staff at the Bureau's Public Information Office at (301)763-4051 or by e-mail to pio@census.gov.

In 1994, *USA Today* reported that a number of San Francisco restaurants, bars and coffeehouses had installed computers that allowed patrons to hook into the Internet. Coin-operated online terminals were being developed by SF Net founder Wayne Gregori where these "pay phones of the future" would give you five minutes on the Internet for a quarter.

Another good source of electronic contacts are local computer bulletin boards. Directories of these by state are published four times a year by *Online Access* magazine, available at large newsstands. Some of the local contacts are amateur genealogists, and their advice and suggestions are free to anyone with a modem.

CALLING IN A PROFESSIONAL

Most novice family historians enjoy the fun of doing their own research, but if you have a particularly difficult aspect of a particular ancestor's history to research, you may want to hire a professional genealogist to perform that task. How much do they charge? John Frederick Dorman, Executive Director of the Board for Certification of Genealogists says there is no standard:

> Fees for genealogical research vary greatly depending on the nature of the work being done and the residence of the researcher.

Some researchers living in small towns in the Midwest charge as little as $7.50 per hour, I understand, while others in major research centers — who act as consultants on difficult problems, are employed to compile major studies for publication, or conduct heirship investigations — may charge between $25 and $50 per hour.

There are several categories of genealogical certification, depending on the kind of research work engaged in. Here is how the Board describes them:

CATEGORIES OF CERTIFICATION

Certified Genealogical Record Specialist (C.G.R.S.) One who searches original and published records, understands all sources of a genealogical nature relating to the areas of his or her specialization, and provides detailed information concerning the contents of the records examined. A C.G.R.S. is not certified to construct a pedigree or prepare a family history.

Certified American Lineage Specialist (C.A.L.S.) One who reconstructs a single line of descent and prepares hereditary-society applications — based upon a sound knowledge of pertinent resources and a skilled appraisal of the authenticity and acceptability of both original source records and compiled printed material. American, in this category, is not limited in meaning to the United States.

Certified American Indian Lineage Specialist (C.A.I.L.S.) One who conducts research to determine descent from a historical Indian tribe indigenous to North America. An individual with this certification will be well versed in the pertinent materials and applicable standards within this specialty.

Certified Genealogist (C.G.) One who is proficient in all types of genealogical research and analysis, is qualified to resolve pedigree problems of all types, and is experienced in the compilation of well-crafted family histories.

To locate a professional genealogist near you, consult with your local librarian or genealogical society. Your local library may have the *Directory of Professional Genealogists*, which is cross-referenced by specialization. The Family History Library in Salt Lake City (801)240-2331 also has a list of accredited genealogists.

AUDIO-VIDEO RESEARCH GUIDES

Your local public library's video center may have a copy of Part I and Part II of *Do Your Family Tree* with research advice.

Two companies that produce do-it-yourself video history kits are Life Stories/A Video Legacy (a notebook of text, a personal history questionnaire and an audio cassette), for information call (800)2R-STORY; and Gift of Heritage, a one hour instructional video (call (800)224-8511).

UNEXPECTED MARKETS FOR YOUR RESEARCH

Ever since her first grandchildren began arriving, Zell Schulman had been telling them "Bubbie's Myseh's" (Yiddish for Grandmothers' Stories). They were stories about her own growing up, interspersed with bits of Jewish history, traditions, customs and foods. When she decided to write some of them down, she found a market for them, periodically, with *The National Jewish Post and Opinion*.

A magazine available in many public libraries that might help with memory recall is *Reminisce*, published at 5400 S. 60th St., Greendale, WI 53129. It's glossy, amply illustrated and, in addition to sparking your memories, may be an outlet for some of your *own* reminiscenses. The only payment is publication, but that may be gratifying to an elderly relative, for example, about whom you've written.

Bob Baxter's experience in creating the videotape of his son (mentioned in chapter two) prompted him to offer his Video Transfer service to others who wanted to trace a family tree through generations, or create some other personal story of a child's growing up or school years or family holidays. For a fee, he assembles up to one hundred photos and slides with music or titles added, if desired, for a personalized gift or keepsake on VHS tape.

While Baxter's video is primarily a collection of still photographs and slides, others who wanted to create a video history of a relative for a special occasion to supplement their written family history have either hired a professional videographer or made their own home movie.

Caring for her eighty-nine-year-old mother-in-law prompted Gayle Wood to establish a video service called Memories: VideoKeepsakes. "I didn't realize until after she had moved into a Tennessee nursing home to be near her other children how much of her life I had shared with her by being here and helping her. I'm sure we talked about things even her own children had forgotten."

Gayle uses professional videographers but she prepares extensively before the "shoot" by interviewing the senior in advance and researching the subject. Gayle is not in view of the camera, only her voice is heard asking questions to prompt the memories. "I also ask clients to surround themselves with a few important pieces of memorabilia that they can talk about."

The interview takes about an hour and is edited to a half-hour final version. For people who want to create their own video family history, Gayle says, "video technique is nowhere near as important as asking thoughtful questions and allowing time for answers. It's fun and meets a deep need of most older ones to tell their story for posterity."

Video "Shelf-Life"

With the advent of the video camera, many families began recording new babies, weddings and anniversary parties on videotape rather than with still photography. But Frank Beacham, a video producer and writer was quoted in a 1994 Knight-Ridder News Service story about the limited life of videotape. Because humidity attacks the binder on the tape, the video image degrades over time. That's why he points out that professional video producers make copies of valuable material every five years. Unless technology changes this situation in the future, you might want to consider periodically checking the important video parts of your history and recopying if you see the picture starting to deteriorate.

JOIN A LOCAL GENEALOGICAL SOCIETY

Most persons researching their family history want to do it themselves and relish the thrill of discovery. Others after months squinting at poor handwriting on microfilm readers or running into dead ends, feel discovery has turned into drudgery.

Joining a local genealogical society can not only renew your energy but revitalize your search with suggestions you might never have thought of on your own. In her book *Genealogy is More Than Charts*, writer Lorna Duane Smith says:

> . . . finding out that your family thinks you've got to be crazy to spend all that time in research, you long for a group that understands you . . . Let me tell you of my first experience. My phone call put me in touch with an enthusiastic person who gave me the address of a school, and mentioned that they meet once a month in the media center.
>
> After attending, signing in the guest book, and receiving a name

badge, I was asked to introduce myself along with other visitors during the business meeting. I felt like one of the group already when I gave the four surnames I was researching. Several members spoke to me afterward. They also directed me to their computerized surname indexes, which have all the names the members are researching, and the locality. I found a member that very night who shares the same ancestor with me. Needless to say, I joined.

The National Genealogical Society, of course, offers not local social contact, but a national conference with seminars and workshops, a Library Loan Service, a Computer Bulletin Board, a home study course in genealogy, a Research Service and extensive publications. For details on publications, membership, and membership and other fees, write the National Genealogical Society at 4527 17th St. N., Arlington, VA 22207-2399.

CAVEAT EMPTOR

Persons researching their ancestors can sometimes become embroiled in expensive but ineffective claims to valuable inheritances. A January 1, 1994, *New York Times* article, for example, describes the experiences of the Pennsylvania Association of Edwards Heirs "whose 3,260 members claim ownership by birthright of about 77 acres of real estate in lower Manhattan. . . .

> "The associations's claim arises from a man it says is a common ancestor, Robert Edwards, an 18th century pirate, who, the group says, held legal title to the tract. Similar assertions, one made as long ago as World War I, have been rebuffed by at least three courts and the New York State Legislature.
>
> "But the lure of a windfall fortune has proved durable and irresistible."

WRITING REMINDER: DRAMATIZING FACTS

In the search for the "facts" about your ancestors, don't overlook the visual images that their lives evoke and your readers want to know about. In this chapter Hannelore Hahn uses a dramatic scene to describe her sudden flight from Germany as a young Jewish schoolgirl in 1937. As you make notes about certain events for your family or personal memoir, keep in mind those circumstances that lend themselves to dramatization with dialogue, rather than straight narration of how grandfather did this and then that happened.

When you see a movie that has been made from a book, do you ever check to see how the author handled the subject and then what the director did? Perhaps by visualizing your memoir as a movie, you can "direct" your writing to show the reader the visual images and dialogue that bring your family to life.

Chapter Eight

Organizing Your Resources

A freelance writer wrote me once to say that her problem in writing was like trying to stuff an octopus in a box. You may begin to feel like that as your library notes, interview tapes, and photocopies of official records are beginning to pile up on a desk or table. How to keep track of what you have and where to find it when you're ready to start writing?

FILING METHODS

If you're writing a family history, you have probably decided to concentrate on your father's and mother's families. A logical way to organize your research would be to create file folders with those names. You would also include a folder for each of your grandparents' families, as well.

Within the family surname file, information may be divided various ways: such as folders for correspondence, newspaper articles about the family, death notices, cemetery photos, photocopies of wills, deeds, and other legal and church documents. You might also photocopy pertinent family photographs for the appropriate folder, then return the original photos to the family photo album.

(If you have sophisticated computer equipment, you may have already taken advantage of its capabilities. For example, one researcher installed a color scanner interface to his computer, which allows him to include photographs within his family history files. Large local computer stores can quote you prices on this type of equipment. Or national photocopy chains, such as Kinko's, may offer this service for a fee.)

Some researchers break down family names into states showing the immigration pattern of the family. Others concentrate on census records for a particular county when ancestors have lived in the same country for generations.

Family tree charts in your files will be more elaborate — showing many lateral connections — than those you would probably write about in your more focused family history.

Your files may also contain beautifully illustrated booklets you've obtained from the foreign area from which your ancestors came. You may have created a mini-map to show the location of your ancestors' houses, schools, churches in their village and its relation to the nearest larger city in that country today.

Indexing Your Resources

You may find it helpful to maintain a running index of names or subject matter with a notation of where the material is located. (For an example of how I do this, see the end of chapter twelve.) You may start out with so few folders that you can remember where everything is filed. But as your research proceeds and you gather information about an increasing number of subjects, without an index you may forget where you filed information.

Background Research Files

Among the folders in your files will be some containing your notes about the times in which your ancestors lived — notes you gathered from reading books about the period. Family history writer Sue Kruse says:

I read a lot and took extensive notes on the places my ancestors came from and what was happening when they lived there.

For example one branch moved from Virginia over the Blue Ridge Mountains and into Kentucky just a few years after Daniel Boone began his settlement in Kentucky. By reading all about Boone, I was able to include in my narrative that my family lived in the same valley where Boone's son was killed just two years earlier; and later that they moved out of Powell's Valley due to Indian troubles the same year Boone's brother was killed by the Shawnees in Kentucky.

Another branch lived in New Hampshire and by reading the history of the town of Exeter, I learned that several members of this branch had participated in a rebellion against the English-appointed governor, and had been arrested in the seventeenth century.

I haven't been to Ireland or Ohio, but by reading both current travel guides and histories, I was able to describe in my narrative what County Cavan was like and what Tuscarawas County was like when our ancestors lived there. I also found reading American history helped me get the feel for the time and place. What motivated a family to pack up and move west at a certain point in time? In one case, by reading history, I learned the country was in a depression that year and maybe that was the motivation. In the case of an ancestor who moved from a mill in Cincinnati to a farm in Indiana, maybe it had to do with the advent of steam power and the closing of mills.

IMAGINED LIVES

But what about the personalities of those ancestors you have never met? Without stories handed down to you by their descendants, you must use your imagination to determine what kinds of people you believe your ancestors must have been, given what you have been able to learn about them and the times they lived in.

In her book *Living by The Word*, a collection of prose pieces, Alice Walker touches on this "imagining" when discussing a black poet and writer's criticism of one of her poems:

> Mr. Cheatwood thinks, apparently, that I should be ashamed to mention, to "advertise" my great-great-grandmother's rape. He assumes an interest, on my part, in being other than black, of being "white." I, on the other hand, feel it is my blackness (not my skin color so much as the culture that nurtured me) that causes me to open myself, acknowledge my soul and its varied components, take risks, affirm everyone I can find (for I, too, have been called everything but a child of God), and that inasmuch as my great-great-grandmother was forced to endure rape and the birth of a child she couldn't have wanted, as well, the least I can do is mention it. In truth, this is all the her story of her that I know. But if I affirm that, then I can at least imagine what the rest of her life must have been like. And this, I believe, has some importance for us all.

YOUR PERSONAL STORY

If your book is not a family history but rather a search for personal revelation, you may want to organize your files in different ways. You'll have a folder for immediate family background, of course, but also a collection of diaries and journals organized by dates, or occupations, or spiritual development, or relationships, or some other unifying theme.

For example, Howard Fast was at the peak of his career as a best-selling author in 1947 when he joined the Communist Party. He remained in the party until 1957 and was sentenced to prison for refusing to give names to the House Unamerican Activities Committee. His book *Being Red* is a memoir, as its book jacket says, "of one man's rise from poverty, his courage in the face of a hostile government, his struggles of conscience and the terrible price paid for good intentions."

Here is an excerpt from Fast's closing chapter which deals with the unifying theme of his memoir:

> What am I to say at the end of these long memoirs? Do I regret those years in the Communist Party? But regret is a meaningless word. Would I do it over again? That is equally meaningless. No human being is given a second time around. It is a time gone by, and most of us who played our roles during that time are dead. We were not a long-lived generation, and we gave of our lives and our strength unsparingly. In the party, I found ambition, rigidity, narrowness, and hatred; I also found love and dedication and high courage and integrity—and some of the noblest human beings I have ever known. I could not finish these memoirs without saying that, even knowing the sneers such a statement will evoke. Be damned to all of that! A man who will traduce those who stood with him in battle is not worth much.
>
> I have tried to tell a truthful story here, but when one writes of the past, one writes of a fluid situation, changed already in the memory of those who lived through it and fated to endless change in the future as each generation rewrites history. Also, there is so much that I left out—as one must, or write endlessly—that this is at best only a small part of the story of the times—indeed only part of my own story. I could write a book of equal length dealing only with the remarkable woman I married and of our struggle to remain married and raise a family during those years.
>
> I was forty-two years old when I left the Communist Party. I had joined it as one of the most praised and honored writers in the United States. I resigned from it as a man whose past had been totally obscured, who had been barred from publishing, who had been slandered and reviled as no other writer in American history. I suppose that in itself is a distinction of sorts. In 1957, when my action became clear to the Russians, they joined in this litany of

hatred and slander—after which they consigned me to nonexistence.

Well, I have lived to see a new America and a new Soviet Union, and the real possibility of peace, not only between these two superpowers, but among all the nations of Europe. Our desperate struggle for peace had perhaps some small effect, as did our struggle for the rights of the poor and the working people of America.

Dealing With Personal Trauma

If a personal story rather than a family history is the purpose of your book, your research efforts may be restricted to your own memory and how much of it you desire to recall. If part of it involves a trauma, you may be interested in the work of psychologist James W. Pennebaker, Ph.D., of Southern Methodist University, who says, "We've studied writing's dealing with divorce, death of a spouse and other problems, and it's typically had a positive influence."

In a 1992 paper presented to the American Psychological Association, Dr. Pennebaker reported, "Since 1986, my students, colleagues, and I have been exploring the value of writing and talking about traumatic experiences. Across several studies, we and others have found that individuals who are randomly assigned to write about deeply personal topics for three to five consecutive days are subsequently healthier than controls who write about relatively superficial topics . . . (as measured by) significant drops in health center visits in the six months after the study."

In conducting other tests to discover *why* writing helped, Dr. Pennebaker and his colleagues discovered that, "The construction of a coherent story together with the expression of negative emotions work together in therapeutic writing."

More details on how the tests were conducted, the kinds of traumas the subjects were working through, and other values of writing in health, learning and creativity are given in Dr. Pennebaker's book *Opening Up: The Healing Power of Confiding in Others.*

STORAGE REMINDERS

Preservation specialists at historical societies remind us that newspapers are very fragile. It might be a good idea to make a photocopy of newspaper clippings that you want to save. Use acid-free paper or a good bond paper. Also, photo albums should be of "archival" materials—acid-free paper, no adhesive mountings, etc. A catalog you might want to investigate is one put out for photographers called Light Impressions (800) 828-9859.

Bulkier items like interviews with relatives recorded on audio- or videocassettes, old photographs too big to fit in photo albums and other materials should be stored in covered boxes and shelved away from sunlight, attic heat and basement dampness. Preferably the boxes should be made of acid-free materials, not metals.

The big old houses of yesterday often had a sewing room or other room not always in use where things could be stored. Perhaps if your present home has a den, you've already appropriated that for your writing corner and can keep your files nearby for easy access. A walk through the nearest warehouse-type office supplies company like Staples or Office Max might give you some storage ideas you haven't thought of. If no store is nearby, you might want to get a catalog by writing Office Max, Inc., 3605 Warrensville Center Rd., Shaker Heights, OH 44122; or Staples, Inc., P.O. Box 1020, Westboron, MA 01581.

One of the most important bits of advice is "Keep Filing Current— Don't Let Data Pile Up!" Whatever organizing method you choose, add new research notes and information to it as you go. That way, you'll always know where you've been and where to go next.

WRITING REMINDER: A PRELIMINARY OUTLINE

At the time you decided on the focus for your book, you began to concentrate your research on topics that would illuminate for your readers those particular people and times.

Now is the time to survey the material you've gathered so far and arrive at a preliminary outline for your book. It might start out as simply a list of topics that you want to be sure to cover. It may still contain some questions about topics you're not sure you want to include.

This initial list may lead to later ones in which you decide on the sequence in which you'll cover your topics. This is particularly important if your book does not follow a chronological order. As Theodore A. Rees Cheney points out in *Writing Creative Nonfiction*:

> A writer of nonfiction will often spend a great amount of time considering structure before ever beginning the composition itself. Some writers claim that they just start writing, and that a structure gradually imposes itself. The trouble with this method is that it may result in a lot of wheel spinning, revision, and rewriting once

the structure magically emerges from the mist. . . .

Faced with the search for structure, sit back and sift, shuffle, and stack. Do any patterns, or things that look like possible patterns, take shape? — even a vague shape that promises structural potential? . . . Consider as many as come to the surface, and think about the possible implications and ramifications of putting each into effect. Don't consider only the problems each presents; think about the positive possibilities. . . . It could go on forever, but at some point . . . you have to fish or cut bait. I believe that the waiting and weighing pay off.

In subsequent chapters in this book you'll see how some authors handled their opening chapters; the devices they used to keep the reader moving through the middle of the book and end their books satisfactorily. Their examples will help you organize *your* material to its best advantage.

Chapter Nine

How Much Research Is Enough?

A dedicated ancestor hunter will say, "It's too much fun to stop now." A researcher whose current interest is only a look at two or three generations back might say, "I'll try to make these relatives into a lively family history my children and grandchildren can relate to *now,* and decide later about researching further back." The writer of a personal memoir may say, "Self-understanding is a continuing process, so this could turn out to be more than one book."

It all comes down to what your original purpose was in writing your book. Notice I said "writing" your book. Playing detective is fun, and historical research is fascinating, but if writing a book is your goal, you have to decide at some point, "Do I have enough information to satisfy my readers or myself *for now?*"

A CHECKLIST FOR WRITING FAMILY HISTORIES

Use this checklist to help you decide if you are meeting the expectations of your book's readers.

- ✔ Are you writing about just your father's family, your mother's or both?
- ✔ If either or both were married more than once, are you concentrating only on the family of which you were a part, or including half brothers and step-sisters?
- ✔ If you've reached a dead end in some area of research, have you asked your local library, historical society or genealogical group for advice? Do you need to, or will readers be satisfied with the information you have?
- ✔ Have you learned not only who some of your ancestors were but also what their daily lives were like when and where they lived?

✔ Can your readers envision your ancestors' values and attitudes toward life — and death?

For some families, blind alleys only mark the end of volume one. They save unanswered questions for future books as new contact sources are discovered.

Others, whose audience is primarily children or grandchildren, confine their books to those specific generations about whom enough is known to make their history relate more directly to our own.

A CHECKLIST FOR WRITING PERSONAL MEMOIRS

Use this checklist as a guide to determine if you are fulfilling your intended goal. Depending on the purpose of your book:

✔ Have you covered the major turning points in your life?

✔ Does your reader understand the educational, social and family framework from which you came?

✔ Does the reader know you as a person — as separate from your role as a husband or mother or professional career person?

✔ If you have included some ancestors, does the reader have a clear picture of them in relation to their times and why they are important to you?

✔ Do your readers know how you feel about your life — what you're happiest about, proud of, regretful of, amused by, unreconciled to, thankful for?

For either family or personal memoir, only you can answer the question: Does the research I have answer my book's purpose for now?

To see if there are some areas of research you may have overlooked, or memories you want to include, let's examine what some others have done.

FAMILY HISTORY RESEARCH WITH MAPS

Grover Buxton has spent forty-seven years researching his ancestors and has eight volumes of their history so far. "My great-grandfather, Jacob Klee, wrote his autobiography in 1893," says Buxton, "and it was his manuscript that got me interested in genealogy." Klee's autobiography describes the family discussions in Munster, Germany, about the opportunities in America vs. the safety of the known at home; the decision to take the seven week ocean voyage; the cramped unventilated steerage sleeping bunks with periodic "fumigation;" the joyous arrival in New

York and subsequent life in America. The government of Muenster-maifeld, Germany, had Jacob Klee's autobiography edited and published as a story of life in America by one of its native sons.

In one volume of his family history, Grover Buxton's research on Maryland ancestor, John Buxton, reveals to us not only the historical background of the time but the way genealogical researchers use maps and other government records. Here's an excerpt from

JOHN BUXTON OF BUXTON'S DELIGHT

The first written record of John Buxton is dated June 13, 1734, at which time he secured a patent for one hundred acres of land in Prince George's County, Province of Maryland.The patent reads in part:

"We do therefore grant unto him the same John Buxton all that tract or parcel of land called Buxton's Delight lying in the aforesaid county and beginning at a bounded red oak standing near the head of a glade of Seneca, and in the main fork of said branch about three miles above the Indian Path. . . ."

Regarding the name "Buxton's Delight" — colonial Maryland farms were often given names, more through tradition than for any legal reason. The naming of each tract of land was a traditional Scottish system.

Some of the other farms in this county bore names that ranged from the whimsical to the downright funny. Here are a few:

Girl's Portion	Let No Man Deceive You
Dung Hill	Trouble Enough Indeed
Bear Neck	Pork Plenty if No Thieves
Easy Come By	Gittings Ha Ha
Dispute	Clean Drinking

On August 4th, 1753, John was granted an additional 760 acres.

Looking at the configuration of the new Buxton's Delight, one wonders how or why he ended up with such a strange looking farm. Was he picking out the good land and rejecting the areas he couldn't use? Or was he merely taking whatever land was left after someone else had appropriated the choice parcels? Up in New England, and later in Ohio, it was the custom to lay out the land in rectangular grids divided into ranges, townships, and sections. But in the southern colonies lands were subdivided among individuals using physical objects such as trees, stones, stakes, ownership of adjoining lands and other things of temporal existence only. This is known as "Indiscriminate Location Plan" or the "Southern" or "Virginia Plan." In terms of real estate John was pretty well-off. The average landholding in this area in 1752 was well under 200 acres, and many a landowner had no more than 20 acres to his name.

Mr. Buxton found a map (see next page) of his ancestor's unusually shaped farm in the Hall of Records in Annapolis, Maryland. He reminds his readers:

> In modern geography this places the location of the farm about two miles north of present-day Gaithersburg along Route 355, the Frederick Road.

ANCESTOR OCCUPATIONS

Which of your family members had occupations that either no longer exist, or are rarely understood by today's young people? Was one of your grandparents a steam locomotive engineer? Did some relative own a livery stable? A streetcar company? Some background details on these and many other older occupations are readily available in libraries.

For example, the only riverboats some Americans know about today are gambling casinos, but in the yesterdays before railroads and automobiles and airplanes, riverboats provided a colorful career for young men. Captain Alan Bates, whose memoir is in the Cincinnati library, here describes his first job on the river:

CAPTAIN L. BIRCH McBRIDE

I met him as a result of friendship with his son, George, and this resulted in my first river employment. Captain Birch had bought the WILLIAM EDENBORN, the SARAH EDENBORN and their auxiliary fleet and he intended to bring them to Harrods Creek from Torras, Louisiana. I begged a job as deckhand. . . .

In addition to the two steamboats the fleet consisted of two transfer barges with high "bridge truss" framing, a derrick boat with pile driver, a floating drydock (really an L-shaped wooden box that could be submerged alongside a boat hull without docking the boat) and a "corking" (caulking) flat. The pile driver hammer was on a flatcar at the top of the levee. . . .

The first thing we did was to explore the boats. The SARAH was much finer than the WILLIAM since she had a lot of turned

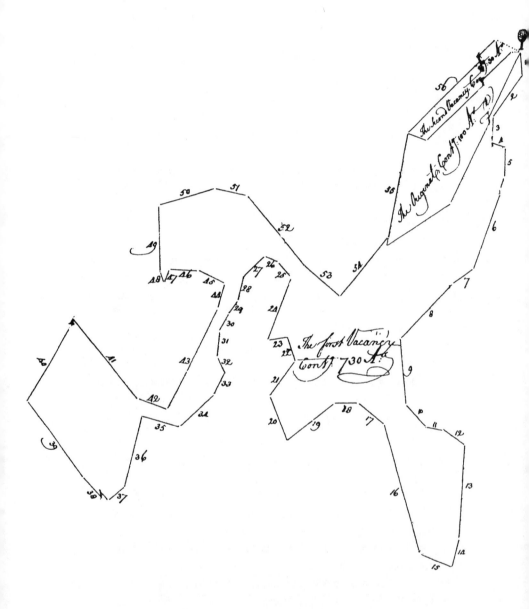

mahogany brightwork railings in her forward cabin. I remember swinging around the after corner of the cabin, hitting a hog chain with my head so hard that my ears rang. These boats were fairly fast, as towboats go, and had large paddlewheels. Both burned bunker C fuel oil. The boats were dusty, but otherwise clean. I found a box of weevily cereal in the pantry, took it to the bow and threw it into the river. G.W. saw me do this and cautioned me, "Don't let the old man catch you throwing anything over the bow — it's supposed to be bad luck for a boat to run over her own garbage — besides, that's the worst place to ever fall in the river. . . ."

. . . And so, up the river we went. All went smoothly until we got just above Greenville Bridge, a notoriously dangerous place. Captain McBride had told me, "Batesy, don't never run on my boat — when somebody runs I think he's in trouble." Right there above that bridge the WILLIAM stuck a drift log through the wheel, cast it up against the stern bulkhead and raised hell generally. I was still in my "watch-the-wheel-turn" days and saw it happen. The chambermaid and cook, who were just inside the stern bulkhead and doing the laundry, went flying up through the boat. I was cool. I walked to the pilothouse and asked, "Does it make any difference if the paddlewheel just fell apart?"

The effect was electric. Bells rang and the engines stopped. . . .

The pilot backed the boat down through the bridge and we tied up to the Arkansas bank. By that time the WILLIAM's paddlewheel was a genuine brushpile. We were prepared, however, for we had loaded enough green oak to build two paddlewheels a couple of days before at Vicksburg.

Captain Bates went on to become master (captain) of steam or motor passenger vessels on the U.S. Inland Rivers and a naval architect who has designed thirty-three of today's river excursion boats. He is the author of six books, including *Do It Yourself: An Autobiography*, from which the above excerpt is taken.

SENSORY IMPRESSIONS

Like any detective, have you used all five of your senses, not just your eyes, to read documents and do library research?

What tastes do you associate with a favorite treat as a child? The first foreign food you sampled on a travel? The salt in your eyes from perspiration working in a hot garden? What sounds do you associate with favorite radio programs, outdoor sports events, the voice of a school playmate?

Dr. Trudelle Thomas, professor at Xavier University in Ohio, has been an advisor to senior citizen groups on how to write their family histories, but she also encourages young people to be part of this activity, too. Her English class in "Life Writing: Journals, Memoirs and Autobiography" focuses on writing in each of these genres. Here's an excerpt from student Meghan Walker's:

MEMORIES OF GRANDMA

Most of my memories of her are sensual images of a woman constantly in motion. The only emotion I remember her evoking in me was one of unconditional love; the rest of my memories of her are based purely on the five senses. Her language was one of the things that amazed me. The mysterious German phrases that were constantly rolling off her tongue were a source of amusement and puzzlement to me; I never understood what she was saying but it was fun guessing what she meant. Her favorite saying was "Osk kish kalish finnemack" or something like that, which, roughly translated, meant "stop messing around." Whenever any of us were bad, she would threaten us with the "kochlefa" (the wooden spoon) but I was never frightened because I knew how soft-hearted she was.

I thought she was magical, not just because of her language but because of her culinary abilities. She brought many recipes with her from Austria-Hungary which produced such wonders as thick, greasy sugar doughnuts, moggstrudel with jelly, and grunskucha, a deliciously thick homemade bread. Her Christmas cookies were even better: linzer cookies in the shape of gingerbread men or reindeer with green and red sprinkles on top and sugar cookies with nut and plum jelly filling. As a small child I was awestruck at how fast her nimble fingers could produce such delectable treats.

While it is easy for me to talk about her life, I often hesitate when it comes to discussing her death. I knew she had lung cancer and the thought that she would "die," whatever that meant, was never far from my thoughts. I must have known she was dead, even before my dad came to tell me.

I have only a dim recollection of timidly entering her room to see her lying pale as a ghost on her bed, but what my reaction was

I can only guess at. Odd that I remember that bed and bedspread. I always had a hard time climbing onto the bed because it was too far up, at least for a nine-year-old. The bedspread was pure white, with long white tassels on the end of it and a diamond pattern throughout. I spent many a happy Friday night sprawled out on it watching the "Dukes of Hazzard"; I was also allowed to watch grandma's soaps with her after school if I did not make a lot of noise.

What aromas or fragrances are associated in *your* memory with certain experiences — freshly mowed grass in the days before air conditioning when families sat on the front porch? The animals on your first visit to an uncle's farm?

What does your sense of touch bring to mind? The fabric of your mother's party dress? Your father's whiskers? A first lover?

What other sensory impressions stick in your memory — and for what reason? I remember my fear as a child of walking across a country railroad trestle the first time my father took me fishing with my brother. I remember the sense of exhilaration when I caught my first tiny sunfish.

MEMORY REINFORCERS

Old movies, now being released on video, can be a source of memories. But VCR owners also have access to "Flikbaks," a series of thirty-minute videos featuring nostalgic film footage of the past. They're set up by years, such as 1930, 1939, 1941, 1950, 1964, etc. If you can't find them in your local video store, call (800)582-2000.

Your car's tape deck is another source of background history. The "Ride With Me" audiocassette series was produced for Interstate highway travelers who want to know the history of the land alongside the Interstate highway network. For example, if you're driving along I-91 or I-95 in Connecticut, you'll learn about that state's colonization, Revolutionary War General Israel Putnam and showman P.T. Barnum. For a list of the tapes and states covered, call (800)752-3195.

Some public libraries may have copies of an audio-cassette series called "Do You Remember," produced by the Great American Audio Corporation. The four-cassette series on the 1940s, for example, cover in one-hour each "The Sounds of the '40s," "American Political Scene," "Life Style," and "Headlines and Sports." Other series also look at the 1950s and 1960s.

Have you ever looked through a family photo album and tried to affix a date to some names inked-in on the white bordered bottom of an old snapshot? Sometimes the locale will be a clue; other times the style of clothes or hair, narrows it to a specific decade. In the twentieth century, newsmagazines like *Time* and *Newsweek* and photomagazines like *Life* and *Look* offer good reminders of "the way we were." Some libraries have a collection of the Time-Life Books series *This Fabulous Century*. Each book is a photo/text compilation of one decade of the twentieth century.

For those writers attempting to recapture the times in which their ancestors lived a hundred years ago, a handy reference is *The Writer's Guide to Everyday Life in the 1800s*. Chapters on household equipment, clothing, transportation, occupations, the Civil War, along with chronologies of events can supplement your own ancestors' records of the times.

The World Almanac is a good place to review a chronology of events. The first edition was published more than a hundred years ago and it has been published annually since 1886. Its current subtitle, *And Book of Facts*, makes it a good general reference source as well as a tool for pinpointing historical events that affected you and your family's lives.

Don't overlook the possibility of just punching in your own family name on the library computer, or looking up your surname in the card catalog. Someone you don't know of may have already done some research on your family. You may also want to just browse in selective portions of the library for contact leads and ideas.

Most public libraries use the Dewey Decimal System in classifying books, while many college libraries use the Library of Congress numbering system. Some numbers in each library type you'll probably refer to most frequently are:

Dewey Decimal		Library of Congress	
929.1	Genealogy	CS 21	Genealogy
929.2	Family History	CS 71	Family History U.S.
973	U.S. History	E 178	U.S. History

A detailed list of other library call numbers—including those for Colonial, Revolutionary, and Civil War periods of American history and those for individual states—appears in *The Genealogist's Companion and Sourcebook*, by Emily Anne Croom (see the Bibliography).

If you are looking up biographies or autobiographies of individuals who may be potential ancestors, you'll find that up until 1965 many public libraries using the Dewey Decimal System indicated biographies with a simple letter "B" designation, and shelved them alphabetically by the last name of the subject of the biography. After 1965 some libraries began to file biographies and autobiographies in the categories related to the subject, which is how the Library of Congress System does it. If, for example, a person were known for his or her activities in the field of education or medicine or science, that's where the biography or autobiography would be located. Family histories that give historical information about the area in which the family is located are classed with books *about* the area (e.g., a family history of a prominent New York City family would be classed with the history of New York City in 974.71). Persons not easily classifiable by those methods would be in the more general family history, Dewey Decimal 929.2 numbers.

There are many specialized genealogical periodicals covering specific family names or localities. Annual features on these and other topics also appear in *Everton's Genealogical Helper*, which is probably in your library.

WRITING REMINDER: CHARACTERIZATION

As you saw in the checklists early in this chapter, the reader wants to know your characters as well-rounded people. Not just what they looked like physically, but what their attitudes were, their values, how they influence you yet today. People reveal themselves to the reader in these ways:

- ✔ by what they say
- ✔ by what they do
- ✔ by what their contemporaries say about them
- ✔ by what we can discern about their relationship to the times in which they lived

In describing a person's physical appearance, you might say: "He was a neatly dressed businessman." Or, you might create a more detailed image, as Susan Lowry Rardin described a character in a *McCall's* story called "Pioneers."

> Listening, he looked down at his feet, narrow in their stylish shoes. Above them were trim ankles in high dark socks, trouser legs tidy and sharply pressed. It was part of a professional appearance that he had developed with care and pride. His feet did not look remotely like a pioneer's.

A family history or memoir writer may choose to incorporate descrip-

tion along with dialogue and other revelations of character in a scene —
at a dinner party, for example.

In her self-published book *Navy WAVE — Memories of World War II*,
Lieutenant Helen Clifford Gunter describes one of her WAVE colleagues this way:

> I told her a story another WAVE in the Supply Corps had
> recounted over dinner at Tabard Inn one night.
>
> Young Ensign Wilma Bangert was a paymaster, and one day
> she'd been sent to pay off the crew of a vessel just returned from
> the war zone. The Navy paid in cash, not checks, she explained
> to her fascinated listeners, and only officers were allowed to handle
> money.
>
> "Of course, I don't actually carry it. A sailor guard goes with
> me, and he carries a satchel full of bills."
>
> Wilma was a petite, curly-headed blond with baby blue eyes
> and a peaches and cream complexion. Always immaculately
> dressed, she reminded me of a Dresden doll in a perky sailor suit.
> I struggled to envision tiny Wilma marching up the gangway of a
> docked warship, followed by a burly sailor with a satchel full of
> greenbacks.
>
> "Aren't you afraid of being robbed?" one of us asked, fascinated.
>
> "No, I have a gun," Wilma explained blithely.
>
> "What's it like? Do you get to talk to the men? Ask about
> battles they've been in?"
>
> "I don't talk to them at all, I just pay them off. Those men are
> rough."
>
> "What do you mean, rough? Do they push and shove, or what?"
>
> Wilma hesitated, then in a shocked tone she explained, "They
> curse." After a dramatic pause she added, "and in my presence,
> too."
>
> She looked bewildered when we laughed.

Whether you've used description, dialogue or narration have you
researched — and thought, or imagined enough — to help us know your
family or yourself as well as we can?

Chapter Ten

Format and Writing Style

N ow that you have gathered your notes and mementos and recalled the decisions you made in the first three chapters about the purpose of your book and its intended readers, it's time to think about the form it will take and the writing style you will use.

FAMILY HISTORY FORMATS

If your goal is to write a more formal family history, then you could consider a *chronological format* that traces the origins of the family down to the present generation.

If your goal is to write an informal memoir for just the immediate family, then perhaps you could consider a format that is simply a *Letter to Our Grandchildren*. It would not be concerned with distant ancestors but rather the daily lives of the previous generation.

If your goal is to write a family history that would be a contribution to your community because your family played an important role over generations in the same region, then your format would be more of a *Community History* — "The Smith Family of Carroll County," for example. Your story would be confined to just that place and time, focusing on the roles of just those people.

Other Formats

Do you have a different idea on how to organize your family history?

One family historian, Laura Tesseneer, chose to combine reminiscences of eight Kentucky sisters along with a heritage of good cooking in *The Wyman Sisters Cookbook*. Here are part of her memories of her mother, Bernice, a teacher of "domestic science" (now called home economics or home arts), and her Aunt Annie:

Alma, Cate and Ruby lived in Lowes during the time many of us were growing up and we have fond memories of the wonderful Sunday dinners served at their homes. The "first table" served ten to fourteen adults while the cousins had to occupy themselves freezing the ice cream and waiting impatiently for their turn at the "second table." The wait was well repaid, however, when we had a chance to start eating the fried chicken, biscuits, gravy, fresh vegetables from the garden, relishes, delicious pies and cakes, and the ice cream often made with peaches from the nearby orchards.

Mother Bernice was the youngest sister. She recalled the gentle life of her rural village with pleasure. She treasured little gifts given her by the tinker who came by occasionally and she remembered events of her early life that centered around the people. During her entire life she continued to show a remarkable joy in the little things of life. To the time of her death, January 30, 1982, at ninety years of age, she would call her children or grandchildren on the telephone and report excitedly, "My amaryllis bloomed today!" "Elizabeth took me shopping today," or "Guess how many points I scored at Scrabble last night," etc.

Annie and Mother were the only sisters who had any formal experience in the preparation of foods. Annie, who was widowed early, went to South Dakota and spent some time as cook for a mining camp. She later returned to Kentucky and for several years was dietitian at Georgetown Baptist College in Georgetown, Kentucky. After her retirement she went to live with her daughter, Lillian, in Mayfield, where she continued to cook delicious foods. The little tea parties she prepared for us when we were young girls (Rebecca Jean, myself, and neighborhood friends) received the attention often reserved for fancy adult functions — tiny sandwiches made with thinly sliced bread, embroidered linens on the table, and a centerpiece of flowers, often bright orange nasturtiums. The table was sometimes placed in a small back yard where tiger lilies and other flowers bloomed.

Here's a recipe for Bernice's Bread and Butter Pickles from the cookbook. Notice the *background family history story* that goes with it:

BREAD AND BUTTER PICKLES

This recipe originally came from a neighbor, "Miss Alice," and is always referred to as Miss Alice's pickle recipe. Mother rarely served a Sunday or "company" dinner without serving some of

"Miss Alice's" pickles and some of her own pickled beets. "Miss Alice" was not really a single lady, but lived with her husband, "Mr. George," and their parrot, "Polly," in the house across Main Street from Bernice and her family. Polly was an interesting bird and would call each of us by name. She could sing several bars of the "Old Time Religion," and professed to be both a Republican and a Cambellite.

1 gallon cucumbers, 8 small onions, and 2 green peppers — sliced thin, sprinkled with ½ C salt, then soaked in ice water for three hours (keep adding ice to water, if necessary). Drain and pat dry with clean towels.
Make a syrup by using:
5 C *sugar*
1½ t *tumeric*
½ t *ground cloves*
2 T *mustard seed*
1 t *celery seed*
5 C *vinegar*
When this mixture boils thoroughly, pour pickles in. Scald but do not let boil. (The cucumbers and onions will begin to look transparent, just before boiling.) Pack sterilized jars with the pickles, then seal. Do not use the pickles for two weeks as this time is required for completing the pickling process.

What other formats suggest themselves to you for your family history? Has the diversity of their *occupations* given you an idea for chapters built around — if not "Tinker, Tailor, Soldier, Sailor" or "Doctor, Lawyer, Merchant Chief" — some other interesting groups?

Do you have a wealth of photographic material but not much ancestral detail and want to create a *Pictorial History* of the Jones Family?

Are you a computer freak who would like to transfer your research into a *Computer Graphics Family History?*

Options open to you are limited only by the information you gather and your imagination. Here is a list of other possibilities discussed either later in this chapter or elsewhere in this book:

✔ the history of the _____ family
✔ an oral history on audiocassette
✔ a community history

✔ a video family history
✔ a photo/text family history
✔ a personal memoir as a book of poems
✔ a family history as a collection of short stories or a novel

FAMILY HISTORY STYLES

If you have accumulated some family histories written by your own ancestors, you've discovered that most of them were written as narratives (the author tells what happened) in the third person and the past tense. But they were not always just long pages of who-begat-who. For example, here is a family history first published in 1842 whose scene describes ancestor Moses Van Campen's first tragic encounter with the Seneca Indians:

Taking possession of the rifle, they marched on with their prisoners up the creek, and soon saw before them the appearance of other settlers. It was Van Campen with his father and brother. Securing their prisoners, they crept cautiously up, and suddenly burst upon this unsuspecting company. The father was thrust through with a spear, and as he fell, the Indian released his hold and it stood upright, from his transfixed breast. The warrior, taking his knife from his girdle, scalped his victim, who was lying in the agonies of death, and then cut the throat of the dying man, from ear to ear. The little brother, who stood by Van Campen's side, as he saw this last act, raised his eyes, and with an agonizing look, said, "Father is killed." In an instant the hatchet was gleaming over his head, and the next moment, the little boy, too, was struggling with his dying pangs. Van Campen was seized by two warriors, who each laid hold of one of his arms, and another coming up, took the scalp from his expiring brother and threw him across the fire. Then the warrior who had killed and had been scalping his father, placed one foot on the body, and drew out his spear. But his thirst for blood was still unquenched; with the reeking blade he came towards Van Campen, and aiming at his body made a violent thrust. But the latter perceiving the movement, quickly shrank to one side, and the spear passed through his vest and shirt, and made a slight wound in his flesh. The Indians, who had hold of him, then seized the weapon and secured his arms behind him, appearing to be satisfied with the number slain.

This was a trying scene for Van Campen. His honored father

lay before him, a slaughtered victim. The dark smoke which went curling up towards heaven, from the fire near, bore in its deep folds, the incense of a brother's blood — too darling a sacrifice to be met with an unblanched cheek. Yet what could he say — or, what do? His little brother had no doubt fallen, because of the agony he had expressed for his dying father; should he, too, allow the deep current of his emotions, to break away from their pent-up channel, and overwhelm him with a flood of grief? This would be to expose himself to certain death. Yet he would as soon die, almost, as live, with the deep sorrow that was pressing him down to the earth. But amid the whole, he preserved his countenance erect — not a single muscle of his face betrayed the agitation within — and there was no sign which gave the least indication of fear. The savages, beholding his apparent indifference, ceased from the fury of their rage and the tumultuous wave passed over, leaving him the one survivor of the wrecks around. They took him prisoner and pursued their march up Fishing Creek, leading along two of his father's horses, upon which they had mounted their baggage.

This account, written by J. Niles Hubbard, grandson of Moses Van Campen, goes on to describe Moses's subsequent service in the Revolutionary War, and further skirmishes with the Indians where his courage and cunning earned him the Seneca name Shenawana (Brave Man, Good Fellow). He was mustered out a Major, and took up a civilian career as a wilderness surveyor for the roads and towns to come.

Addison Van Campen, his Midwest descendant says, "I have a poster which advertised a pageant presented by the boys of YMCA Camp Shenawana to commemorate the life of Major Moses for whom the camp was named and have visited his old homeplace in Angelica, New York."

Writing Reminder: Notice in the quoted history excerpt above that in addition to reporting the facts of the encounter with the Indians, the author takes us briefly to the viewpoint of the young boy to tell us what he must have felt at the time he saw his father and brother killed.

The style of this excerpt, as mentioned earlier is in the third person narrative form (*they* marched on, *they* crept cautiously) and the past tense (the Indian *released* his hold, *scalped* his victim). The viewpoint is "omniscient," in that we can see not only what is happening but what the young boy is thinking as well as doing.

Most family history writers find that the third-person narrative form gives them the most flexibility in telling their stories. As to what their ancestors were thinking, if that had not been revealed by the ancestor himself, then the author must decide whether to let his imagination become that "omniscient viewpoint," and let the reader know (perhaps in the Preface to his book) that he took such liberties.

As you can also see, this 1842 family history is written by a person in the voice of his time. *Your* family history will reflect *your* natural voice, not some adopted "literary" voice. You'll prefer the plain word to the fancy, keeping the sentences and paragraphs simple and easy to read. No one expects or even wants the family history to read like *War and Peace*.

To guide *his* organization of his mother's family history, Grover Buxton used a fan chart (page 133) to help him keep track of where ancestors fit into the chronological order of family.

But as you saw in the excerpt in chapter nine, Buxton combined a *past tense* historical account of the lands of one of his forefathers with a *present tense* description of the same land in modern Maryland.

MEMOIR FORMATS AND STYLES

How does the writer handle the first person memoir? To present a persona different from that perceived by those who only know him or her in one aspect? To settle old scores? To search for his or her real self? Or to just tell it all, as it happened, was felt and thought? That's what writer John Cheever did. What will be *your* choice for the style and content of your personal memoir?

When John Cheever died in 1982 he left behind journals estimated between three and four million words. When some of them were first published in *The New Yorker*, Cheever's son, Benjamin, reports in his introduction to the book, *The Journals of John Cheever*, "Most of the people I know reacted with enthusiasm . . . but a few were hurt and bewildered by what they found. Those who broached the subject with me had two questions: Did John Cheever really want this material published? And if so, why?"

Bernard Cheever says yes, his father wanted them published because his father told him so; and "I also think I know why. . . . For much of his life he suffered from a loneliness so acute as to be practically indistinguishable from a physical illness. . . . He meant by his writing to escape this loneliness, to shatter the isolation of others. . . .

"A simpleton might think that bisexuality was the essence of his problem, but of course it was not. Nor was alcoholism. He came to terms with his bisexuality. He quit drinking. But life was still a problem.

Format and Writing Style 133

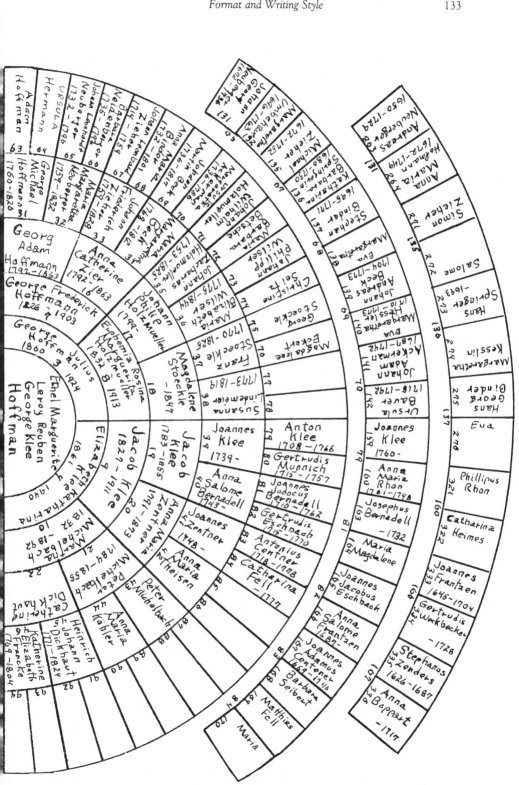

The way he dealt with that problem was to articulate it. He made it into a story, and then he published the story. When he discovered that he had written the story of his life, he wanted that published, too."

Are You a Poet?

Have most of your observations about your life and those you love taken the shape of poems? If writing a personal story in the form of a series of poems appeals to you, why not do it? There's no rule that says a memoir has to be in a certain literary form. I remember hearing on the radio a poem by Richard Wilbur called "Digging for China." It could have been part of an autobiography of many of us as children. In fact, I found it later in a collection called *New Coasts and Strange Harbors: Discovering Poems* selected by Helen Hill and Agnes Perkins. It's part of a chapter called "When I Was a Child." There are other chapters of poems about people, poems of love, the seasons, aging, singing and dancing, death.

When poet Rod McKuen wrote his first book of prose, *Finding My Father*, about his lifelong search for the father he never knew, his author's note at the beginning of the book points out:

> Since poetry has for so long been one of my main elements of expression I have at times included in this work certain excerpts from poetry triggered by an incident I was attempting to describe. This seemed to me more sensible than the tendency toward needless elaboration.
>
> Some of the poems are new and were written expressly for this book; other poetry and song lyrics have been published before.
>
> A list of sources and first lines for the selections appear at the end of the book.

Maybe the death of a loved one was the reason to start writing a family history and a poem seems a good way to close the chapter on that person. Here's a poem by Pollyanna Sedziol that closed a book of memories her mother wrote about her own mother:

REVERENCE FOR LIFE
By Pollyanna Sedziol
"The good Lord wasn't ready for me yet."
How many times we've said those very words
knowing well, whatever comfort we get
from them, we've no more knowledge than God's birds

about how flight takes place or life takes wings
to leave the body here and move on There.

But something in the heart of faith still sings
that life and death are one eternal stair.
The loved ones who go on Ahead are still
alive in loving hearts and memories;
sometimes an afternoon will seem to fill
with that "great crowd of witnesses" to seize
imagination's fruitful fantasy
assuring life as an eternity.

FICTIONALIZED FACTS

If you are writing a personal memoir rather than a family history, you may choose to use a collection of short stories as a format. Here's the way one Irene Schwartz wove memories of her North Carolina home into a short story:

HOMECOMING

Mist lay in pockets over the Carolina flatlands. The twilight brought chill and spreading darkness. I was driving, lost somewhere on dusty backroads that bordered miles of tobacco farmland. When attempting to follow the shortcut shown on my map, I must have taken the wrong turn at one of the numerous crossroads. This whole venture steeped in nostalgia had proven catastrophic. My solitary trip to the seashore where our family had spent vacations a million summers ago proved a disaster. Old landmarks had fallen. In their places banal high-rise hotels claimed the water's edge. Empty spaces of soft sands had been packed down to accept crowded facilities built for play in the carnival weeks of summer and winter vacations.

Pulled out of my depressed musing, I suddenly became aware that the widely spaced farm houses I was passing appeared vaguely familiar. That chinaberry tree in one yard—I know I had climbed it once long ago. The porch that almost wrapped around another house was where I had huddled mesmerized at the violence of a summer storm. Before the next house I slammed on my brakes. Smoke coming from its chimney blended into the dusk. Two huge oaks flanked the house and from one hung an old tire. I had played on that homely swing many times.

As I started up the house's wooden steps, the front door opened and an inquisitive middle-aged black woman peered from behind the screen door, obviously waiting for an explanation of my uninvited visit. In using my initial excuse of the need for directions toward town, her fears seemed to ease. I then offered my name.

At hearing it she threw up her hands with a baying "whoo-eee" and screamed back into the house, "Aunty, she's here, she's here!" I almost toppled backwards. An aged woman shuffled through the doorway. Her glassy eyes scanned my face, and beckoned for me to come inside. A mixture of fear and suspicion rooted me to the porch.

As a soothing remark, Aunty offered, "I declare, don't she favor her daddy?" Then she began to reel off the names of my entire family. I was in shock.

"Here, come inside. I have something to show you. Sit by the fire and Luella will make us some coffee."

After leading me to a creaking rocker, the elderly woman smugly pointed to a battered trunk in a far corner. I let my eyes adjust to the dimly lit interior. My head floated. I recognized it as having once belonged to my mother. On rainy days of my childhood I had spent hours rummaging through its contents heaped with letters and faded photographs.

After my father's sudden death, mother seemed pressured to move immediately from her large home, out of the small town and into one of the distant cities where her married children lived. Before we were alerted, half of her furniture had been sold and half given away at a house sale. Chancing by it, Aunty had been offered the trunk as a gift. She accepted it and for years filled long winter nights by the fire as she and Luella matched letters with photographs to recreate our family's history. They were ready to return the gift. I received it with tears filling my eyes. My search of years had ended on a forgotten road that delivered carefully nurtured portions of the past.

Dialogue in Anecdotes

Have you ever watched a book buyer browsing through the latest novel to see how much of it was long pages of description and very little "talking?" The look of a printed page that is solid text turns some readers off. They want to hear the characters themselves. Dialogue in fiction takes the form of anecdotes in a family history.

The dictionary defines anecdote as "a short entertaining account of some happening, usually personal or biographical." One of the ways Sue Kruse found to enliven her family history was to ask older relatives to recall some of their experiences. Here, in this brief excerpt — incorporating an anecdote — the structured life of our ancestors is brought home to those of us living far different lives:

> Grandma Minnie Davis Casey always wanted to be early, especially when catching trains, and since she didn't drive, she was at the mercy of others. When family gathered on vacations or holidays, she was the first to bed and admonished everyone that it was time to quiet down. Her children, lively and fun-loving, liked to stay up late playing cards and telling stories.
>
> Margaret Casey Chabot, her daughter, remembers: "Years ago when we were all gathered in Austin, Mama went to the kitchen about five o'clock to get dinner. Mabel yelled, 'Mama, what are you doing?'
>
> "Why I'm getting dinner of course.'
>
> "Mabel reminded her that we had had lunch only a couple of hours ago. Mama said, 'Well, we ate too late.' Mabel urged her to come on in and sit down for awhile. Mama stuck her head into the dining room and declared, 'When it's mealtime, it's mealtime. It's time to get the meal!'
>
> "We became hysterical. Ever after when Mama suggested getting food on the table, someone in the group would start up the chant, and we'd all join in. 'When it's mealtime, it's mealtime! It's time to get the meal!"

"A family history," says Sue Kruse, "is a long-range, never-ending commitment and, although I think they should tie in with what was happening historically, using as many anecdotes as possible makes the story more readable."

One of the handiest examples of anecdotes to study is *Reader's Digest*. In fact, it might be a market for some of your own amusing stories. Take a look at how those writers have — within three hundred words — written brief anecdotes about "Life in These United States" or life at college ("Campus Comedy") or experiences in the armed services ("Humor in Uniform") or humor on the job ("All in a Day's Work"). Notice how each of these anecdotes is a little story, complete with a beginning, a middle and an end. (Of course, not all of your anecdotes' endings will be "punch lines," as they are in *Reader's Digest*. Indeed, some of your little stories may deal with serious or somber occasions.)

Anecdotes can relate either a personal experience or result from an observation of human behavior that illustrates a point.

Television news anchor Dan Rather, in his autobiography *I Remember*, describes in this anecdote growing up in gun-worshiping Texas where:

> Something deeply imbedded could quickly wipe away neighborliness when a Texan felt angered or threatened, and — pop! — he would be "going to the iron". . . .
>
> Local students of violence blamed the trend on our Texas past and, in consequence, the cavalier attitude of grand juries in handing up indictments and the custom of judges to go easy on killers.
>
> "I don't understand Texas justice," an eastern lawyer allegedly told an old Texas judge. "You'll suspend sentence of a convicted murderer, but you'll hang a horse thief."
>
> "Sonny," the old judge is supposed to have replied. "I reckon that's cause we got men that need killin' but we ain't got no hosses that need stealin.' "
>
> Funny? I never thought so.

You'll notice in this anecdote the use of the words *allegedly* and *is supposed to have replied*, which is the device some writers use to report a handed-down story for which there is no known source.

Description

While Rather makes good use of *dialogue* in this story, he doesn't hesitate to use *description* as well to tell us about an overseen moment with his parents and the social mores of an earlier Texas where guns were ready to hand, but dancing "was for sinners only:"

> Late one night when I was five or six years old and had long been put to bed, I woke up and heard music . . . in the kitchen. This was unusual for such an advanced hour, so I got up, cracked my door open quietly, and peeked to see what was going on.
>
> They didn't see me, but I glimpsed what looked to me like a magical sight. I didn't want to disrupt it. My parents were dancing.
>
> They danced for a long time, maybe an hour, off and on, sometimes stopping to fine-tune the radio through the static, trying to bring in one of the outlaw stations across the Mexican border, the ones that carried slow and fast tunes. These outlets were also

home to "Doc" John R. Brinkley, once candidate for governor of Kansas, who promised rejuvenation with a "goat gland" treatment that cost $750, which made us laugh our heads off. He was our Johnny Carson.

Doc Brinkley was not on the air that night, so Mother and Father danced through the static, ballads, and all other kinds of music, and they were plainly happier than I'd ever seen them. Mother hummed along much of the time and both were smiling a lot. It was especially sweet and remarkable to see the delight on my father's face. The pressures of the workday had been lifted from his features; I remember that distinctly.

They never did spot me and I never asked them why they chose to go dancing in the kitchen that night. I suspect they felt an urge to relive their courtship years. They also must have felt safe, which was important, for as I grew older I learned that even the most respectable dancing was still somewhat controversial in Texas when I was very little, although it was becoming acceptable.

Characterization

What did our ancestors look like when they were not posed formally in their Sunday best, but toiling under a midday sun on a farm cleared out of the wilderness? Or fighting a war to end all wars? Or welcoming home a new baby? Or celebrating a promotion?

What were their thoughts and feelings, as well as how they looked?

Readers learn about characters by what they say and do as well as what the author tells us about them.

Here is the opening of *The Confessions of Jean-Jacques Rousseau*. What is your impression of this man from his words?

> I am commencing an undertaking, hitherto without precedent, and which will never find an imitator. I desire to set before my fellows the likeness of a man in all the truth of nature, and that man myself.
>
> Myself alone! I know the feelings of my heart, and I know men. I am not made like any of those I have seen; I venture to believe that I am not made like any of those who are in existence. If I am not better, at least I am different. Whether Nature has acted rightly or wrongly in destroying the mould in which she cast me, can only be decided after I have been read.

Notice that this passage from a journal is written in the *first person* and *present tense*. If your personal story is taken from a series of diaries or journals, you may want to preserve that same sense of immediacy. On the other hand if your journals are only a research source from which you wish to distill the person you are today, a *first person, past tense* viewpoint may be your choice. Here is such an example from Thomas Griffith's book *How True: A Skeptic's Guide to Believing the News*:

> To choose a career is to choose how life is going to happen to you. As long ago as I can remember I wanted to be a journalist. While my schoolmates were wise in hubcaps and fender treat-ments that marked this year's Buick from last, I studied the charac-ters of whatever newspapers I could lay hands on, and found ro-mantic the very type-shapes of their front page logotypes — the proud Gothic dignity of the *New York Times*, the plain square-cut legend of the *Kansas City Star*, and the brassy patriotism of any Hearst paper, its name enwrapped in American flags while from a ferocious eagle's beak trailed ribbons improbably celebrating pa-triotism, freedom and truth.
>
> If every choice of career is a limiting, it is in the beginning a freedom, a zest of potentialities. Just as in that other crucial roman-tic decision of one's life — that of marriage — one acts with a show of reason but under the ordering of illusion.
>
> I thought journalism meant to live in the actual, to see and then to describe, to seek the truth, to show the way. Other careers might be valuable, but to me too narrow, insufficiently encompass-ing, too physical, beyond me (music or mathematics), too messy (labs), too routine (office work), unworthy (public relations), self-ish (business), false (selling), fusty (scholarship). Illusion sustained me through the apprentice discovery of how dull, grubby and triv-ial much of journalism can be; sustained me until I became surer again that journalism was where I was meant to be.

What do your readers want to know about the characters in your family history or memoir? They want to know their outerselves: What they looked like, how they dressed, the habitual gestures, how they talked, their social manners. But they also want to know their inner selves. Proud? Self-effacing? Pessimistic? Temperamental? Loyal?

As mentioned before, these aspects of your characters are revealed not only in how they appear to others, but in what the characters them-selves do and say.

Although she was talking about the short story, Hallie Burnett points out in *Writer's Digest Guide to Good Writing* that while styles of writing have gone through many changes over the years, one thing has stayed the same. And it is true for readers of family histories and personal memoirs as well. Burnett quotes Robert Gorham Davis, who said a story asks a question: "What is it like to be that kind of person going through that kind of experience?" Your answer to that question will be what *your* readers are looking for, too.

TRANSITIONS

How the writer decides to blend the present with the past may only come through writing and seeing what makes the most seamless version of the story. While a prepared outline may give you the main highways to get from the beginning to the end of the book, there will be many opportunities along the way to choose, momentarily, a side road that offers some new vista—but always connects up again with the main highway.

Transitions that writers have successfully used to move readers back to an earlier time could include the sound of certain music, the smell of a freshly painted room, the touch of a jacket being packed for give-away to the needy. One *sensory reaction* in the present leads the author to a similar memory of the past.

In addition to the use of *sensory transitions*, some others that are useful to memoir writers include:

Time Transitions: "Ten years earlier we were in an even smaller town, but one that had great promise for me. . . ." This gives the author a chance to *flashback* to an earlier time that illustrates a personal experience that affected her later life.

Another author might use a time transition to *foreshadow* a topic to come later: "It was John's first meeting with a man whose path would cross his with disastrous consequences in the years to come."

Phrase Transition: Repeating a word or phrase from a previous paragraph may bridge a movement to another topic. For example:

"My sister used to say that some of the Southern whites she knew were 'too poor to paint and too proud to whitewash' their houses.

"Poor and proud was something the Smith family knew from experience. . . ."

Question Transition: This is one that if overworked can call attention to itself, so use it sparingly. At the end of a chapter or paragraph, the author might say: "What possible explanation was there for that sudden decision to move?" giving an opportunity to change locale and discuss another phase of family history.

FREEDOM TO GUESS

That hypothetical question in the last paragraph leads us to raise the issue of just how much freedom the author has to guess at unrevealed reasons for why ancestors made certain choices, to make judgments about their actions. Must the writer just "stick to the facts?"

I think these are decisions each author must make individually. The author can tell his readers in the preface what rules were followed in the writing. An author might say that throughout the text, wherever he does not have authenticated facts, he will say that he is making an assumption or offering an opinion and invite other family members to come to their own conclusions.

For an example of how one author phrases these remarks, see the excerpted foreword to *The Story of the McGuffeys* in chapter twelve.

A CHECKLIST OF WRITING REMINDERS

- ✔ *Anecdotes*: Have you included these "human interest stories" which give the reader insight into the people in your memoir?
- ✔ *Characterization*: Can the reader see your people not only in terms of their physical attributes — height, hair, complexion, facial structure — but also any personality traits that may have been revealed in letters or diaries or memories of relatives who knew them?
- ✔ *Conflict*: Are there points in your story that show family members in conflict with nature (drought, floods, fire, the sea) or their environment (poverty, a political regime) or other people (religious persecution, ethnic wars) or their own families (loyalty vs. ambition) or themselves?
- ✔ *Description*: Is there enough concrete detail, but not so much that it slows down the story? Is it woven discreetly into the text?
- ✔ *Dialogue*: Are there enough scenes involving real or imagined conversations between the people in your story?
- ✔ *Time and Place*: Do we get a clear picture of the places in which your ancestors lived — or where you and your family grew up? Do we know the historical context of their lives?
- ✔ *Transitions*: Have you moved smoothly from topic to topic? Chap-

ter to chapter? If not, do you need some bridge sentences or para-graphs to carry the reader along in your story avoiding any abrupt left turns or dead end digressions?

You may want to add some other reminders to this list to help you create the effect you want your book to have on its readers.

Chapter Eleven

Establishing a Writing Schedule

I n her book, *Biography: The Craft and the Calling*, Catherine Drinker Bowen quotes William Stubbs, a Church of England bishop as saying, "If a man wishes to learn something of a subject, his best policy is to write a book upon it."

There's nothing like the prospect of a published book to stir some of us to organize our random memories, treasured artifacts and new explorations into a story about where we came from and why we turned out the way we did.

If you have done some preliminary research and decided on the focus of your book, your next move will prove how serious you are about getting it written.

Your research efforts may have been accomplished casually whenever you felt like writing to a distant relative or visiting the local library. But you'll make greater progress on gathering those loose threads into a marvelous story if you set yourself a schedule.

To paraphrase Laurence Peter of *The Peter Principle*, "When faced with an important task the competent person simply begins."

To that I would add, "and begins again each day—preferably at a certain time."

THE BEST TIME TO WRITE

Are you a morning person or a night owl? The best way to get your book written is to take advantage of that corner of the day or evening when your energy level is highest. If you're an early bird, get up one hour earlier than the time you usually do for your job or your family and spend it at your "writing place," wherever you have decided that will be. Spend at least one hour a day there, working on whatever part of your book is the easiest place to start. Do it every day, so that you get into the writing habit.

If you're a night person, be sure to pick a spot away from any noisy distractions. You'll be surprised how the pages will mount up, even though you're only working one hour a day.

The discipline of writing is a little like the discipline of exercise. One study reports that people who exercise and those who don't each have the same amount of leisure time — about twenty-five hours a week. The difference is how each person decides to use that time.

If you start out doing the easy parts of your book, you'll build momentum for tackling the harder sections. Setting yourself a goal of working one hour a day will be more productive than trying to set a goal of *x* pages a day.

Some writers, like joggers and walkers, need a teammate for incentive and support. If you don't have a spouse or housemate who shares your interest, membership in a local writers' or genealogical group may provide ready and willing ears. They may also provide able suggestions when you're stuck at a particular point in the manuscript.

Some women writers find it easier to set aside one day a week rather than schedule one hour each day. They let the beds go unmade, forget the dust. If there are small children in the family, they make a deal with a neighbor to trade off babysitting for one day a week.

If you are able to set aside a greater part of the day than just one hour, how long can you maintain concentration without a break? For example, I find that if I work straight through from seven, eight, or nine in the morning until early afternoon, stopping only for a cup of soup or other quick, low-fat snack, I can get more accomplished than if I take a long lunch break and try to come back to work. Afternoons I save for library work or interviews. Night writers have probably worked out their own ways to get more actual writing done without distractions or loss of creative energy.

MAKING THE TIME TO WRITE

The struggle for space and privacy for the woman writer — especially with preschool age children — was described accurately by Pat Schneider in *The Writer as an Artist*:

> On a particular winter afternoon I felt as if I would lose my mind. It was a day when all three babies were fussy, and nothing I could do was enough. We were all in the kitchen, which was cluttered with toys, baby formula, laundry and breakfast dishes. Condensation on the windows closed all access to the outside

world. A very painful kind of cry began in my mind. It was rhythmic, like a chant. In that desperation where one does not observe oneself, I ran out of the kitchen, up the stairs two at a time, grabbed the typewriter, brought it down, and slammed it on top of the throbbing washing machine — the only cleared surface in the kitchen. With two babies playing on the floor and one strapped to the changing table, I pounded out a page-long poem. Although it did not say so directly, the meaning was, "I will never write again." When I finished, I stood in a kind of shock, knowing three things: I had been writing; what I had written was not bad; and nothing, as long as I lived, would keep me from writing again.

When you cannot, as Virginia Woolf writes, have *A Room of One's Own*, you must find ways to cope until you can.

Writers who face both small children at home and a long commute to work may try a variation on the example of this man. A consultant by profession, he explained in a *Prevention Magazine* article, entitled "Celebrate Solitude" by Jeffrey A. Kottler, why he refused to install a telephone in his car:

> "I can't imagine having a phone in my car. I sit perched on my seat, watching the scenery flow by, a landscape that is forever changing. I love to sing along with the radio. And I love to talk to myself. If I ever feel the urge to talk to somebody else on one of my long trips, I like to make tapes on a recorder I carry with me. I conduct these long monologues. I feel so uninhibited talking to someone who is not really there. I can easily fill up a ninety-minute tape just chattering away about what is going on in my head or my life. My friends appreciate getting these tapes in the mail because they are so honest and spontaneous."

Even a half-hour commute could offer the opportunity to record some memories for a family history or personal story.

MINIMIZE DISTRACTIONS

If you're going to be working at home, let people know you're writing a book and you'd prefer not to have phone calls until such and such a time each day. Most people respect the discipline required of writers working on a book and will keep your schedule in mind. But, if you have forgetful, talkative friends, just turn on your telephone answering machine.

At the end of your writing time you might want to make a list of one to three topics you'll want to concentrate on next. This will give you a specific goal to accomplish when you next sit down to write.

Sometimes something as simple as closing a window drape can add productivity to your writing schedule. I have a second bedroom that I use as an office. My desk faces a window that overlooks some trees and a pool for residents of the apartment building nearby. Watching birds in the trees or people around the pool is very relaxing—but mightily distracting if you're trying to write. I keep the drape closed and my thoughts on the manuscript in progress.

But okay, I'll admit it—when I get stuck, I'll walk to the front of the house and look out a different window for a few minutes!

As a matter of fact, researchers at the University of California say that if you've tried everything else to solve a problem, stand up. You can improve your chances of solving the problem by twenty percent if you're standing instead of sitting. Why does it work? Standing boosts your heart rate by about ten beats per minute. And the increase in blood flow stimulates your brain.

In her book *The Writing Life*, Annie Dillard says that:

> Jack London claimed to write twenty hours a day. Before he undertook to write, he obtained the University of California course list and all the syllabi; he spent a year reading the textbooks in philosophy and literature. In subsequent years, once he had a book of his own under way, he set his alarm to wake him after four hours' sleep. Often he slept through the alarm so, by his own account, he rigged it to drop a weight on his head. I cannot say I believe this, though a novel like *The Sea Wolf* is strong evidence that some sort of weight fell on his head with some sort of frequency—but you wouldn't think a man would claim credit for it. London maintained that every writer needed a technique, experience, and a philosophical position. Perhaps the position need not be an airtight one; London himself felt comfortable with a weird amalgam of Karl Marx and Herbert Spencer (Marks & Sparks).

In *The Writing Life*, Dillard describes her own working methods, including the graveyard shift in a Virginia college library carrel, and comments on the role of schedules in a writer's life:

> How we spend our days is, of course, how we spend our lives. What we do with this hour, and that one, is what we are doing.

A schedule defends from chaos and whim. It is a net for catching days. It is a scaffolding on which a worker can stand and labor with both hands at sections of time. A schedule is a mock-up of reason and order — willed, faked, and so brought into being; it is a peace and a haven set into the wreck of time; it is a lifeboat on which you find yourself, decades later, still living. Each day is the same, so you remember the series afterward as a blurred and powerful pattern.

RESEARCH VS. WRITING TIME

If you start writing before your research is complete, you may want to organize your time so that some days will be devoted to library research or interviews, and others to correspondence. There's nothing like a new discovery in the mailbox or at the library to bring you back to the typewriter or computer with renewed interest. But no fair counting letter-writing as part of your one-hour-a-day writing commitment. That time is only for actual writing on the book!

AVOIDING STRESS

Be realistic about what you can accomplish without adding more stress to your life. The finished product will be enjoyed by the whole family, and you'll have fun doing it too — *if* you just tackle a little bit at a time.

Adair Lara, a San Francisco columnist once wrote, "My mother used to wash our clothes in a wringer washer and then hang them on the line. As she pinned up each garment, she said, she thought about the child it belonged to. (It was a wonder she knew; there were seven of us kids.) She never wanted a dryer, even after we could afford one, because it would steal this from her, this quiet contemplation."

Lara asked her readers, "What do *you* do? What's *your* version of hanging out the wash?" The baskets of mail she received turned into a book called *Slowing Down in a Speeded-Up World*. Here's just one excerpt from that book that might spark some ideas or memories of your own:

> I read somewhere that a tribe of Americans-who-came-wandering-in-about-forty-thousand-years-ago had small pouches in which they kept fragrance memories. When anything remarkable happened, they would pick a plant or collect some pebbles to save. When they wanted to re-create that memory, they would take out the talisman.

For me the smell of laundry drying in the breeze is one, as is the smell of barbecued ribs in the oven on Saturdays. Irresistible!

In trying to set aside specific hours or days to work on your book, you may have to learn how to say "no" more often. A survey by *McCall's* magazine found that more than half its readers admitted that "no" was one of the hardest words to say. The next time someone asks you to serve on a committee or do some volunteer work for a "really worthy" cause, consider whether you'd rather spend those hours working on this book that means so much to you. You can always be diplomatic in thanking the person for asking you, but be sure to say "no" and not "maybe." "Maybe" leaves the door open for another claim on your time.

HANDLING YOUR INTERNAL CRITIC

Maintaining consistent work on a regular schedule will give you a manuscript you can shape into your final book. Avoid the urge to constantly revise as you work on your first draft; that compulsive search for perfection will keep you from ever completing a manuscript. You must let your creative self be in the driver's seat and put that critical editor partner in the back seat until you're ready to review the manuscript as a whole. Dr. David D. Burns, a psychiatrist, did a study with a test group of one-hundred-fifty salesmen a number of years ago and roughly forty percent of them proved to be perfectionists. But they were not any more successful than the rest. "There was not one shred of evidence that they were earning any more money." Dr. Burns, who described his results in his book, *Feeling Good: The New Mood Therapy* says:

> Perfectionists are people who strain compulsively toward impossible goals and measure their self-worth entirely in terms of their achievements. . . . you may find that you do some of your most outstanding work when you aim for good solid performances rather than one stress-producing masterpiece.

> This strategy proved useful to me when I was writing for educational journals and had been stymied by writer's block. "This has to be outstanding," I would tell myself every time I sat down to prepare a draft. Then I would agonize over the first sentence until I gave up in disgust.

> When, instead, I told myself, "I'll just crank out a draft," I found that my resistance to writing diminished and my output improved substantially. Moreover, I was struck by the fact that the quality

of my writing improved when I wasn't trying so hard to impress other people.

SUPPORTING YOUR WRITING SCHEDULE

One way to force yourself to complete a certain amount of writing in a set period of time is to take a writing course. Most colleges and some high schools offer continuing education courses in writing and home study courses are available from Writer's Digest School and other companies that advertise in *Writer's Digest* magazine. Some universities also offer home study creative writing courses.

BREAKING WRITER'S BLOCK

If you're having trouble some days getting into the memoir-writing groove, you might just simply type a list for yourself something like this:

Do you remember:

- ✔ The first day of school?
- ✔ Your first date?
- ✔ Your first job?
- ✔ The day you got your first library card?
- ✔ Your most embarrassing moment?
- ✔ The most interesting person you ever met?
- ✔ The scariest moment of your life?
- ✔ What made you happiest as a child? a teenager?
- ✔ How you met your spouse?
- ✔ The best game of _____ you ever played?
- ✔ The first prize you ever won?
- ✔ The birth of your first child?
- ✔ The death of your nearest relative?
- ✔ Your introduction to war?
- ✔ The books that have affected your life?
- ✔ The funniest movie you ever saw?
- ✔ The people who influenced your career?
- ✔ The writer you admire most?

Answer each question as you go through the list. You'll discover later a place where the paragraphs just fit in the manuscript. Even if you don't, the exercise will get you back in the writing mood, ready to tackle another part of your memoir.

In a hospital newsletter on "Procrastination—The Thief of Time," Dr. Dale E. Turner commented that:

People die prematurely because they delay in making changes in their lifestyles. Students fail because they postpone study. Business people experience losses because they put off key decisions. Marriages disintegrate because little irritations aren't dealt with when they're little.

Ours are busy lives and no one can do everything; priorities are a must.

But if we can't do everything at once, we can at least do something at once.

The most important thing is to begin.

Chapter Twelve

The First Part of Your Book

E ven though the pages in the very front of your book will be the last ones to be typed, you must collect information for them almost from the start. You might set up folders for this "front matter" so that you'll have the material handy when you're ready to type it. "Front matter" is the first pages of your book, even before page one of text. It includes:

- ✔ title page
- ✔ copyright page
- ✔ dedication page
- ✔ acknowledgments page
- ✔ permissions page
- ✔ table of contents
- ✔ preface
- ✔ foreword
- ✔ prologue

Publishers call those pages following the actual text of your book "back matter." This could include:

- ✔ epilogue
- ✔ appendix
- ✔ bibliography
- ✔ index

Let's look at each component.

FRONT MATTER

Title Page

The title page has no page number. It includes your book's title, placed about one-third down from the top of the page, and is centered.

After a double space, the word "by" is centered. Then, after another double space, the author's name is centered.

Copyright Page

The next page — again with no page number — will be printed on the back of the title page. It contains the copyright information. This is simply a line such as the word *Copyright* or the international copyright symbol: © 1995 by Robert Smith. List the copyright year as the year your complete manuscript was ready for the printer.

If you are self-publishing the book for resale, you may want to type below the copyright line the name of your self-publishing company, such as Smith Family Books, and then your address, city and state below that. This allows people to order books directly from you.

Although your copyright exists as soon as you have created the manuscript and put your copyright notice on it, you may choose to formally register your manuscript with the Copyright Office. Write or call them at the Library of Congress (Washington, DC 20559-6000, telephone: (202)707-3000) and request an application form for a book. The number above is for the Public Information Office; specialists are on duty from 8:30 A.M. to 5:00 P.M. Eastern time Monday to Friday except holidays. Or, use the Forms Hotline Number (202)707-9100, which is available twenty-four hours a day. Leave a message with your name and address, requesting a copyright application form for a book.

When you receive the application form, fill it out as explained on the form. Then return it to the copyright office with your check (cost was twenty dollars in 1994) and two copies of your book. As long as your copyright notice appears in your book, your copyright is valid for your life plus fifty years, whether you had filed a registration or not. The main reason to register your work is that registering legally proves your ownership. It is necessary if you want to collect statutory damages and attorneys fees in the case of an infringement suit.

Another bit of information that appears on this copyright page is your ISBN number. The International Standard Book Number is used by book publishers, booksellers and librarians for both ordering and cataloguing purposes. If, for example, you self-publish your book and regional bookstores become interested in selling it, you'll need this number to further identify your book beyond its title and your name as author. In addition, if a regular trade publisher becomes interested in your book for distribution, the ISBN will be one other measure of your professionalism.

To obtain your ISBN number, write to R.R. Bowker Company, 121 Chanlon Rd., New Providence, NJ 07974 Attn: ISBN Agency.

Dedication

The next page (still unnumbered) is the dedication page, where you may choose to dedicate your book to some particular person (such as a family member). You can either center the word *Dedication* or just type *To*, or *For*, and the person(s) name(s) centered about one-third of the way down the page.

Of course, some writers use the dedication to make a point, which may tie in with the theme of the book to come. For example, Rita Rudner, whose book jacket describes her as an ex-dancer turned stand-up comedian, dedicated her book, *Naked Beneath My Clothes: Tales of a Revealing Nature*, this way:

> This book is dedicated to my parents
> Abe and Frances Rudner,
> who always told me I could do anything
> but never told me how long it would take.

Acknowledgments

The next page (unnumbered) is the acknowledgments (centered about one-third down the page), in which you thank individuals or institutions that were especially helpful to you in some way, such as research, writing, or who encourage you to tell your story.

Here, for example, is the acknowledgments page to a family history called *The Spencers of Amberson Avenue: A Turn-of-the-Century Memoir*, by Ethel Spencer, edited by Michael P. Weber and Peter N. Stearns, historians in the Department of History and Philosophy at Carnegie-Mellon University:

ACKNOWLEDGMENTS

The editors wish to acknowledge the important role of Elizabeth Ranney, Ethel Spencer's niece. She first recognized the value of this remarkable memoir and called it to our attention. During the editing process she served as an important source of information. Her penetrating questions regarding our interpretations of the Spencer family greatly improved the Introduction. We also thank the members of the Spencer family, especially Mrs. Elizabeth Spencer Blue, for their willingness to share their family experiences with outsiders. We are all indebted to them.

With a few exceptions, such as those dated after 1912, all the photographs in the text were taken by Charles Hart Spencer. They come from the family collection, kindly made available through the generosity of Elizabeth Ranney, Mrs. Charles H. Spencer, Jr. and Anne Spencer. The captions are adapted from those written by Ethel Spencer.

(Charles Hart Spencer, father of the author, was one of the growing number of middle-management employees in American industrial cities in the 1880s and 1890s and the memoir looks at one kind of urban life of three generations ago. This is an example of what can happen when family memoirs are well-written and interesting enough to capture the attention of historians. The book was published by the University of Pittsburgh Press. More about this in chapter sixteen.)

Permissions

This is the place to acknowledge excerpts from others' works. If you incorporated into your family history or personal memoir some material from a previously copyrighted poem, song, article, story or book, you would list that source, such as: *Title of Work*, Copyright 1993 by John Smith. If there are only a few copyrighted excerpts, you might include them on the Acknowledgments page. If there are many, you would have a separate page titled "Permissions," on which you recognize your sources. For an example, see the permissions page in this book.

How Much Can I Quote? There is no set number of words that can be copied from another's copyrighted work without infringing on the original author's copyright. A scholar might reprint several hundred words from another scholar's book without infringement, but reprinting just one verse from a copyrighted song's lyrics might be considered infringement by its publisher.

The law allows fair use of copyrighted material for the purposes of criticism, comment, news reporting, teaching, scholarship or research. But it also says "fair use" depends on these factors:

✔ The purpose for which the copyrighted material is used — is it for commercial purposes (you intend to sell the book that uses the appropriated copyrighted material), or is it for nonprofit educational use (you intend to give away copies to your family and friends)?

✔ How much of the copyrighted work is used in comparison to the length of the entire work? (Were you quoting just a few paragraphs about a particular branch of your family from another relative's six hundred-page book? Or reprinting his sixteen-page pamphlet in your fifty-page booklet?)

✔ The nature of the copyrighted work itself—is it a song, a poem, an article, a book, or is it a news item, a fact from an encyclopedia? (Facts and news are uncopyrightable.)

✔ How does your use of the previously copyrighted material affect the potential market for or value of that copyrighted work? (Would your use of an author's copyrighted material keep people from buying your source's book?)

Gathering Permissions: If you want to incorporate a substantial quote from another's copyrighted work, you must, of course, obtain permission in advance from the holder of the copyright. (This is usually the author, his or her heirs, or the work's publisher.) To do this, write to them in care of the work's publisher, or directly, in the case of family members or friends whose addresses you know. A letter requesting permission might be worded something like this one:

> Dear (author's name):
> May I have your permission to quote the passage I have marked on the enclosed photocopy from (*title of copyrighted work*) in my book, (title), which I am self-publishing for my family and friends?
> I am including a copy of the preceding paragraphs from my own manuscript so you can see how it is used in my book.
> Please let me hear from you via the enclosed stamped, self-addressed envelope whether I may have your permission.
> I will be sure to carry your copyright credit line on the acknowledgments page of my book.
>
> *Sincerely,*
> *Your Name and Address*

It would be a courtesy to that person to send, on publication, a photocopy of the quoted passage, along with a photocopy of the title page and acknowledgements page for their file.

If you wanted to request permission from a commercial publisher to reprint a poem or song lyric or passage from other copyrighted material in a self-published book you planned to sell, your first paragraph might say something like this:

> Dear (author's name):
> I am self-publishing a book about the Smith Family of Central

Kentucky and hope to find distribution for it among bookstores in the Kentucky/Tennessee/Virginia area where other branches of the family live. May I have your permission to quote the passage I have marked on the enclosed photocopy from your (title of copyrighted work) in my book (title)?

The next three paragraphs would be the same as the letter on page (156).

You will probably discover that even with limited distribution from your book, if you choose a popular song or well-known poet, the fee requested of you might be more than you care to pay to include the quote. On the other hand, the publisher may assess only a modest fee, given the limited potential sale of your book, or even grant permission without a fee.

Table of Contents

If you have given titles to your individual chapters, list them here in the sequence in which they appear in your book. This page is also unnumbered.

If you have grouped certain chapters into a Part I, for example, because they have some unifying element — such as "Revolutionary Ancestors" or "Early Days on the Prairie" — and subsequent chapters are grouped into other parts, the contents page would show . . .

Part I
with individual chapter titles and page numbers
Part II
with individual chapter titles and page numbers
. . . and so on.

You can't list the actual page numbers, of course, until the book's pages have been typeset and printed. If you are producing a book from your own pages of camera-ready typed copy, however, then you'll be able to type the contents page with the correct page numbers before submitting the book to the printer.

Preface

The next page (still unnumbered) in the front of the book could be a preface, in which you set forth for the reader a statement of your purpose or the theme of your book. Suppose, for example, that your family was among the earliest settlers in your county and no one had ever written down where they originally came from and what other early families helped found the community. In their book *All Our Yesterdays: A Century of Family Life in an American Small Town*, authors James Oliver Robertson and Janet C. Robertson used the following preface to describe their purpose in writing their book:

> It is our hope that this book gives significant voice to ordinary people who are now dead, and who can therefore not tell their own stories. The memory of human beings is never dependable. We all forget the horrors and pleasures, the accomplishments and failures of our own lives. How much more do we forget about people who lived and died in other times and places? Without some memory, some record, and some stories told, we are all deprived of pasts that not only belong to us, but that shape us, our beliefs and ideals, and our acts.
>
> In what follows, we have tried to honor the aspirations, fears, hopes, orneriness, endurance, and even the despair of the many members of the Taintor, Bulkeley, Davis and other families of Hampton, Connecticut, whose stories we have come to know. We have written in admiration and respect for hundreds whose lives have touched ours profoundly, over separating distances of three, four, five, or six generations.

Their book was the outgrowth of the Robertson's purchase in 1965 of an eighteenth-century house in Hampton, a small town in northeastern Connecticut. This young couple with two children discovered that the former owners of their 150-year-old house had saved a vast quantity of papers — personal and business letters, bills and business files, visiting cards, playbills, newspapers and other periodicals. Their further research produced a 512-page book that became a Book-of-the-Month Club selection.

Does your book have similar commercial possibilities because of its unique historical value?

Foreword

Some writers combine a preface and an acknowledgments page into a single foreword. Alice McGuffey Ruggles, in the foreword to her book *The Story of the McGuffeys*, explains what is and is not known about the family whose name is synonymous with the *McGuffey Reader* schoolbooks of yesterday:

FOREWORD

This is a story—not a documented history. The first American McGuffeys were too busy or too illiterate or too lacking in self-consciousness to write of themselves. They left no family records, and firsthand material on their background is scanty. When facts were available, I followed them scrupulously. What traditions I could gather, I handed on. Failing both, I fell back on probabilities—with apologies to my forebears, who seem to have been very matter-of-fact.

Information on the Scottish emigrants, William McGuffey— "Billy" in the story—and his wife, Ann McKittrick, I owe to Mr. George A. Ostheimer of Indiana, whose wife was descended from Catherine, sister of "Sandy the Scout."

Dr. Daniel Drake, one of the first Westerners to develop a sense of the regional history, left an account of the youthful exploits of "Sandy" (the first Alexander McGuffey) told to him by the Scout himself. The journal of Dr. Drake's brother, Benjamin, and certain Drake letters give glimpses of young Alexander Hamilton McGuffey, who collaborated in the compilation of the *Readers*. And the unpublished autobiography of Charles D. Drake, the doctor's son, contains vivid pictures of life in southern Ohio in the early nineteenth century.

A sketch of Dr. Henry McGuffey of Kentucky, who was the baby on the horseback trek of Sandy and Anna to northern Ohio in 1802, was written for me by Miss Jennie McGuffey of Seattle, the doctor's granddaughter.

Miss Katherine Walker Stewart of Dayton, last surviving grandchild of William Holmes McGuffey, turned over to me her collection of family photographs and papers. And from her lips I wrote down her own recollection of her maternal grandfather and his second wife, Laura Howard. The description she gave me of William's earlier married life with his first wife, Harriet Spining, she had received from her mother, Mary McGuffey Stewart.

In my interview with my cousin Katherine, she urged me in whatever I might publish about the *Readers*, to bring out the *human* side of the story. For many years, she had been meeting McGuffey devotees who paid tribute to her as a granddaughter of the educator but who knew little about the real personalities behind their beloved old schoolbooks.

Of Alexander Hamilton McGuffey in his later years, I have my own recollections. He was the indulgent grandfather *par excellence*, associated with trips, treats, and marvelous Christmas parties under his hospitable roof. For his earlier married life with Elizabeth Drake, the grandmother I never knew, I have used the recollections of my mother, Anna McGuffey Morrill.

Secondary sources, mostly articles in magazines and newspapers, are too numerous to list. Two invaluable books of reference are *A History of the McGuffey Readers*, by Henry M. Vail, written from the publisher's angle, and *William Holmes McGuffey and His Readers*, by Dr. Harvey C. Minnich.

My aim in this little volume has been to make these old-fashioned Americans and their world come to life.

In a commercially published family history or personal story, the foreword may be written by someone other than the author, such as a well-known person whose name adds prestige and credence to the book. That person may be someone engaged by the publisher to read the book in advance of publication (who the publisher hopes will offer a complimentary assessment of the value of the book for readers). If you know someone who might be a candidate for writing your book's foreword, suggest the name(s) to a potential publisher when you make your initial book proposal.

Prologue

Some writers of family histories use a prologue to present the reason for exploring the past. Here are the opening paragraphs of the Prologue to *All Our Yesterdays: A Century of Family Life in an American Small Town*:

RELICS OF THE PAST

Wherever one goes in New England — in farm country, suburbs or really deep woods — there are stone walls. People ask about them. Tourists speculate about them, sometimes wonder whether they were built by Indians. The stone walls are, in fact, the boundaries of fields first created by settlers.

Those fields were cleared of trees, often plowed and planted, and certainly "rock-picked." (Rock picking is every New England farmer's spring time misery. During the winter as the earth freezes and thaws, rocks rise to the surface of the fields; they must be removed before plowing can proceed. Stacked at the edges of the fields, they are the raw material for all those stone walls.) Wherever there is a wall, there was once a field, even in what is now a forest. Those walls stand as evidence that in the days settlers built them many more people lived off the produce of New England's rocky soil than do today.

Such relics of the past—along with old houses, churches, and fences where there are no walls—stand mutely insistent that all America started out rural and agricultural. Even Manhattan and Chicago were farmed at one time, and Los Angeles was ranch country. Only in the twentieth century has the United States become an urban nation. The small-town world of stone walls, old houses and churches and fences, has been left far behind. The life that produced them is totally gone. What follows is an excursion into one of America's old towns, an old house still standing there, and through that house into the lives of people and families who lived in the world where they built those stone walls.

This prologue immediately precedes chapter one in a book that describes the Revolutionary Americans who lived in the same house occupied by the authors today.

THE TEXT

The first page of the first chapter of your actual text is where you should begin numbering your pages. Pages are numbered consecutively from page one to the end of the book.

If you are going to use your manuscript pages as camera-ready copy for printing or photocopying and also plan to bind the pages to read like a regular book, then your pages would be set up as follows: Page one would be a right-hand page, so the page number should appear in the upper right-hand corner. Page two would be a left-hand page and the page number would appear in the upper left-hand corner. If you are using a computer, you have (or can get) a software program to set up your pages in this way.

On the other hand, if you plan to submit your book to a regular trade book publisher, then you would not use that method. Simply type the manuscript double-spaced as you would any book manuscript; place your last name in the upper left-hand corner and page numbers in the right corner. The book's publisher will take care of these pagination concerns.

For additional details on preparing a book manuscript for submission to a trade book publisher, you may want to refer to *The Writer's Digest Guide to Manuscript Formats*.

BACK MATTER

Epilogue

Some writers may use the epilogue to indicate that this book is only the first of a planned series. If it is a family history, for example, you may indicate you are seeking further information for your future volumes and invite knowledgeable readers to share data with you — giving an address where they may write you.

Appendix

There may be some special photographs, maps, fold-out pages showing family-tree charts, reproductions of special ancestral documents, or other artifacts that you want to print here, rather than within the text of the book for manufacturing cost considerations or other reasons.

At appropriate pages within the manuscript you would refer your reader to the appendix.

Depending on how many items are involved, you may want to label them as *Appendix A*, *Appendix B*, etc., with an identifying title at the top of the page, such as "Appendix A: Map of The Virginia Military District of Ohio, 1787-1849."

Bibliography

If in your research you have found a number of sources that you think other family or personal historians would find useful, you may want to include a bibliography to aid their searches in libraries or bookstores.

The usual citation for such a reference is: author's last name, first name, title of the book (in italics), city of publication, name of publisher, year of publication. If there are two or more authors, only the first author's name is reversed such as Polking, Kirk, John Smith and Bob Jones.

Punctuation of the book citation would be:

Clark, Thomas, Bruce Woods, Peter Blocksom and Angela Terez. *The Writer's Digest Guide to Good Writing*. Cincinnati: Writer's Digest Books. 1994.

If the citation is to a magazine article it would be: author's last name, first name, title of article in quotes, name of the periodical in italics, volume or serial number and date of issue, page numbers.

Punctuation of the magazine citation would be:

Carlisle, Andrea. "Writing Stories from Life." Writer's Digest 74 (July 1994) 30-32.

For other specialized citations, you may want to refer to the latest edition of *The Chicago Manual of Style*. (Because readers of this how-to book on Family Histories and Memoirs may more likely be searching the Bibliography by *title* rather than *author*, I set up my Bibliography that way.)

Index

Nothing frustrates me more when picking up a nonfiction book than to discover it has no index. Some writers argue that certain types of books — humor, for example — are published for enjoyment, not reference. If yours is a family history, however, you may want to include an index — especially if this is the first of a multi-volume series.

While there are some computer software indexing programs (see your local computer software store or write The American Society of Indexers, P.O. Box 386, Port Aransas, TX 78373 and ask about their *Guide to Indexing Software*), most of us do our indexing the old fashioned way.

That means keeping a running A to Z list of the important names and topics in our manuscript, so we can fill in the correct page numbers later on the final proof before printing. I usually take a legal pad and cut out the right side of each page to make a thumb-indexed A to Z group of pages on which to list my notes.

Chapter Thirteen

That Very Important First Chapter

I n a time when the life and death of a television series is subject to the mass clicking of remote controls, the book author's challenge is to deliver — on page one of chapter one — something that will make the reader want to keep reading.

Your opening chapter, of course, must be in keeping with both the scope and style of the book you decided to write. It must enthrall readers and propel them forward into the book, but it must also set up realistic expectations for what is to follow. Don't, for example, use a slam-bang action chapter to lead into what otherwise is a book of gentle reminiscence.

OPENING DEVICES

What techniques do writers use to capture the reader's attention? Some of the examples that follow show the use of:

✔ A startling statement
✔ A family as symbol
✔ A photograph and a family assumption about it
✔ An unexpected revelation
✔ The author's place in time

When you sit down to write your book's opening, look for scenes that could involve:

Action: Is it our ancestor trying to cross the snowy Donner Pass right after that fateful party had to resort to cannibalism to survive? Is it a grandfather narrowly escaping an accident in a steel mill? Is it relatives enduring an Indian attack on their isolated homestead?

Suspense: Is it your grandmother facing the unexpected death of her young husband and the prospect of needing to support herself and three children in the days when women did not work outside the home?

Character: Is it your own story of confronting and then coping with a discouraging diagnosis of your first child?

A Sense of Place: Do you, or your family, identify so strongly with where you were born or grew up that, even though you don't live there anymore, you maintain an unbreakable bond to this place?

Anecdote: Is there a story about an incident in your family that has been handed down for generations that synthesizes how you feel about what your family's attitudes or values are?

The News Peg: Is there something in today's news that parallels a previous time in history in a corner of the world where your ancestors came from?

Inspiration: Did someone you knew affect you so intensely that your life has never been the same since?

You may have already thought of a dozen other ways to capture your reader's attention, given the specific material you'll be working with. But let's examine some published works to see how other successful authors did it.

THE OPENING PARAGRAPHS

Few of us have the opportunity to use a first chapter opening line like this:

"It's not easy to cut through a human head with a hacksaw."

That's from author Michael Crichton, who in four opening paragraphs of his autobiography, *Travels*, describes that assignment of his as a medical student.

Crichton goes on to explain that he had gone to college planning to be a writer, but early on a scientific tendency appeared.

In the English department at Harvard, my writing style was severely criticized and I was receiving grades of C or C plus on my papers. At eighteen I was vain about my writing and felt it was Harvard, and not I that was in error, so I decided to make an experiment. The next assignment was a paper on *Gulliver's Travels*, and I remembered an essay by George Orwell that might fit. With some hesitation, I retyped Orwell's essay and submitted it as my own. I hesitated because if I were caught for plagiarism I would be expelled; but I was pretty sure my instructor was not only wrong about writing styles, but poorly read as well. In any case, George

Orwell got a B minus at Harvard, which convinced me that the English department was too difficult for me.

Michael Crichton's revenues from his novels and films like *Jurassic Park* and *Disclosure* proved his career change from medicine to writing was a profitable one.

Is there some aspect of *your* story that illustrates an unexpected fact about your family or yourself?

A Family as Symbol

John Egerton's meeting with a 105-year-old South Carolina woman made him see that a single American family, whose lives spanned several generations, could be seen as a microcosm of our national experience. His chapter one of *Generations: An American Family* begins this way:

> We were perfect strangers when we met, but I had been looking for Burnam and Addie Ledford for a long time.
>
> The search had begun in my mind on a summer day in 1976. By chance, by sheer good fortune, I found myself sitting on the cabin porch of a 105-year-old woman in the marshy low country of South Carolina. At the beginning of the nation's third century, she could remember the start of the second — and in her vividly drawn impressions of nineteenth-century Carolina there was a sense of timelessness that could have belonged as well to the eighteenth-century birth of the nation. In the clarity of her recollections, in the specific detail of her observations, in the grace and eloquence of her language, the old woman was spellbinding; it was as if she had taken me on a personal tour of the past.
>
> I came away from that experience with a heightened awareness of the treasures that waste away in the minds and memories of the elderly. The greatest gift they have to offer — their vision of the past — is too often unappreciated, neglected, ignored. The very old ones lived in a world unseen by the rest of us, a world long since vanished. Their memories evoke the sight and smell and feel of homespun clothes and handmade tools and candlelit cabins by the creek. And when they were young, they knew old people from a time when England claimed most of this continent and the United States was still a revolutionary dream. There remains a remnant of elderly Americans who have seen and heard every generation of citizens in the history of this nation. They are the last connecting link between our ancestors and ourselves. When

their time is gone — and it will not be long — there will be none who remember the nineteenth century.

From my encounter with the South Carolina centenarian, an idea evolved. It began as a succession of questions: How accurate are the stories of the elderly? How typical? How complete? Can they be drawn out in conversation? Can they be verified? Are they consistent enough and lively enough to sustain interest? In the recent works of other writers — Alex Haley, Irving Howe, Theodore Rosengarten, Ernest Gaines, Studs Terkel, to name a few — I subsequently found both fiction and nonfiction that appeared to be inspired by the same kinds of questions. Looking beyond the power-wielders of history — the kings and presidents and generals — these writers had found among the uncelebrated masses, about whom history is seldom written, some portraits from the past that glowed with realism and authenticity.

Thinking of these efforts to explain us to ourselves, and thinking of the very old among us, I began to wonder whether a true story about continuity and change in four or five living generations of one family would add anything of value to our understanding and appreciate of our evolution as a people. Could I find a family whose collective life stories were sufficiently diverse to be typical or representative of the majority of Americans? Could I find an elderly couple with accurate and detailed recollections of their lives since the nineteenth century, and older stories passed on to them from an earlier time? Would there be enough people and enough variety in the couple's succeeding generations to form a complete picture? Could I gather and assemble this family biography in such a way that it could be seen as a social history of our national experience, a mirror of our times, a metaphor of America?

I became convinced that a careful search would turn up such a family, perhaps many such families — indeed, it seemed to me that almost any family would produce a representative portrait if its elders were old enough and clear-headed enough and if their descendants were numerous enough. The story of any large family, I thought, would give those who read it a glimpse of their own history, a better vision of themselves. One family could be a prism through which the shape and texture and resonance of American life could be transmitted — and the more carefully the family was

chosen for its typicality, the more universally recognizable the
resulting portrait would be.

The first step was to draw up a descriptive outline. I wanted to
find a family that had been a part of the middle-class mainstream
of national life for at least a century, a family securely anchored
between the extremes of wealth and poverty. There must be a
hundred or more people in at least four generations, beginning
with elders born in or around the 1870s in a rural or small-town
environment in the mid-American heartland. Ideally, the elders
would still live in the same county — or at least the same state —
in which they were born. Typical of the national majority, they
would be white, Anglo-Saxon, mainstream Protestant, Democratic or Republican citizens — she a retired homemaker or perhaps
a schoolteacher, he a retired farmer or teacher or preacher or
merchant. They should be in good health, living at home rather
than in a nursing home, and they should have lucid and detailed
recollections of the past — and an untiring fondness for talking.

From such a couple, if they had produced a half-dozen or more
children, would inevitably come succeeding generations progres-
sively larger and more diverse than the first, until in the third or
fourth generation they ranged across the spectrum of occupations,
income levels, places of residence, political preferences, religious
beliefs. Given sufficient numbers, they would have been almost
everywhere, done almost everything; given even modest numbers — say, a hundred past the age of eighteen or twenty — they
would have been to enough places and done enough things to tell
a collective tale of the evolution of a nation. And in that story, I
was confident there would be a true and accurate image that any
American would recognize.

Aristocratic Ancestors?

Is some handed-down painting or portrait photograph the starting
point for a family history? In his book, *Ancestors: A Family History*,
William Maxwell's opening chapter reveals this:

> My Grandfather Maxwell was a lawyer in Lincoln, Illinois, and
> one of his clients, out of affection for him, brought back from a
> visit to Scotland a sepia photograph of Caerlaverock Castle. This
> ruined fortress is the ancestral seat of a Scottish family of some
> importance, members of which have held the titles Earl of

Morton. . . . and Lord Maxwell. . . . During my childhood it hung over the horsehair couch in my Aunt Maybel's sitting room. . . . It was referred to in the family as the Maxwell castle—proudly, but also as if that was all there was to know about it. I didn't think to ask somebody where it was. . ...

There is no evidence that any ancestor of mine ever lived in (thirteenth century) Caerlaverock Castle, even in the capacity of a kitchen boy or swineherd. Tenant farmers commonly took the surname of their landlord, and so it does not follow that every Maxwell is a blood relative of every other person of that name. . . . But the photograph was all the proof the older generation required that the loins from which they had sprung were ultimately aristocratic.

How many other handed-down stories about our ancestors have made us want to know who we *really* are?

A Lost Mother

Personal memoirs do not always begin the way you might expect them to, given the present image of the author. Here's the opening of Art Buchwald's *Leaving Home: A Memoir*:

Shortly after I was born, my mother was taken away from me or I was taken away from my mother. This was done because she was mentally ill. She suffered from severe chronic depression, which required that she be committed to a private sanitarium. She never recovered and, eventually, when my father ran out of money, she was placed in a state hospital in upper New York for thirty-five years—the rest of her life.

Buchwald's opening very quickly sets the stage for a narrative that recounts his own bouts with clinical depression, his life in foster homes before enlisting in the Marines during World War II, and his subsequent life as a writer. Even a quick glance will tell readers that this will not be another of Buchwald's humor collections.

Historical Time

Placing the family in the context of history is another way to start. Jim and Jodie Armour decided to continue a family history that Jim's father, John H. Armour, had begun but then abandoned because of illness. "I keep a journal myself," says Jim, "and I think it's important

to look for the significance of events as they happen and write it down
as it happens. Family histories help us understand what our own life has
been about and what we have contributed. It helps our readers know
us better."

Here's an excerpt from the opening chapter of Jim's father's memoir:

> 1913 A.D.! What was happening that year? For one thing, the
> Constitution of the United States has a new amendment, the 16th
> Amendment. It brought the people the joys of Federal Income
> Tax. It was ratified in January 1913, and on the 9th of January in
> 1913, I was born. Of these two events I like to think that I have
> brought more joy to mankind! . . . In Europe by the year 1913 the
> fuse was being lit for World War I which made the world "safe
> for democracy." The Berlin to Baghdad R.R. was the dynamite,
> Serbia was the fuse, and the Junkers of Central Europe lit it.
>
> By the time I went from diapers to Buster Brown suits, the
> Armistice was signed, the Armours had moved from Homestead
> Park, Pennsylvania to Knoxville, Pennsylvania, and the world (and
> Homestead Park) was safe for democracy. Someone invented the
> radio and someone invented Buster Brown suits. In 1919 my dad
> built one, a crystal set, and my mother put me in the other and
> sent me off to school.

In another passage, John Armour gives us not just the facts but the
personal feelings that accompany historical events he lived through like:

DEPRESSION DAYS

> If you have read the statistics from the volumes written, and
> the many accounts both factual and fictional, about the Depres-
> sion days, and even though you listen to many tales told by those
> who survived these years, you cannot possibly feel these times.
> Inside of us there was a feeling; it was at once frustration and
> courage, anger and patience, hope and resignation, bewilderment
> and faith, and the whole gamut of human confusion; and it was
> with you every minute of every waking hour, year after year. Every
> man, woman and child was a casualty to some degree, and the
> impact upon our society is still a factor in today's culture.
>
> I do not remember the statistics, only the people. The old lady
> with her Packard limousine and chauffeur who came every week
> to stand in the dole line for her ration of potatoes and coal. The
> same as Nick Cindrish, Punks Tagmier, and others of the steel

mill families. It was said her husband had committed suicide when their fortune was wiped out. The old chauffeur stayed on because there was nowhere to go, and there was no one buying limousines, mansions or the like. But they always helped the elderly along their way home by giving them a ride with their burdens from the dole line. And along the banks of the rivers at the railroad terminals the destitute built villages of cardboard and tin shanties. Homeless and always hungry, when summer was gone, they were cold and sick for lack of clothing and proper heat. They existed only because others cared enough to share their meager sustenance with them.

Chapter One as Author's Plan

Instead of writing a preface or introduction to their books, some writers simply tell us in their first chapters how they plan to develop their books. Here's what James Michener said in the opening paragraphs of chapter one of his *The World Is My Home: A Memoir*:

> This will be a strange kind of autobiography because I shall offer the first seven chapters as if I had never written a book, the last seven as if that were all I had done.
>
> I segregate the material in this way for two reasons: I want the reader to see in careful detail the kind of ordinary human being who becomes a writer and then to see the complex and contradictory motivations that enable him to remain one.

A Letter From Abroad

If your personal story is a recounting of a special experience you had, you might format your book as a collection of letters that you wrote to describe over a period of months or years what happened and what it meant to you. For example, personal stories often grow out of interesting jobs we've held. Elaine Reed is an American business consultant with the Peace Corps in Albania. Her letters to friends and professional colleagues back home are part of the personal story, that she might want to edit into a book one day. Perhaps it will focus on what she learned that will be useful to other professionals now working in our new global environment. Here's an excerpt from a recent letter:

> I'm living on my own now in an apartment after seven and a half months with host families. Being the only female American business consultant here, almost everyone knows me. Unfortu-

nately, some people think since I'm American I have tons of money. Attempts have been made twice now to break in to my apartment.

Work here is challenging and frustrating. The culture is respectful of women and very male dominated so a woman in business (rare) is still called a businessman. In articles I write I tried to introduce the expression "business people" but had to explain that people included men and women.

My work revolves around providing consultation in the form of marketing, financial planning or general business plan development. I work in conjunction with a credit giving organization fifty percent of the time. In the current economic climate with huge demand for all products and little supply, a lousy decision still yields a huge profit. But I focus my energy on those people who want to plan for the future when there is more competition.

A personal story might start something like this and then flash back to how she happened to get the job; move to Albania; what it was like living with the different host families and getting to know the business people she would be consulting with.

FICTIONALIZED HISTORY

Those writers considering a fictionalized version of a family history or personal memoir might want to review Doris Ricker Marston's book *A Guide to Writing History*. In the chapter "Four Types of History in Fiction," Marston compares the straight biography to the biographical novel, such as Catherine Drinker Bowen on John Adams vs. Irving Stone's story of John and Abigail Adams in *Those Who Love*. She discusses the "factual novel," *In Cold Blood*, in which Truman Capote explains in his acknowledgment page that:

All the material in this book not derived from my own observation is either taken from official records or is the result of interviews with the persons directly concerned, more often than not numerous interviews conducted over a considerable period of time. . . .

She also cites several historical novels in which the historical figures and background may be accurate, but the central characters around whom the story unfolds are imaginary. More contemporary examples of such fictionalized histories are books by John Jakes and James Michener.

ENDINGS OF CHAPTER ONE

The end of the first chapter should not mark the end of the reader's interest in your subject. What special problem can you pose for your protagonist to face at the end of the first chapter: This "cliffhanger" will make the reader want to know "What will he want to do now?," "Where can she find help?," "Will they find a way to fulfill their dream?" *and* keep reading.

Here are two examples of how professional writers do it:

The opening chapter of Finis Farr's book *Margaret Mitchell of Atlanta* describes the excitement in Atlanta surrounding the premiere in December, 1939, of the movie *Gone With the Wind* — made, of course, from Mitchell's famous novel. Readers see the parties, the arrival of the movie's stars, the costume ball, and the premiere screening itself, after which the movie's stars and Mitchell were called on stage.

Here's the closing paragraph of chapter one:

> Miss Mitchell bowed, and waved a white-gloved hand as the applause again crashed over her. She had indeed experienced incredible success since the publication of her magical book, and now stood at the high point of her life. Had the fame, the adulation, and this evidence of genuine love from a whole city made her a happy woman? Those who knew her best would have been most hesitant in offering a ready answer; for there was much, very much, in Margaret Mitchell and her life that did not meet the eye.

The author thus lures us into chapter two where she explores Margaret Mitchell's family background and childhood.

Here is the second example. "The Outsider," the opening chapter of Richard J. Whalen's book *The Founding Father: The Story of Joseph P. Kennedy, A Study in Power, Wealth and Family Ambition*, describes in a brief anecdote the unusual method by which Joe Kennedy got his coveted baseball letter at Harvard — "one prize in a lifetime spent in quest of success, a pursuit bound up with a grandfather he never knew, for whom success was the humble certainty of a full stomach." The first chapter then goes on to explore Joe's Irish tenant farmer grandfather, the immigration of his father, and *his* rise in the Irish business and political community in Boston. Here are the last three paragraphs of chapter one:

> With the fortunes of many improving, the Irish were inspired to invent such classifications for themselves as "shanty," for the

luckless, and "lace curtain," for the up and coming. Close questions of precedence were decided by the year (even the month) of a parent's arrival, the "older" the family, the higher the rank.

Patrick Kennedy had been courting pretty Mary Hickey, whose family stood a rung or two above the Kennedys' but Kennedy, a state representative at twenty-eight, had only begun to climb. They were married in 1887, and on September 6 of the following year, their first child was born. He was named Joseph Patrick.

The first Irish Mayor of Boston, Hugh O'Brien, had been elected only three years before, and the Irish were whooping across the threshold to political power. But it soon was clear that the Yankee would not be easily overcome. He had, as it were, simply retired from the ante-chamber and double-locked the doors beyond, which, by reason of their peculiar construction, could not be forced. For Joseph Patrick Kennedy, life would center on the search for the key.

Chapter two describes the early childhood of Joe Kennedy and the beginning of his search for that key.

Chapter Fourteen

How Writers Avoid Middle Book Sag

W riters of family histories and personal stories have to use the same techniques novelists and other writers do to keep readers turning the page. There are many such devices available to you; the dozen outlined below are particularly appropriate to family histories and memoirs. No matter what devices work in your story, however, the goal is the same — to maintain the reader's interest in your story.

The research you've done and the notes you've made already include the answers to most of the questions I'll pose concerning these devices. If not, you may want to keep these ideas in mind for additional research, which will help you flesh out your final draft.

Let's examine some possibilities in your book for employing each of these devices.

- ✔ *Conflict.* Were or are there internal (or external) clashes between family members, between different families, even within a specific character? Was the integration of Old World societal traditions into New World life smooth or jarring?
- ✔ *Emotion.* What is your character's reaction to the death of a loved one? To betrayal? To injustice?
- ✔ *Character.* Do you know what makes your ancestors who they are? How do you find out more than just their names?
- ✔ *Action.* What wars, revolutions, terrorist acts, floods, earthquakes, forest fires put your ancestors or your family to the test?
- ✔ *Suspense.* Are your characters facing choices that could affect their future — and yours?
- ✔ *Self-Image.* What are your values and do they differ from those of other members of your family? What were your ancestors' politics, religion, outlook on the world?

✔ *Crises.* Have you or your family faced some personal crises? Are they matters you feel belong in a memoir or not?

✔ *Social Mores and Sex.* Was it an Old Country "arranged" marriage or a love match? A shotgun wedding or a single parenthood? Was a dateless Saturday night the fate worse than death? Should schools give out condoms?

✔ *Secrets.* What are the family skeletons and do you want to dig them up or let them rest in peace?

✔ *Atmosphere.* Does a strong sense of place run through your memoir? Is the setting as much a "character" in your story as the people?

✔ *Humor.* Are there funny stories that reveal as much about a family as historical facts do? (The reader often prefers this.)

✔ *Tying Present to Past.* Does a Mother's Day or Father's Day or some other holiday celebration prompt a memoir for your book?

Writing Reminder: Each of these elements can be used to enhance reader interest in your story. Since each author's book and purpose is different, I can't give you a master recipe that tells you when to add a dollop of drama or a pinch of humor. You have to decide what makes the pace and flow of your story move best.

In a play, for example, we refer to the first stage of the plot as "rising action." This is the presentation of essential information that rises as the protagonist encounters some conflict or opposing force (this is called "complication"). Rising action peaks at the climax — the moment of highest intensity — and is resolved when a decision is made or an action taken to solve the conflict.

Of course, a play usually concentrates on only a couple of characters and a brief period of time. Your book-length family history or memoir, on the other hand, may be a panorama of characters and events. You can, however, use this storytelling device of rising action-climax-resolution to tell multiple characters' stories throughout the book.

Let's look at some published family histories and memoirs to see how some of these storytelling devices were used. You might then want to read one or two of these books to see how these middle-book excerpts fit the book as a whole.

FAMILY RELATIONSHIPS

Were there conflicts between generations or within a single family unit that disrupted the orderly flow of family life in your history? The choice of a career may cause friction in some families. For example, Katherine Wyse Goldman, whose mother is a successful advertising executive and writer, was brought into her mother's business. In this middle-of-the-book excerpt from her *My Mother Worked and I Turned Out Okay*, Goldman uses the story of a potential conflict to give us a clearer picture of her mother:

> Your children may not remember you for your pristine bathrooms, flaky pie crusts, and collection of needlepoint pillows, but they will remember you for helping steer them in the right professional direction.
>
> As everything else involved in raising children, nobody says it's going to be easy.
>
> First, there's a lot of wincing, grimacing, shrieking, whining and complaining. Who wants to take *her* advice? Who wants to do what *she* says? Who wants to *be* her?
>
> Yes, I went through all of it. I clearly remember grudgingly agreeing to go work for my mother, as if I were doing her a big favor. After all, it's tough to follow in your mother's footsteps. Is this what boys have gone through all these years in going into their fathers' professions and their fathers' businesses?
>
> Having an achieving mother can make you want either to be president of the United States, to be better than she ever was, or to work alone in the basement of a university library cataloging doctoral theses for the rest of your life, to escape forever the possibility of a matchup.
>
> It's nerve-wracking to think you'll never measure up to her professionally. It's hard to be introduced as her daughter when others have clear ideas of who she is, her levels of competency and authority, when you're a little pipsqueak.
>
> The first day I worked for my mother was unbearable. I had to write a sixty-second radio commercial that I couldn't possibly compress to less than three minutes. I didn't understand, couldn't believe, that I could ever, ever, ever be as good as the worst copywriter there ever was, much less even close to my mother. At the end of the day, I walked into her office and burst into tears, "I can't do it," I blubbered.
>
> "Close the door," she said.
>
> "Kathy," she told me, "I never would have hired you if I didn't think you could do it. I know your work. I know how you think.

I have absolute confidence in you. I don't want you to fail. I'm not going to be your boss. I'm not going to teach you how to write. You have somebody else to report to. I want you to believe you can do it." Then she told me the story of a famous woman in business who used to go home every night and cry when she first started working because she didn't think she could make it through the obstacle course. She rose to the occasion, my mother told me, and became a model businesswoman. I felt a lot better.

Isn't that just like a mother? And who's to say that's not how you're going to treat your children when they are ready for career advice? You'll be just like you are when they need help drinking out of a cup, tying their shoes, or tackling a term paper.

A mother is a mother is a mother.

Sibling Relationships

How close are you to your sisters and brothers? How have your relationships changed as adults from when you were kids together? Marian Sandmaier, a writer on psychological and family issues, says in *Original Kin: The Search for Connection Among Adult Sisters and Brothers* that sisters seem to make the most effort to maintain an intimate relationship. Brothers, on the other hand, may care about each other but often don't make the necessary overtures to stay in touch. Brother-sister relationships fall somewhere in between, usually because the sister works harder at it.

How do these conclusions fit your own family relationships? Does a large family make a difference in how children relate to each other later as adults, or not? What caused friction between your family's siblings? Resentment over a parent's "favorite"? Jealousy of a sibling's greater material success? Dislike of a sibling's spouse or in-laws? An "unforgivable" insult? A feeling of "being taken advantage of"? Invitations ignored or never returned? Mistreatment of a parent?

The relationship between siblings can be deep and loving as well as shallow or confrontational. Siblings who are very close sometimes have a sixth sense about each other, as described in this personal memoir by college student Beth Mrea Hillerich:

> I woke up suddenly on July 25th at 5:00 A.M. I had been up late with friends at Amy's house, in St. Paul, Minnesota. Home from college, enjoying the summer, we had talked (as twenty-year-olds often do) until 3:30 A.M., but I had awakened with a deep

feeling of alarm only an hour and a half later. I should have been sound asleep, but I wasn't. Something was wrong — very, very wrong.

I tried to wait until 6:00 A.M. before I called my mom. I only made it until 5:45. She was startled by my call. Little did I know she was just about to pick up the phone to call me.

"What are you doing up, honey?" She asked.

I explained to her how I had woken up suddenly and just wanted to talk to her, to make sure everything was OK. If she was surprised at my question, I couldn't tell. She asked me if she could come and get me since I was already awake. "I need your help with something," she said. Mom always woke up very early and always had one project or another going on, so this request wasn't the least bit odd or out of character for my mother.

"Of course," I said, "I'll wait for you outside."

I calmly went and woke up my friend Amy. "Amy, something's wrong with my brother Bart."

"What? Why do you think that?" She asked.

I repeated the conversation I had with my mom.

She replied, "What does that have to do with Bart? Did she say something was wrong?"

I told her no, she hadn't even mentioned him, she had merely asked me to help her with something. Amy thought I was overly exhausted and probably a little crazy, but I knew I wasn't, and that something was wrong with Bart. I had always had an amazing connection with my older brother who was two years older than me and somehow this connection caused me to sense that something was wrong with him.

I sat on the porch steps outside Amy's apartment. Staring off into space, I didn't really see my mom until she was walking up the steps. As soon as I saw her I knew I was right; just looking into her eyes I could tell something was wrong. "What's wrong with Bart?" I asked her.

She immediately asked me if I had called home again and talked to Dad.

"No, I haven't," I answered. "But what's wrong with Bart?"

She replied by saying, "Let's get in the car and go home, honey."

"No, because you're going to tell me something's wrong with my Bart. Where is he?" I wanted to know, "How badly is he hurt?"

She kept saying, "Let's get in the car" and I kept refusing, insisting that she tell me what was wrong.

Finally, exhausted with trying to maintain her facade, she broke down, "Beth," she began, "Bart's not just hurt, he was killed in a car accident early this morning. . . ."

We made it back to our house in Woodbury, Minnesota, in approximately twenty minutes. When I entered the house, I stood in the foyer without moving; I glanced towards the kitchen, in the direction where the voices were coming from. My dad was sitting on one of the kitchen stools, with friends circled around him. His face was filled with a pain I had never seen before on my father. I will never forget hearing what they were talking about . . . "the body." They kept referring to "the body" and what to do with "the body." The words seemed to be on a megaphone, a loud service speaker. That was it, enough. I was done with this nightmare. I wanted out and I definitely wanted to be away from this house and this insane talk of "the body." I left and I ran — literally. I have never before and never again run as long, and as far, as I did that day. I ran until I fell and then I got up and I ran again.

Beth's memoir continues with her remembrances of her childhood, high school and college days with her brother and her sense of loss at his death at twenty-two.

What are the most important relationships in your family now? What were they before? If you were an only child, or an adopted only child, what was growing up like? What is it like now, if your parents are dead and you have no siblings?

Family Feuds

What were the relationships of your ancestors to each other? Did family feuds separate family members for years? What brought them back together? Or did they die unreconciled?

Writing Reminder: If there are several sides to a story and you can't prove one side is truth, tell all the sides. Or tell the stories and then point to the one your research indicates is most likely true.

A chronicler of a famous family feud, *The Hatfields and the McCoys*, Otis K. Rice, handles the facts vs. the myths of this Appalachian family this way in his preface:

Without question, the Hatfield-McCoy feud has excited more interest than any of the late nineteenth-century vendettas of the southern Appalachian Mountains. Scores of books and articles have related its history, and novels, motion pictures and outdoor dramas have drawn their inspiration from it. Unfortunately, too many of the depictions have been more given to sensationalism than to accuracy and objectivity.

At the outset, it must be recognized that the origins of the feud were complex and cannot be identified with one particular event. Moreover, many of the details of events in the feud may never be known with certainty, for accounts, even by participants, were often so contradictory that there is no way of determining precisely where the truth ended and fabrication began. In addition, many newspaper accounts were so biased or so grossly inaccurate that they must be used with considerable discrimination. Reminiscences in which long conversations were recalled verbatim, used by some writers, are by their very nature suspect.

The present study makes no claim to the discovery of the ultimate truth of every detail of the feud. I have tried, however, to separate myth from known facts, to present as dispassionate and balanced an account as available sources will afford, and to place the feud in the social, economic, political and cultural context in which it occurred. I have drawn as much as possible from contemporary sources, including court records, public documents and other materials, including newspapers, that offer a degree of reliability. Above all, I have sought to weigh evidence carefully and to avoid the partisanship and condescension that have characterized much of the writing on the feud.

CHARACTER INSIGHT

In both family histories and memoirs, the book as a whole is an insight into a family's or a person's character. Who a person is—his or her essential being—is the quality responsible for the actions that person takes. Insights about a family or persons come to the reader throughout the book.

People who are writing family history narratives (as opposed to those who are simply putting names and dates on tree branches) have a real challenge in trying to add personality to their ancestors. What can we know about our great-great-great grandparents beyond what they did, wrote in a letter or diary, or said to someone else who wrote it down?

We can learn what times were like when they lived; we can examine the public record of their lives in marriage documents, deeds, wills.

As a Penn State University librarian pointed out in a press release some time ago, "Your town librarian can probably point you to a number of specific histories, available to anyone, that can let you know how life was where and when your ancestors lived. For example, if your great-great grandfather lived in Penns Valley, Pennsylvania, during the Civil War, there's a strong possibility that he was a Democrat with pro-Southern sympathies. Why? Because those were the beliefs of many of the people living in that region at that time. This information isn't reserved for scholars alone. If you know your ancestor's occupation, religion, when he lived and where, with some digging, you can make generalizations about his life."

But what about their special quirks of personality that also made them who they were as individuals?

The first book dealing in psychohistory that I remember reading about was *In Search of Nixon: A Psychohistorical Inquiry*, by Bruce Mazlish. When it came out in 1972, I thought to myself, "How can anyone presume to know what a person's thoughts, motives, influences have been?" I had the same reservations that were expressed in a *Virginia Quarterly Review* review of the book: "Mazlish's sources are confined almost exclusively to Nixon's writing and public statements, as well as to several journalistic biographies. . . . Mazlish raises a host of important and provocative questions. But without personal interviews with the President, his family, his colleagues and his associates — and such intimacy is not likely to be forthcoming — these questions will remain unanswered."

The debate continues. In a 1987 book, *Psychohistory*, edited by Geoffrey Cocks and Travis Crosby, there is an interesting chapter on "Why did Van Gogh cut off his ear?" Thirteen possible explanations, based on some things known about Van Gogh's life and relationships, are suggested. But William McKinley Runyan points out that each, all or none of the explanations may be true.

In another chapter, John Klauber is reported as noting "that while the idea of science is unitary explanation of multiple phenomena, history and psychoanalysis attempt to find multiple explanations for single events." And psychoanalyst Erik Erikson developed the distinction that "In a case history we learn what went wrong and why . . . a life history in contrast describes how a person managed to keep together and to maintain a significant function in the life of others."

There is no easy answer to the question of how you add personality to names in a census record. Novelists have the freedom to use their

imaginations. Family historians don't. You will not know all the heredi-
tary and environmental influences on your ancestors, so can only make
assumptions — which you honestly admit to your readers as you write
them.

For example, in his book *The Edward Clark Genealogy: 1676-1988*,
Walter Burges Smith says:

THE ALLISON THEORY

One hypothesis is that Edward was brought to Middlesex
County by his future father-in-law, David Allison. There is no
clearcut evidence suggesting this. Still, it is worth examining.

(A) Ann Allison turned fifteen exactly one month before she
and Edward were married in 1681. Her family would not have
allowed the marriage if they had not known Edward well. . . .

(B) Another possible hint is the fact that Edward in middle age
bought land in next door Essex County and moved there for the
rest of his life; Edward's attraction to Essex may have stemmed
from his having lived there as a child. David Allison also has a tie
with Essex County and may conceivably have lived there before
settling in Middlesex as will be seen below. Hence, one may speculate that Edward was an orphan, was brought up by David Allison,
and came with David to Middlesex not long before 1662.

Of course, every family history author's viewpoint is subjective. I
am reminded of Carolyn Heilbrun's comments on how *she* selected the
pseudonym Amanda Cross for the first detective novel she wrote and
the reasons everyone *else* came up with for why she did. In *Writing A
Woman's Life*, she writes:

The question I am most often asked is how and why I chose
the name "Amanda Cross." This was, or seemed at the time, a
matter of no significance. My husband and I had once been stran-
ded in a deserted part of Nova Scotia; while we awaited rescue,
we contemplated a road sign reading "MacCharles Cross." My
husband, attempting cheer, remarked that if either of us ever
wanted a pseudonym, that would be a good one. I remembered
that moment in 1963 when I finished my first detective novel, but
was told that my book had obviously been written by a woman
and that I should use a woman's first name. I chose "Amanda,"
under the (as it turned out, entirely mistaken) impression that no
one since Noel Coward's early plays had had that name. In recent

years, I have heard many other explanations of my choice of pseudonym: that I stole Agatha Christie's initials; that the word *cross*
carries many meanings of conflict, tension and choice, which I
wanted; that the phrase *a-man-da-cross* is not without significance,
and so on. I accept all of them, even the one claiming it was after
Katherine Hepburn's role of Amanda in *Adam's Rib*. I didn't see
that movie until a few years ago, on television. Certainly if I had,
the name would have appealed to me for that reason. A word or
name must bear, I agree with Coleridge, all the meanings that
connotations attach to it.

Using Action to Reveal Character

Action takes many different forms in family histories and memoirs.

Writers who have access to original letters or diaries from ancestors
can use these to give readers a deeper understanding of the characters
by using the relative's own words to show readers what the character
thought and felt about the experiences he or she was going through. In
her book *The Box Closet*, Mary Meigs quotes from letters of her uncle
Arthur Ingersoll Meigs (AIM) at the end of World War I, while inter-
spersing some contemporary comments of her own:

> AIM had in his nature the necessary toughness to be a soldier;
> he could shut off feeling in order to get through the horrors with-
> out going to pieces. Edward could never have toughened himself;
> he would have gone to pieces. He could not excise his loving
> memories of Germany any more than Arthur could prevent himself
> from feeling sorry for the pale undernourished prisoners under his
> authority. Yet both could speak of the "Huns," the "Bosche,"
> the faceless monster that had to be defeated and deserved to be
> punished, and Arthur could write, "A lot of the Germans' best
> men have been killed, which is satisfactory." The best men were
> faceless like the monstrous war; multiple deaths were "satisfac-
> tory." The satisfaction of the body count, once one has assented
> to the necessity of war, this abstraction in contrast to Arthur's
> compassion when he looks at his prisoners and sees real men. "A
> thing happened that embarrassed me awfully," he writes to his
> cousin, Ed Ingersoll, in July. "One of my sergeants, the nicest man
> in the world, was taking things out of the prisoners' pockets —
> they had no arms when we got them — and being a little short on
> German, commanded — 'Out, Down,' making a gesture of taking

things out of the pockets and throwing them on the ground. The two poor devils on the end of the line understood only the last part of the gesture and immediately dropped on their knees, in the most abject manner. They looked as if they wouldn't have been in the least surprised if the next command had been to bow their necks preparatory to having their heads cut off. It embarrassed me, and it embarrassed my very nice sergeant."

It is strange that the enemy is transformed into a human being when he becomes a prisoner. He does not feel the change in himself; he is certain that he may still be seen as the enemy and be killed. His life depends on a convention but also on the shock of recognition between captured and captor. Even now, in our merciless time, prisoners are not always killed, and we see them on television, dirty and unshaven, herded behind barbed wire with the kind of heart-breaking look in their eyes that AIM saw. Perhaps the ability to see that look comes from being in the state of love that AIM was in almost continuously in 1918. At the end of the letter about the prisoners, there is a P.S. Arthur had been sitting in the still evening, "smoking my pipe with my back against a fence post." "When, like Lycidas, 'At last I rose and twitched my mantle blue,' (brown in this case) a great big moon was sailing up over the shoulder of the hill, and standing in the lane, in the dust, was a funny little French fox, who took a look, and disappeared in the oat field. So you see, it's a land of contrast. A big six inch gun, firing on one side of the hill, and in this particular instance, complete silence between times, and on the other side of the valley, a ripe oat field, a big moon, a small fox and a country lane."

A LIFE TURNING POINT

When we spoke earlier about "rising action," we mentioned that a story rises to a climax—the point at which the character must make some decision. Each of us has several points in our lives when we must make decisions that affect our future, and examining such points can be revealing and fascinating for readers. For example, the fiftieth anniversary in June, 1994, of World War II's D-Day in Europe brought to newspapers, magazines and television numerous retrospectives on that Allied effort that marked a turning point in the war.

In the middle of his book, *The World Is My Home*, James Michener describes an incident in his Pacific theater service that became a turning point in his life:

> While we were executing these routine maneuvers for avoiding a hazardous landing, twilight had darkened, and as we made our approach in minimum visibility my nerves tensed, my muscles tightened. No go! Visibility nil! Again the roar of the engines, the sickening swing to the left with the wing dipping almost vertically, and the swerving away from the mountains ahead. Then back out to sea and another wide swing over waves barely visible below for a third approach.
>
> I cannot now recall whether Tontouta had night-landing radar at that time — probably not, but if it did it was undoubtedly insufficient. During the third approach I was extremely tense but not panicked because I had flown thousands of dangerous miles in small planes in the Pacific and had learned to trust Navy pilots. I remember telling myself: It's got to be this time or we don't make it, and I did not care to speculate on whether we would have enough fuel to carry us back to Fiji or north to Espiritu Santo.
>
> With skill, nerve and determination our pilot brought his heavy plane into perfect alignment with the barely visible runway and eased it down in a flawless landing. We applauded, but he gave no sign of acknowledgment, because he, better than we, appreciated what a near thing it had been.
>
> That night I had no appetite, for the tenseness in my stomach banished any interest in food, but neither was I ready for bed. In what was to become the turning point of my life, I left the transient quarters where travelers like me stayed until they could get back to their home base, and unaware of where I was wandering, I found myself back on the long, dark airstrip with the mountains at the far end visible whenever the low, scudding clouds separated momentarily to reveal them.
>
> For some hours I walked back and forth on that Tontouta strip without any purpose other than to calm my nerves, but as I did so I began to think about my future life and to face certain problems: What do I want to do with the remainder of my life? What do I stand for? What do I hope to accomplish with the years that will be allowed me? Do I really want to go back to what I was doing before?

Important Moves

Persons who keep diaries already have a head start on a family history or personal story. Diana Cooke, currently studying for a master's degree in counseling psychology, says, "I have kept a diary, on and off, over a period of forty-six years, so a personal memoir seems like a good way to pull together some of my life experiences. A personal memoir would also help me find out some things about myself—provide a means of self-evaluation for where I've got to in my journey. My life has been interesting. If I record it, there is more hope of remembering details. Writing it down somehow—even if I fictionalize it to some extent—would jog my memories of people I've known and exotic (as well as common) situations I've experienced. It would be my written photographic album of how I experienced my world."

Here is a brief excerpt from her memoir, describing their family move to Caracas, Venezuela, when her husband was transferred by Procter & Gamble from England to that country. "This unforgettable experience," says Cooke, "incorporated some of the best times of our lives, as well as some of the worst." The latter were due to the eruption of a wave of terrorism as Communist Cuba attempted to expand its influence within the Hemisphere:

On All Souls' Night (or Halloween)—October 31st, 1960— when we landed at La Guaira, Venezuela's airport, there was a riot in full swing. Enrique, the P & G local company courier and greeter, was there and helped us through the arduous entry formalities, nevertheless our culture shock cranked into high gear. Due to bombings, gunfire and car-burnings on the main highways he said we had to take the old road through the hills to get to Caracas. (This is where all the poor folk live, we later discovered. Their homes, the so-called *ranchitos*, are mostly made of cardboard cartons.) Luckily by using that route, and avoiding the main thoroughfares, he managed to deliver us to our hotel, and so we came to the end of our long, weary journey.

Bob's worst forebodings were justified by this hazardous beginning to our South American adventure. His intuition told him to get the next plane back to England, but it was too late. His old job was now filled, and we were cut off.

The insurrection continued and the government suspended constitutional rules, giving themselves overriding powers (to search homes and detain people without warrants, etc.). Somehow

we adjusted to these frightening aspects of foreign living. Bob
fortified his plant with barbed wire and gun emplacements, and
had sentries patrolling with fierce guard dogs to protect it against
attack. Fire bombings had devastated Sears, and several other U.S.
companies in the area. Worst of all were those times when the
school buses bringing Sue and Alison home from school were
delayed due to outbreaks of rioting in the streets along their route.
I felt terribly anxious when an hour's delay stretched out to ninety
minutes or sometimes longer, and no one knew where they were.
I was incredibly relieved when they came home safely at last. Then,
along with the relief, came a crushing feeling of guilt for submitting
them to danger, and this persisted. Fortunately, they seem none
the worse for having had these experiences.

SELF-IMAGE

If you wanted to define for the readers of your family history or personal
story what it means to be an American today, what would you say? How
would you define for your readers what you think were the good and
bad things that the people we elected to Congress and the Presidency
did for the country and the world? My guess is most families, like mine,
are far from unanimous in their choice of elected officials and opinions
about their decisions.

What did your ancestors think about *their* political leaders?

If you know what your ancestors said or wrote about the politics of
their time, your readers would like to know. Your descendants will want
to know what *you* thought about politics today, which they'll be reading
about in a future we don't know yet.

You might want to compare how three different living generations
view a particular event. For example, a friend's daughter brought home
a list of questions for the family from school, one of which was "What
did you think of the demonstrations surrounding the 1968 Democratic
National Convention in Chicago?" The child's mother, remembering
her own self-avowed "hippie" reactions of the sixties differed completely
from her seventy-two-year-old father in regard to those "crazy kids."

What is the image of Americans to others? For twenty-six years,
Alistair Cooke was the American correspondent for the *Manchester* (England) *Guardian*, interpreting the U.S. to his British readers. A collection of those essays called *America Observed: From the 1940s to the 1980s*
was published in 1988.

A different approach was taken by James Simmons, an American adventure travel writer, who collected *his* observations of non-U.S. citizens into a book *Americans: The View From Abroad.* Here's what Jane Walmsley of London, England had to say:

> The single most important thing to know about Americans . . . .
> is that Americans think that death is optional. There's a nagging
> suspicion that you can delay death (or — who knows? — avoid it
> altogether) if you really try. This explains the preoccupation with
> health, aerobics, prune juice, plastic surgery and education.
>
> An Amsterdam college student told the author: I am of neither
> Dutch or European culture, I am of the Coca-Cola culture.

Books like these that we read often give memoir writers new insights about ourselves and the generations from which we came. Your book's readers will have a deeper understanding of your characters as you learn more about them yourself.

Foreign Cultures

Have you, or any members of your family lived or worked for a while in a culture quite unlike that of the U.S.? Are their observations of interest to readers of a family history? For example, a relative of mine lived for a while in a country whose religion governs much of its law.

Here is an excerpt from the English language newspaper *Arab Times* I received from my relative, in which Saudi Arabia's executioner, Saeed Al Sayef, described his work which involves cutting off hands (of thieves involved in serious robberies) and the heads (of murderers, rapists, drug traffickers and other persons convicted of serious crimes):

WHAT ARE THE TOOLS OF YOUR JOB?

To chop off the heads of men I use a special sword, following the writings of the Prophet Mohammed, while I use the gun to execute women. The reason for using the gun is to avoid removing any of the cover on the upper part of the woman's body. To cut the wrists of those involved in robbery, I use very sharp-edged knives to ensure that the wrist is cut cleanly in one stroke.

WHICH IS MORE DIFFICULT: CHOPPING HEADS OR CUTTING OFF HANDS?

Frankly speaking, it is easier to chop a head since this act means the end of the story for the criminal. Chopping off a hand needs more courage, since you are cutting a part of the body of an individual who is to survive. The cutting itself needs very skilled attention to assure that the chopping tool does not slip or cut in the wrong place. Psychologically, I feel some reluctance in these cases.

Travelers and workers in countries outside their own have a great opportunity to educate their families through the journals they keep, the letters they write, the clippings they save that explain one culture to another. And those resources may be an integral part of a future memoir.

PERSONAL CRISES

Diaries and journals offer family historians and biographers the best view of what our ancestors thought. Sometimes they surprise us. Thomas Mallon, in his *A Book of One's Own: People and Their Diaries*, tells us that Leonardo da Vinci worried in one of his notebooks about "wasting time, doing too little and doing it so badly that no impression of him will be left."

What doubts and fears did your ancestors reveal in letters or diaries that belied their ultimate accomplishments?

What personal crises have you or some of your family members had to face? Kitty Dukakis's autobiography *Now You Know* describes some battles she fought:

> Late in the campaign, I began to think about what I was doing, how drawn I was to the vodka, how necessary it was for me to have a drink. I tried to dismiss the thoughts, but they would not completely vanish. For many years I had lived with the guilt of taking diet pills; now I had this small voice inside warning me about the drinking. Small, indeed; I reduced the sound to a feeble squeak.
>
> During September and October, I was very down. The polls were not in our favor; everything seemed to be tinged with melancholy. While in St. Louis, I talked to a friend for hours. He saw my despondency and was concerned enough to telephone Bonnie. He told her he thought I was in very bad shape and headed for a real depression. In truth, I already was suffering from depression. Bonnie was wonderful all during those trying times. Officially, she was my executive assistant and took care of all the campaign details. Beyond that, she was a good and true friend and tried her best to look after me. Before she could take any action to help me, I managed to pull myself together. Activity kept me on the go. I could run away from my thoughts, from my feelings, and from

my fears. And so I did, until November 8, 1988. On that day I ran right into the brick wall of defeat.

The day after the election on November 9, my staff had a party for everyone who had worked for me during the campaign. The day after the party, on November 10, I became an episodic, binge drinker. An alcoholic can contain himself for only so long. When a crisis hits, the restraints snap. . . .

Statistics show alcoholism progresses much faster with women. Men produce a stomach enzyme that allows them to metabolize alcohol more quickly. Within weeks, I absolutely had to have a drink every two or three hours. Though many believed it was the campaign that started me drinking, the campaign actually had had a restraining influence. During that period I had been high on activity. The campaign was wonderful in almost every way. There were ups and downs as there are in any kind of roller-coaster experience, but the presidential race was a very positive undertaking. Then it was over. I began drinking when I was faced with a gaping emptiness I could not endure.

Writing a truthful personal or family story may be difficult for women for several reasons:

✔ a deep sense of privacy or loyalty
✔ the trauma in reliving a certain part of our lives in memory and on paper
✔ a historical tradition of women's autobiography, which is often nostalgic and romantic and hides any pain and anger

Carolyn Heilbrun makes that last point in her book, *Writing a Woman's Life*. In it, she describes the experience of American poet and novelist May Sarton whose autobiographical writings fell into, and then transcended the traditional trap.

Her *Plant Dreaming Deep*, an extraordinary and beautiful account of her adventure in buying a house and living alone, published in 1968, eventually dismayed her as she came to realize that none of the anger, passionate struggle, or despair of her life was revealed in the book. She had not intentionally concealed her pain: she had written in the old genre of female autobiography, which tends to find beauty even in pain and to transform rage into spiritual acceptance. Later, reading her idealized life in the hopeful eyes of those who saw her as exemplar, she realized that, in ignoring her rage and pain, she had unintentionally been less than honest. Changing times helped bring her to this realization. In her next book, *Journal of a Solitude*, she deliberately set out to recount the pain of the years covered by *Plant Dreaming Deep*.

For some of us, the understanding comes in early childhood that nothing lasts forever and life isn't always fun and games. Here's a personal memoir from college student Glory McLaughlin:

> When I was three and a half my father converted from a Bible-thumping Southern Baptist to a more rational Presbyterian, and so we moved to Clinton, Indiana.
>
> After we had gotten settled into our new home, we soon met the Dorrells. Phil Dorrell was a Methodist minister who had also recently moved his family to the rather obscure little town of Clinton, Indiana. He and his wife were about the same age as my parents, and they had a daughter one year younger than me. I had turned four by this time, so Rachel would have been three when I met her. My parents invited the Dorrells over for dinner one night, and as I became acquainted with my new friend, we sat on the yellow-carpeted steps in my house, playing with my Bristle Blocks. I knew right away I liked this girl. I don't know how I knew — maybe I sensed that she was intelligent; maybe I sensed that she would do whatever I told her to — whatever the reason, right then and there Rachel Dorrell became my best friend.
>
> We played Private Eyes a lot. This was our favorite thing to do. We used to draw maps to hidden treasures. We walked around outside, searching for "clues." One night we somehow talked my mother into letting us use flashlights to walk up and down the block in the dark, searching for clues. We took along our treasure map and envelope to collect our treasures. We picked up anything shiny. And then there was the ultimate Private Eye challenge: Details. Don't ask me how we got this name, but that was what we called eavesdropping on our parents and writing down whatever we heard. Of course, we couldn't write as fast as they talked, so the jumbled snippets of conversation we ended up recording were ridiculously funny. We lived on the edge, in constant fear of being caught with that incriminating evidence in our hands, perched on the landing of Rachel's stairwell. How brave and fearless we imagined ourselves to be.
>
> I don't remember exactly when I found out that Rachel's family

was moving, but I do remember the confusion I felt upon hearing the news. My world was about to be shattered. Who cared that the hostages had been released, or that Reagan was about to get shot? What about my best friend? Why did she have to move? Our family didn't have to move, so why did theirs? And why did they want to move? I felt very angry towards Rachel's mother, who couldn't wait to move out of the quiet little town of Clinton, Indiana, and go back to her hometown of Indianapolis. Didn't she care that I didn't want Rachel to leave? Did anybody ask Rachel if she wanted to move? This was the first time in my life that I remember really feeling as if things were out of my control. No matter how much I wanted my friend to stay, she wouldn't. She couldn't. So we talked about the new place where she was going, and tried to imagine what it would be like there. My mom told me that it would be easier for Rachel, because she got to go some-place new and make new friends, and I would be left behind by myself.

Vaguely, I remember going over to her house on the day they were leaving, walking around inside after everything had been taken out, and thinking how empty and different it looked. It made me sad, because that house had become a second home to me, and suddenly all the things that my memories were made of were gone. I felt a strange, empty feeling. I walked outside and stood with my parents as Rachel's family finished packing their last-minute things into the car. When everything was ready to go, I said goodbye to my best friend, and watched her get into the car, shut the door, and wave at me as she slowly drove away.

An era in my life had just ended.

SOCIAL MORES AND SEX

The conflict between Old World ways of doing things in Italy and the actions of native sons visiting from the New World is aptly described in this mid-book excerpt from Gay Talese's book *Unto the Sons*:

Gaetano Talese's first visit home to Italy in more than six years was made memorable a week after his arrival, when, while standing one evening beneath the balcony of a young woman with whom he was having a prolonged and lightly flirtatious conversation, he was grabbed and choked from behind by a man who, before stabbing him with a knife, whispered: "You have no right to speak to this woman."

As Gaetano fought the man off, then felt the blood flowing from his right temple, the assailant disappeared into the shadows between two buildings, never to be taken into custody. The woman later swore to the police that she could not identify the attacker; nor could she suggest the name of any man in whom she might have encouraged such impassioned possessiveness. But at that time it was not unusual for a woman in Maida not to know that a particular man had laid private claim to her, since such a man felt compelled to inform only his close male acquaintances, whose noninterference he sought and required while he watched her window at night, and frequently followed her during the day, learning all that he could about her until he was ready to reveal his ardor and marital intentions to her family.

This ancient rite of remote courtship, which still existed at the turn of century in southern Italy, was seen as both natural and proper: the woman was secretly desired and pursued; her family was later informed and consulted; and finally the nuptial terms were agreed upon by mature representatives of both parties — devoid of the ambiguous utterances, the furtive liaisons, and the fickle dalliances of a young couple in love. A stable society was founded on pragmatic matchmaking.

But recently the return of many native sons visiting from the New World who presumed the right to speak to any woman who caught their fancy was causing agitation among the population. While most people publicly expressed regret at what had happened to Gaetano, in private many believed he had gotten what he deserved.

Other offenses by returnees had gone unpunished. Several naive maidens, swayed by the men's exaggerated tales of their wealth and accomplishments overseas, and believing their promises would deliver them from poverty and stagnation of the village, later found themselves pregnant and abandoned by their persuasive lovers, who returned alone across the sea. Even when a young man was honorable, and wanted to marry his *inamorata* in Italy, he was sometimes rebuffed by her parents, who feared that if she joined him overseas they would never again see her. For the first time in local history, it seemed that the closeness of the large Italian family could be weakened and fractured by its transoceanic extension.

Therefore these visits home by workers from abroad were viewed apprehensively by many elders, who saw the migrants not as returning sons but as young men on the prowl, soldiers of the economy who were here today and then gone forever as men with a personal role in the village's future. Their American experiences had desensitized them to local customs, made them another in the long line of invaders. And during the *passeggiata* they were conspicuous in their foreign-made clothes, pridefully striding arm in arm with their more modest relatives, often failing to tip their hats to the passing priests or to members of the aristocracy, as if *they* were now the new aristocrats.

Financially generous as many of them undoubtedly were to their relatives in Maida, and thus an asset to the local economy, they nonetheless by their very existence prompted questions about the worth and courage of those hometown bachelors who had shunned the opportunity of enriching themselves overseas. The choice of local men to remain at home would not have become an issue had so many local women not become attracted to the travelers, and to the idea that a woman's life might be improved by taking chances and deviating from the path chosen by her elders. Even if she remained at home, the typical village maiden was no longer contented with what she had—her horizons had been widened, options were in the offing; the hometown boulevardiers, walking in circles, now lacked the mystery of the men visiting from abroad.

Teenage romance in America a couple of generations ago was a simpler matter, as seen in this memoir by Evelyn Weber:

A LOVE STORY?

Mother did not approve of Easter finery; she thought it irreligious. But on the Fourth of July she indulged us; we could have brand-new dresses, material and pattern chosen by us.

One year when I was about fifteen I chose a flowered voile that she sewed into the prettiest dress I ever had; princess style with a bertha collar.

I wore it that glorious Fourth of July on my date with the first love of my life. We went to the movies where we sat holding hands enjoying ourselves when suddenly there was a thunderstorm. The lights went out. The storm raged on and the lights were still out. So we started home. To protect me from the chill of the rain, Herman took off his jacket, wrapped it around me, lifted me into his arms and proceeded to carry me home. So very dark, one could not see the pavement. Then it happened! He stumbled stepping down from a curb. Desperately he tried to regain his balance when he dropped me in the dirty, swirling water in the gutter. I was furious! My beautiful Fourth of July dress all muddy, dirty, utterly ruined. I got up and started running towards home with Herman following calling out to me "Wait, Evelyn." I stopped. He caught up with me and we walked on. I was so angry with him, I would not talk to him. Quietly we walked through the rain. When we got home, I dashed into my house slamming the door in his face.

Attitudes and actions about sex were one aspect of life in the "silent generation" described by Benita Eisler in her book *Private Lives: Men and Women of the Fifties*. She followed a group of her contemporaries from their post-war growing up to the 1980s. Here's a passage from a middle-of-the-book chapter:

> In any market situation, value is always the *perception* of value. The worth of a commodity is as high or low as most people think it is and are willing to pay. Heroic independence of mind was required to escape a market psychology that described a woman's sexual favors in terms of "giving it away" or "saving it" (as in what-are-you-saving-it-for?). And this was only the realm of perception. The real danger — getting pregnant — was both public proof of and punishment for the nasty stuff you had been up to.
>
> "Everybody was doing it," Cass Hunnicutt says. "But it was the Big Lie that nobody was." Of all the secrets of coming of age in the fifties, sex was the darkest and dirtiest. As sexual beings, people became underground men and women. For some, leading a double life was no metaphor.
>
> In his third year of medical school, Mike DiStefano became engaged.
>
> "Terry came from a rich family. She was very spoiled and a terrible student, but she really enjoyed life. I was attracted to her because she was all the things I wasn't. She was attracted to me because I was all the things she wasn't; disciplined, serious, hardworking. We were infatuated with each other.
>
> "On Valentine's Day in my senior year, I went to her apartment with my little two-dollar packet of violets. Her roommate let me in. There were a dozen red roses on the table with a card. The card was from the married man she had been seeing. He was a

forty-two-year-old pediatrician with three children.

"For a guy like me, who was so naive and inexperienced," Mike says, "it was like the whole world had ended. We were only lovers in the emotional sense. There was never any consummated sex. At that time, I was one of those idealistic sort of males who was still a virgin.

"I realize now that Terry had been involved sexually with all kinds of men. But because we were planning to get married and because of the way I was, she had to let me believe she was a virgin."

Young people from immigrant cultures had sanctions coming from all directions—religious and social, the old world and the new.

"It wasn't so much that I consciously believed in virginity for its own sake," Mike says. "It was a combination of other factors: the fear of pregnancy was a big one. But also respecting a woman's view that if she were not a virgin, she wouldn't be respected. That was the basic thing.

"I felt that if I were sexual with someone, that indicated that I didn't respect them. I could be sexual with someone I didn't care for, but not with someone I did care for. The fact that I was never sexual with anyone is because I never dated anyone I didn't care for."

SECRETS

Some aspects of our families' lives we can only learn about belatedly and they sometimes surprise us. For example, in his memoir, *Patrimony*, Philip Roth describes this visit with his 76-year-old mother:

> Just the summer before her death, during a weekend visit to Connecticut, when we two were alone having a cup of tea in the kitchen, she had announced that she was thinking of getting a divorce. To hear the word "divorce" from my mother's lips astonished me almost as much as it would have if she had uttered an obscenity. But then the inmost intertwining of mother and father's life together, the difficulties and disappointments and enduring strains, remain mysterious, really, forever. . . .

Roth accurately portrays the problems in some families when a successful business executive husband retires and "settled down to become Bessie's boss—only my mother happened not to need a boss. . . ."

HUMOR

One of the devices writers use to keep their readers' interest is the use
of anecdotes. As Kathryn Murray pointed out in the introduction to
her book *Family Laugh Lines*, "In every household there are certain
remarks that live on through the years because they apply so well to
everyday situations. Some of these phrases are the punch lines of jokes.
Others come from true happenings, but they all become a frequently
used means of family communication."

Kathryn Murray, wife of the celebrated dance impresario, Arthur
Murray, and former star of her own weekly TV show, took her husband's
suggestion and collected a number of such family anecdotes from well-
known people into her book, *Family Laugh Lines*. Here's just one brief
excerpt:

> Victor Borge is a Dane by birth but a dean of American show
> business, with a huge and devoted following of TV viewers and
> theatergoers. Like all well-known stars, Mr. Borge is frequently
> greeted by people who are not even vaguely familiar to him. If his
> wife, Saana, is along and asks him, "Who are they?" he answers
> as his son did in this true incident.
>
> The Borges have five children and when their youngest boy
> was four-years-old he was invited to a swimming pool birthday
> party. When the little boy returned, his father asked him, "Did
> you have a good time?"
>
> " 'Yes, father.'
> " 'Did you have ice cream and cake?'
> " 'Yes, father.'
> " 'Were there lots of boys and girls in swimming?'
> " 'Yes, father.'
> " 'Were there more boys than girls in the pool?'
> " '*I don't know. They didn't have clothes on.*' "

Humor in family histories can take many forms. It could be a kids-
say-the-darndest-things anecdote. It could be an embarrassing moment
of your own that *now* you can laugh at. It could be an ancestor's funny
experience that has been handed down in the family for years.

What makes you laugh? I had a friend who was a past master at the
pun. Although she died recently, every time I see a funny one in the
newspaper or magazine I think of her. Other people like slapstick or the
sight gag in a movie.

Do you cut out jokes like this one from *Reader's Digest* and mail them to friends?:

> At age twenty, we worry about what others think of us. At forty, we don't care what they think of us. At sixty, we discover they haven't been thinking about us at all.
>
> —*Jock Falkson,*
> *quoted in* Frontline, *South Africa*

What would amuse your book's readers? Make sure that your family history or personal story's more serious memories are leavened with some humor.

FAMILY MEMENTOS

One of the ways to break up solid text and please readers at the same time is with poetry or verse. Are there any interesting samples among your family mementos?

Jim Hogue, a Vermonter who combines the unusual occupations of farmer and performer of Cabaret Shakespeare and mystery dinner the-ater, is the son of an actor on Broadway and in film. But his ancestors were Scotch who shipped coal *from* Newcastle to Australia in the early 1800s. Among his family documents is a eulogy to his grandfather by Sir Joseph Carruthers, ex premier of New South Wales, and this poem by an uncle, war hero and poet, Major Oliver Hogue, who fought at Gallipoli in World War I:

AN EPIC FROM EGYPT
by Trooper Bluegum
It ain't no use a-swearin',
  It ain't no good to fret;
There's little gained by grousin'
  Or getting all upset.
This wilderness is rotten—
  All flies, and dust, and tears,
But the Israelites they stuck it
  For years and years and years.

The Willie-Willies choke yer,
  The dust-storms get yer down;
The red sun robs yer beauty
  And burns yer black and brown.

The drought is something shocking;
  The thirst, our squadron fears,
Can only be abolished
  By beers and beers and beers.

But war won't last for ever,
  This scrap'll soon be done,
An' we'll have done our little bit
  A-strafing o' the Hun.
An' when we get back home again,
  An' meet our little dears,
All thought of Egypt will be drowned
  In cheers and cheers and cheers.
                    (From "London Opinion")

TYING PRESENT TO PAST

Tying the present to the past is handled in different ways by different writers. Establishing a sense of place is the way one writer did it. Writer Sham Eden, whose first name is a shortened form of the Biblical name Shulamith as found in the Song of Songs, captures the feeling of a city in the newly formed state of Israel—the sights, the sounds, the climate, the varied peoples arriving from around the world—in this personal memoir:

RISHON LE ZION 1952

It is a city of contrasts and contradictions, of early extremes and human differences. This city is at the crossroads of an undying past and a newly awakened present, of the exotic orient and the dynamic occident.

Here in the throes of nature, a gentle ocean breeze tempers a blazing sun, a bountiful crop is withered by a parching khamsin wind, and the desert sand is nourished and blooms.

Against a cloudless Mediterranean sky, stand vast trenches of glistening new white houses, interspersed by wooden huts, clay houses, and endless rows of new immigrant tents.

High above, and overlooking the area, is a synagogue. It seems to guard over a city of earthliness and holiness, of want and plenty, of despair and hope.

Down the bustling main street come the speeding jeeps and motorcycles, the stray goats, the tractors, and the cycling youth, the buses, the pack-burdened donkeys, and fruit-bearing trucks, the luxurious taxis and the jaunting horses.

And here on foot, are the multitude of men and women ingathered in Israel from the four corners of the earth. There are the tiny dark-skinned Yemenites, the Shoah survivors of Hitler's Europe; the crafty, temperamental North Africans; the serene, white-garbed Bnai Israel from India; and western democracy's British, French and Americans; the strong-willed, arrogant Sabres (native born); and the healthy well-cared-for infants.

The perfumed, habitués of the shaded, sidewalk cafe are oblivious of the people around. They are savoring the aroma of their Turkish coffee and Hungarian pastries.

Across the road, the air is heavy with the perspiration of men and women standing in the blazing sun, waiting for the arrival of an overcrowded bus. The street vendors approach them with hot pita, spicy falafel, freshly roasted peanuts, popcorn, corn on the cob, and delicate cactus fruit.

The sandy side streets fill the air with smoldering firewood, (lit beneath the laundry tubs), with the aroma of freshly plowed earth, heavenly palms, ancient vineyards, tropical fruits, and a gentle ocean breeze.

Eden points out that when her grandparents settled in Rishon from Ohio in 1920, "it was mostly sand. Water was delivered three times a week. There were no paved roads or sidewalks. Life in 1952 was luxurious compared to that."

The use of concrete detail that helps the modern reader see and smell something of the past they never knew personally is important to keep the story moving. Here's how Marian Young shows the difference between today's American supermarket and her relatives' corner grocery and meat market of yesterday:

A typical cracker-barrel General Store, it had a movie-prop pot-bellied stove, jars of rock candy and cinnamon sticks on the counter, bucket scales with slotted iron weights, and a hand-cranked phone out in the hall. Along one wall marched a row of wooden bins where dried beans, peas, rice, barley, coffees and condiments were stored . . . then measured out to-order with tin and wooden scoops. Plunging my hands in to stir up coffee-bean dust produced clouds of heady, musty aroma.

Behind the counter in Uncle Frank's corner, wood shavings

covered the floor to absorb drippings from the butcher blocks. Each night after closing, and armed with a wire brush, he scrubbed the blocks clean, then swept up the day's shavings and laid down fresh for the next day's mess. The aroma in Uncle Frank's corner is better forgotten.

Tying present-to-past was accomplished this way in the last paragraph of Marian Young's tribute to her deceased mother of nine children:

> Before she left us, she gave me her set of Charles Dickens and one of her favorite houseplants. It still hangs by a window in my living room. It bloomed a few years back, delicate waxy pink spheres all up and down its curly-leafed ropes. It isn't the kind of plant any of us ever expected would bloom, so when it did, I ran to the phone with, "Wow! I've got to tell Mom." When reality hit, I burst into tears. Even today, those beautiful gnarled hands are there whenever I feed and water that patiently-waiting greenery. I miss you, Mom.

THE ENDING

What effect do you want to leave your readers with at the end of your manuscript? Admiration for what our ancestors endured and survived? A keener insight into you as a person separate from your profession or station in life?

You may have planned your ending when you opened your book; many writers finish a book by returning to some point they made in their opening chapter. Perhaps you described a painting of an ancestor that got you started on family history research in the first place. And in your last chapter you realize the portrait's subject turned out not to be an ancestor at all, but you met lots of other interesting people along the way.

In chapter twelve, we reprinted the preface of the book *All Our Yesterdays: A Century of Family Life in an American Small Town*, by James Oliver Robertson and Janet C. Robertson. Here's how they ended their last chapter:

> We have sought roots in a past that did not seem to belong to us. Can you buy into history when you buy a house? Only in America, perhaps. We would like to feel that we have provided the next best thing to Roger Davis's desire that the house continue in the hands of Mary Taintor Davis's descendants. We have given

the house good care and an active life. We have done our bit to keep the community that is Hampton going. And we have endeavored to tell the stories that made Mary Taintor Davis's house so important to her.

We have tried, with respect for the realities of their lives, to find our own roots in the Taintors and in Hampton and to understand that other people's pasts can be all our yesterdays.

Benita Eisler whose book, *Private Lives, Men and Women of the Fifties*, we excerpted earlier in this chapter, discussed "The Way We *Were*" early in that book on "the silent generation." For her final chapter she summarizes "The Way We *Are*," and concludes with these paragraphs:

> Starting out as a no-choice generation, we compensated for our stifled beginnings—and then some. For all of us—and there are many—who have remained "hugging the shore," to borrow John Updike's title (among whose ranks I count myself), or who "went in up to our knees, but not over our heads" in Dan Ross's formulation, there are scores (including several of the men and women in this book) who, to their own amazement, went off the deep end!
>
> How hard it was for us is summed up in a phrase used, remarkably enough, by dozens of people I interviewed about very different events in their lives: leaving marriages, changing careers, marching for abortion rights, "coming out," even looking for a job or going back to school. It was first said to me by a psychiatrist describing his feelings when, in the early fifties, as a young medical student with a government scholarship, he refused to sign a loyalty oath. "I felt," he said, "like I was walking off the edge of the world."
>
> Every generation is transitional, a social and genetic link between the past and future. Ours may be more transitional than any in our history—perhaps the one respect in which we are extreme.
>
> We are the last men and women in America to have expected to live the way our parents lived, only to be cast into uncharted terrain, with neither compass nor maps.
>
> Yet, unlike those generations whose coming-of-age was marked by the Depression, World War II, or Vietnam, we lack a common crucible of social and economic upheaval or the dislocations of war. In talking with veterans of the Korean "conflict," I was surprised to learn how little effect—moral or psychological—their experiences seemed to have had on the rest of their lives. In

marked differences to those who participated in the D-day invasion, or who were dropped by parachute into Vietnamese jungles,
they expressed no feelings of continued community with fellow
combatants.

In further contrast to our seniors and juniors, our lives were
characterized by constant contradiction. We got the best and
worst of everything in this century: the prosperity and political
repression, the "sheltered and gradual coming-of-age" and the sexual hypocrisies, the plentiful jobs and the miseries of suburbia.
And finally, after doing as we were told for most of our lives, we
were exhorted to "get with it" — to find out who we were and what
we really wanted!

Our generational bond is not to be found in bread lines, fox-
holes or sit-ins, or in the broad experiences many of us share —
college, early marriage and parenthood, and our steadily improved
standard of living — or even in the ways feminism, divorce, psycho-
therapy, sex or success did or did not change our lives.

Like former prisoners, we connect in the knowledge of our past
constraints and in a cautious sense of new freedom. It's the veiled
joke, the glint of triumph, or the rush of sympathy. Still silent, we
connect most of all in the unspoken question (and answers) of
underground men and women: And how was it for you? We trade
survival tactics and even a few secrets. We hope that having rolled
with too many punches doesn't show. Still putting "best foot forward" in our public selves, we're ready to role-play the part of
tribal elders.

Perhaps your book was a question to yourself: Who am I? What have
I learned about myself through my life experience? And now you have
come to some conclusions about those questions. Here's how T.S. Matthews closed his autobiography, *Name and Address*:

> Is there any hope that in my remaining years I will pull myself
> together, keep my desk clear, really learn French and Spanish,
> breathe properly when I swim, become a graceful and witty
> speaker, recover my forehand drive, write one good poem, love
> anyone unselfishly, make up for lost time and fulfill the unkept
> promise, whatever it was, of my life? I have just enough sense to
> know that there isn't any hope of my accomplishing any of these
> things. And yet I live hopefully; I am glad — more than glad, thank-
> ful, full of thanks — to be alive.

My life has been a good deal like this book. I set out to become a first-rate man, or at any rate a good one, and instead turned into—me. In this book I meant to write the truth, even more of it than was decent about my life; and I discovered that I didn't know the truth and that there were a good many things that I didn't want to tell. This record is incomplete — partial in both senses of the word. As it stands, probably, it has neither given me away nor made my case, whichever you like, any more than a newspaper succeeds in telling you what actually happened to the human race yesterday. A better journalist might have made this book more of a journal. And I have told almost nothing about my personal weather, which, like everyone's, is continuous, ever-changing and unrememberable. Like everyone's, that weather has at times been shockingly bad, "unbearable" or at any rate extremely painful, at other times hopeful, halcyon, unspeakably pleasant.

I have left out almost all the "small things" that fill the days of a man's life, those 25,000-odd days (the Biblical threescore and ten) of which I have now used up nearly 22,000. If I had really tried to describe myself, wouldn't I have confessed that my besetting phrase isn't a phrase at all but an incoherent sound, the same nervous clearing of the throat that I thought so annoying, ludicrous — and, in retrospect, endearing — in my mother? Why haven't I given some indication of the extent to which tennis (and, for fifteen years, its bastard little brother, squash rackets) has both lightened and darkened my life?

In short, I have failed to do what I set out to do. I thought I could paint a self-portrait, warts and all — and found I couldn't. (Why didn't you catch him shaving, or asleep, or when he thought he wasn't being watched? Ah, if only I could have.) So the book has turned out as it has — me again.

This is not a satisfactory conclusion, nor in fact a conclusion at all. I neither can nor want to imagine the ending of my own story — which, like the story itself, I have lived through with mixed emotions and no clear understanding. My world, my family, my nature have not taught me clarity. To my pent-up way of thinking, which has no more sense nor reason in it than a dream, in every good man there is a rascal, in every rascal a good man, struggling to get out. I can only be sure that in us, in me, something is struggling.

Chapter Fifteen

Self-Editing Your Final Manuscript

I n writing your first draft, you may have followed the advice of Andre Gide, who wrote in his *Journals*, "I too often wait for the sentence to finish taking shape in me before writing it. It is better to take it by the end that first offers itself, head or foot, without yet knowing the rest, then to pull: the rest will follow along."

If your first draft's goal was to "just get it down on paper," now's the time for that self-editor to climb out of the backseat and take over.

Now's the time to go through the manuscript chapter by chapter, sentence by sentence, to check for things like:

- ✔ organization
- ✔ what's missing
- ✔ what should be deleted
- ✔ clutter
- ✔ clarity
- ✔ dialect
- ✔ color
- ✔ cadence
- ✔ spelling
- ✔ subject-verb agreement
- ✔ tense sequence
- ✔ pronoun usage
- ✔ mood
- ✔ active vs. passive voice
- ✔ punctuation
- ✔ word usage

Here are a few tips for using this checklist as you revise the manuscript before final typing:

ORGANIZATION

If your first draft writing was guided by an outline, keep a copy of it in front of you as you review each chapter. Make sure you covered the points you intended.

If you discarded your original outline and rearranged some chapters as you got further into the writing, you might want to make up a table of contents showing the order of the manuscript as it now stands. See if this order seems to strike a good balance between devices to hold reader attention and logical sequence. Are action scenes and less-active descriptions interspersed? When you find places where the pacing is off, you might need to cut or add material. Are readers smoothly carried from chapter to chapter?

Before you begin your editing, read the manuscript through for subject content, reader interest and overall effectiveness. Then go back and tackle the potential problems you may uncover.

ADDITIONS AND DELETIONS

Let's consider first what might be missing. Have you included everything you think might fulfill your original purpose in writing the book? If you haven't, is it because you have decided to pare down your focus to a more limited time frame or a narrower branch of the family tree? Have you kept in mind who your intended readers are and what they will expect to find in your memoir?

Does your manuscript give the reader a clear picture of your or your family's time and place in relation to the world in which you or they lived?

Have you included some dramatic scenes with dialogue as well as straight third-person narration? Is the humor you've included consistent with the subject matter and not offensive to your potential readers? Are your transitions smooth or a speed bump on your reader's highway?

Sometimes it's not a matter of what's left out but what's still in. Howard Wells, a literary consultant who works on both commercial manuscripts and personal stories for clients, says, "Two problems I see in manuscripts that writers need to watch out for involve both 'putting in' and 'taking out'. Too often, writers fail to put in the emotion: How did they *feel*, not just what did they do? And they can't bear to take out the factual overkill on some aspects of their lives that is more than the average reader wants to know. Never lose sight of the needs and interests of your reader."

Don't be afraid to set aside some manuscript pages that may have value for some other work, but don't belong in this book. In *The Writing Life*, Annie Dillard puts it this way:

> Several delusions weaken the writer's resolve to throw away work. If he has read his pages too often, those pages will have a necessary quality, the ring of the inevitable, like poetry known by heart; they will perfectly answer their own familiar rhythms. He will retain them. He may retain those pages if they possess some virtues, such as power in themselves, though they lack the cardinal virtue, which is pertinence to, and unity with, the book's thrust. Sometimes the writer leaves his early chapters in place from gratitude; he cannot contemplate them or read them without feeling again the blessed relief that exalted him when the words first appeared — relief that he was writing anything at all. That beginning served to get him where he was going, after all; surely the reader needs it, too, as groundwork. But no.

On the other hand, freelance writer Rick Zabel says: "I'd rather criticize myself for something that I've written than to later criticize myself for not having written anything at all."

How much to tell in a family story? C. Vincent Wright, who self-published his family history, *The Wright Stuff: Descendants of Brigham C. Wright and Urania Murray*, says, "It was my choice not to include marriages that ended in divorce, and from which there was no issue. This seemed to be appreciated."

A friend whose family members have created family histories says, "My advice is to tell the myths as well as the truth, but do not leave out any truths!"

Of course, others will say some truths are better left out of family histories! Only you, the author can decide.

CLUTTER

William Zinsser sums it up well in his book *On Writing Well*:

> ... the secret of good writing is to strip every sentence to its cleanest components. Every word that serves no function, every long word that could be a short word, every adverb that carries the same meaning that's already in the verb, every passive construction that leaves the reader unsure of who is doing what — these are the thousand and one adulterants that weaken the strength of a sentence.

Eliminating clutter is a primary self-editing rule. Politicians, bureaucrats, corporate big-wigs all use too many words to tell us (usually painful) things: *Revenue enhancement* (taxes), *decentralizing, reorganizing* and *downsizing* (you're fired).

But we, too, add unnecessary extra words (see, I just did) in our sentences. Go through your manuscript with a thick, black pencil and eliminate those extra words.

CLARITY

A goal of good writing is this: Each sentence's meaning is clear with the first reading. "No one should have to read a sentence twice," says Wilson Follett, "because of the way it is put together."

In his book *How to Make Your Writing Reader Friendly*, Richard Dowis points out how the placement of a comma can affect the meaning of a sentence. Notice these two sentences:

She did not accept the transfer because she wanted to earn more money.

She did not accept the transfer, because she wanted to earn more money.

The first sentence means that she accepted the transfer, but she did so for a reason other than the money. The second says that she did not accept the transfer, and it implies that the reason she did not accept it was that it would not have paid her more money.

Ordinarily, a dependent clause such as *because she wanted more money* would not be preceded by a comma. When a *because* clause follows a negative statement, however, a comma may be needed. A thoughtful writer will consider carefully whether a comma is needed to express the desired meaning.

The nonfiction writing course at Writer's Digest School points up an even more important legal reason for putting your commas in the right place:

How important can omitting such a small thing as a comma in a series be? In one case it was worth $2,500:

Some years ago, a lawyer handled a will that read: "To my daughter and sons: Mary, John and Mike, I leave the sum of $15,000."

The lawyer then gave each of them $5,000. Mary sued. She

claimed that by the way her father wrote his will, he intended her to have $7,500 and John and Mike together to have $7,500. The case went to court. And the judge ruled in her favor.

He stated that if Mary's father had written, "To . . . Mary, John, and Mike, I leave the sum of $15,000," it would have meant that he intended each of them to share the money equally. But because he wrote, "To . . . Mary, John and Mike, I leave the sum of $15,000," it meant that he intended John and Mike to be considered as a single unit, and therefore to share together equally with Mary.

Because of the judge's ruling, Mary got $7,500, and John and Mike got $7,500 to split between them.

With luck, you will never have a comma cost you $2,500. But this incident does point up the importance of using commas to establish exactly the relation you intend in a series of items.

James J. Kilpatrick's *The Writer's Art* includes a chapter on Faith, Hope and Clarity. In it, he skewers a few newspapers for mistakes like these:

> A staff writer for *The Miami Herald*, reporting the mugging of a British couple who had just arrived in Florida, said the hoodlums "beat both he and his wife" . . . . United Press International describes Washington National Airport as "surrounded on three sides by water." It is an interesting trick, to surround something on three sides. *The New York Times*, great newspaper that it is, often errs. The *Times* has reported upon "falsely padded expense accounts," upon a playwright who was a "lifelong native of New York," upon a man "shot fatally three times."
>
> Most of these goofs, gaffes and blunders are the result of a single cause: haste. If there is one sin against clear writing more serious than all the others, it is the sin of careless copyreading. . . . Careful editing would have eliminated the *falsely* in "falsely padded expense accounts." Even a moment's scrutiny would have caught the beating of "he and his wife." The more we read our copy after we believe we are finished with it, the more we will catch obscurities in expression, roughnesses in style, mistakes in spelling, and inexactness in our choice of words.

DIALECT

Capturing the flavor of conversations in the different regions of the United States is a challenge to any lover of language, but too much dialect is very hard to read. A happy compromise might be to render an initial few sentences or the occasional phrase in, for example, the Appalachian or Pennsylvania Dutch dialect to show the idiom. Then let the rest of the conversation proceed without any unusual spellings to slow down the reader.

Family history writers might have more temptation than other authors to indulge in dialect (especially when trying to capture the Old World flavorings of grandparents or great-aunts). You'll notice that in chapter eight, Meghan Walker avoided the problem by not using foreign words in dialogue. Instead, she incorporated them into a third-person narration, which also gave her the opportunity to explain the terms at the same time. To see how author Harry Crews used the dialect of his sharecropper-poor Bacon County, Georgia, background in his autobiography, see his memoir: *A Childhood: The Biography of a Place*.

ADDING COLOR

Color might take the form of apt simile, or a vivid characterization, but the simplest of all forms (using the actual colors of the things we're describing) should not be overlooked. Writer Fanny-Maude Evans points out these color writing examples in her book, *Changing Memories Into Memoirs*:

> *Clumps of wild iris grew beneath the pines.*

We know pines are green, but if you've never seen wild iris, they're only black print on white paper.

> *Clumps of wild iris, in shades of deep purple, pale lavender, and white, grow beneath the pines.*

See how adding color brightens the picture?

> *I would see the hunter's cap bobbing in and out among the trees.*

What color is a hunter's cap? And we assume the trees were green. But were they?

> *I could see the bright red hunter's cap bobbing among the aspens wearing their fall shades of orange and gold.*

Besides looking at your picture, we want to hear how things sound. We respond in one way or another to the blare of rock music, the throb of marching drums, or the slow rhythm of a waltz. Sounds can be harsh and irritating or pleasant and relaxing. The cheerful chirping of crickets, the noon blast of a factory whistle or the monotonous drip of water can help us hear as well as see the story you're writing.

What do you hear in this sentence?

My daughter sat up in bed as she heard the ambulance in the street.

If your imagination is active enough, you may imagine the sound of the ambulance. But you can't definitely hear anything. Listen again.

My daughter sat up in bed as the shrill siren of the ambulance shattered the silence of the street.

Now the siren is a clear sound, isn't it? Here's another noise you often hear. Yet, no matter how much you hate it, you don't hear it in this sentence.

On Saturday mornings I awoke to the sound of lawn mowers cutting the grass.

Revise it something like this?

On Saturday morning I groaned awake to the sound of lawn mowers chattering back and forth across the grass.

I groan, the mowers chatter, and you hear them.

In *The Writer's Art*, James J. Kilpatrick devotes a chapter to "The Things We Ought to Be Doing." One of those things is mastering our tools, and one of those tools is the simile. "Effectively used," says Kilpatrick,

> good similes can light up a paragraph as a smile lights up a face; the image comes alive. The first rule is that similes must be accurate. The things compared or equated have to be genuinely alike. . . . Good similes depend upon close observation. . . . A good many years ago I happened to be covering some hearings on labor racketeering. Among the witnesses who took the Fifth Amendment was one especially repulsive fellow, dressed in a suit of bilious green. He was short and fat and his vocal cords had been smoked in the gas of ten thousand cigars. I wrote that he sat at the witness table "like a frog on a lily pad, dripping hostility from hooded eyes, and repeatedly croaking, "duh privilege."

As you'll remember, a simile is when we say something is *like* something else. A metaphor is when we say it *is* something else. *Webster's Collegiate Dictionary* defines a metaphor as "a figure of speech in which a word or phrase literally denoting one kind of an object or idea is used in place of another to suggest a likeness or analogy between them."

After reading a relative's correspondence, for example, you might make an observation about its content using a metaphor such as, "Aunt

Emma was a transplanted Southern flower trying to survive in a wintry northern landscape of Yankee relatives."

CADENCE

Kilpatrick gives a lot of other good writing advice in his book. He reminds us of an important ingredient this way:

> The best writing—the writing that is quotable, that zings and stings and packs a wallop—depends on many elements. It depends on having something to say and on saying it clearly; it depends upon fresh metaphors and lively similes, and of course the grammar and syntax and spelling have to be right. But when all those elements have been raked and weeded and watered, our prose gardens demand something more: cadence.
>
> We ought never to be embarrassed, in the privacy of our chambers, to "sound out" a sentence. Fingers were made to count feet. As Barbara Tuchman has said, "An essential element of good writing is a good ear: One must listen to the sound of one's own prose." If a sentence lacks cadence, the sentence collapses like an overcooked souffle.

Reread your writing aloud and listen to its cadence, its rhythm. Does it synchronize with the subject matter and like a piece of music offer variety and not monotony?

Now that you have looked at the "big picture" of your story, let's go back and tackle its individual parts to make sure it adds up to a correct and readable whole.

SPELLING

If you're using a computer with a spell-checker, you've already learned you can't rely on it totally. Take, for example, homonyms such as *their* and *there*; if you've typed in the wrong one, your spell-check won't catch it. If you have misspelled a word, but your spelling is itself a word, then spell-check won't catch it. For example, you may have meant to type *kind* but you left off the *d*; since *kin* is also a word, the spell-check will let it stand without question. If you typed *other* but meant *brother*, the word *other* would stand.

Be sure to watch out for that smallest spelling problem of all: *it's* with the apostrophe means "it is"; *its* without the apostrophe is the possessive, as in "Each language has its own peculiarities."

Those of you with unusual ancestor names may find the same difficulties Joseph Kastner did in his August 1989 *Smithsonian Magazine* essay about his then word processor's spelling methods:

> Things went along nicely at first. It told me to take out the extra *t* I always put in *Cincinnati* and to insert a *c* that had slipped out of *occurrence*. When it came to *Jean Jacques Audubon*, it went along with *Jean* but stopped at *Jacques* and then offered me *jocose* or *jackass*, both of which I rejected. Going on to *Audubon*, it paused and then proposed *Autobahn*. Dubiously I pressed on to the abbreviation *Mme*. It gave me *mew, moo, meow*. Confronting *ows*, it came up with *ewe, ass* and also *owl*, which is what I had meant to type.

A spell-check has its place, of course. But the only way to proofread your manuscript is to do it yourself, word by word, to see if what you typed is what you meant.

SUBJECT-VERB AGREEMENT

Some of the trouble in this area comes about when the subject is separated from the verb by other words. For example, "A history of the Smith and Jones families is important to Clark County residents." The verb *is* agrees with the sentence's subject, the singular noun *history*, not the nearer noun, *families*.

On the other hand, when one part of a subject is singular and the other part plural, and they are joined by the words *or*, or *nor*, the verb agrees with the nearer subject. The plural word preferably should be closest to the verb. For example, "Neither my father nor his ancestors *were* ever bothered by social conventions." To some the sentence might seem a little awkward if it read "Neither his ancestors nor my father *was* ever bothered by social conventions."

When a plural noun is actually singular in meaning, a singular verb is called for. For example, "The data about my ancestors is inconclusive." *Data* is plural but in common usage takes the singular is. When in doubt, check the dictionary. Webster's defines *data* as a "n.pl." (plural noun) but adds "often construed as singular."

TENSES

In a family history you may be moving from the present to the past or past to present and must be sure to keep your tenses appropriate. For example, "As I look at the faded photograph, I remember the family event it captures. My grandfather had gone north during the Klondike Gold Rush of '98 and. . . ."

The author *looks, remembers*, in the present tense, but switches to the past perfect, *had gone*, when referring to the earlier time involving her grandfather.

After recounting what happened when her grandfather was prospecting, she might return to the present this way: "Now, as I *tuck* the photograph back in its folder, I *wonder* what our lives would have been like *had he succeeded* and we *became* Canadians instead of Americans."

PRONOUN USAGE

How many times have you winced when you heard a radio or TV person say, "This is strictly between you and I"? Of course, it should be "you and *me*," since *me* is the object of the preposition *between*. Or have you stumbled yourself in not matching up a pronoun to its antecedent. For example: "General Grant and my grandfather arrived at the same time and then he left immediately after the meeting." Who left — General Grant or your grandfather?

A collective noun could require a plural pronoun if the group is considered as individuals; but take a singular pronoun if considered as a unit. For example: "The jury filed into the courtroom and took *their* seats. Then the jury foreman, when queried by the judge, presented *its* decision."

Remember that *who* and *whoever* are used as subjects; objects take the words *whom* and *whomever*. For example: "Give credit to whoever deserves it." (While it seems as though *whoever* is an object of *to*, since it is the subject of an entire clause — "whoever deserves it." So *whoever* is correct, not *whomever*.) Another example: "She is the candidate whom most people prefer." (*Whom* is the object of *prefer*.)

MOOD

This word has two separate meanings for writers. As a grammatical term mood refers to the form of the verb. You'll remember that the indicative mood states a fact ("My father is six feet tall."), expresses an opinion ("He needs help."), or asks a question ("What kind of help does he need?").

The imperative mood expresses a command: "Call 911 right away!"

The subjunctive mood expresses desire or suggestion or hypothetical condition: "The family feud would have been settled sooner if it had been more openly discussed." This last sentence illustrates a rule that says to use *would* or *could* only in the main clause of a conditional statement. You would not say, for example, "The family feud would have been settled sooner if it would have been more openly discussed."

The other meaning of mood refers to the predominating tone or atmosphere in a literary work—somber, evil, witty, romantic, etc.

A family history's or memoir's mood could be informative, entertaining, inspirational, revelatory, startling or all those things, depending on the subject matter. For examples, reread the various excepts quoted in this book.

ACTIVE VS. PASSIVE VOICE

The active voice usually provides a more vigorous style. Sentences gain strength from "action" verbs, which are more engaging for readers than the more passive "to be" verbs (*is, was, were*, etc.)

A historian using the passive voice might say: "The British tax on tea *was thought* by American colonists *to be* an unjust import restriction." An active-voice version might be: "American colonists *protested* the British tax on tea as an unjust import restriction." (Even better would be to show the colonists' protest: "When word of the tax on tea reached Boston, angry colonists *disguised* themselves as Indians and *threw* the tea into Boston harbor.")

Passive voice is necessary, however, when the doer of the action is unknown: "John Brown's blood-stained body *was found* the next day in a ravine miles from his camp." Also, when the object of the action is more important than the doer, passive voice is useful: "Although *discovered* by accident, pencillin remains a most useful antibiotic."

PUNCTUATION

They may be tiny little marks on the page, but punctuation marks are as important as road signs in helping your reader travel through your book. Some areas to watch out for that you may have forgotten since English classes include these:

Comma Splice. When two sentences are joined (spliced) by a comma instead of a semi-colon and there is no coordinating conjunction such as *and, but, or*; the result is a comma splice. Remedy:

Add a conjunction after the comma.

Substitute a semi-colon for the comma.

Use a period and make the sentences separate.

Make one of the sentences a dependent clause of the other.

Fused Sentences. When two sentences are run together with no punctuation at all, the fused sentence is hard to read. Example: "Human motivations are seldom as simple as they appear hasty judgements are therefore often wrong." Remedy:

"Because human motivations are seldom as simple as they appear, hasty judgements are often wrong."

Sentence Fragment. Sometimes sentences start out with a subject but lose a verb along the way. Or start out with a subject and a dependent clause and the author forgets to finish the sentence. For example, "Writers who merely tell who begat who without giving interesting details." The subject "writers" has no predicate and is a sentence fragment. Remedy:

Remove the period and add "will bore their readers."

In dialogue, however, when the meaning is clear from the context, sentence fragments are acceptable. For example,

"Was your brother ever married?"

"Yes. Once. A long time ago."

Quotation Marks. Most writers remember to use double quote marks when directly quoting another writer and no quote marks if they are paraphrasing what another person said. What usually causes writers to pause is considering the use of quotation marks with other punctuation.

Commas and periods go inside quotation marks at the end of a sentence.

Colons and semi-colons go outside end quotation marks within a sentence.

Dashes, question marks and exclamation points go inside quotation marks only if they belong to the quotation. If they apply to the larger sentence of which the quotation is only a part, then they go outside the quotation marks. For example: "Do you remember — I think it was Henry Ford — who said 'History is bunk!' "?

Quotation marks are used in manuscripts to indicate titles of articles, stories, poems, songs, essays and chapters. (Italics are used for titles of longer works.) If a quotation or dialogue is longer than one paragraph, quotation marks are used at the opening of each paragraph but only at the end of the last paragraph. If the quotation includes the words of another speaker, that interior speaker's words are set off by 'single quote marks.' Some books (like this one) use a block indent form without opening and closing quotes for longer excerpted passages.

WORD USAGE

One of the words that I use unnecessarily is *that*. For example, the previous sentence reads just as well as, "One of the words I use unnecessarily is *that*." The first version isn't incorrect, but to my ear the second just flows easier.

Whether to use *that* or *which*, however, is a problem for some writers who remember some vague English teacher caution about "restrictive and nonrestrictive modifiers." For example, take the sentence: "The family that keeps good records is a joy to the genealogical researcher." The modifier "that keeps good records" is necessary (and restricts the meaning to the particular family). The sentence contains *no* commas around the modifier.

On the other hand, look at the sentence: "The Smith Family, to which I'm related by marriage, was among the earliest settlers in the Midwest." The modifier, "to which I'm related by marriage," adds some information, but is nonrestrictive — it isn't necessary to the meaning of the sentence. It *is* set off by commas.

Two words you frequently see blurred in usage are *loan* and *lend*. Preferred usage is to use *loan* as a noun and *lend* as a verb. It's not "Loan me your pen." but "Lend me your pen." It's not "He loaned me his briefcase"; but "He lent me his briefcase."

A couple of trouble-makers for some writers are *lie* and *lay*. *Lie* is an intransitive verb and takes no object. The past tense is *lay* and the past participle is *lain*. (My grandmother always lay down for a nap in the afternoon.) *Lay* is a transitive verb and does take an object. The past tense is *laid* and the past participle is also *laid*. (No one knew who had laid the will in such an unlikely place.)

Another stumbler for some writers is the difference between the past tenses of *hang* (meaning to fasten or suspend) and *hang* (meaning to execute). Proper usage is: "The criminal was hanged, but his picture had hung in every post office as one of the Ten Most Wanted."

A printed announcement I just received in the mail from the Federal Aviation Administration reminded me of one of the smallest booby traps in the English language. The announcement said, "You are invited to take advantage of an unique opportunity to land at Wright-Patterson Air Force Base." The "Glossary of Usage" in my copy of *The Little Brown Handbook* says:

> Use *a* before words beginning with consonant sounds, including those spelled with an initial *h* and those spelled with vowels that

are sounded as consonants: a historian, a one-o'clock class, a university. Use *an* before words that begin with vowel sounds, including those spelled with an initial silent *h*: an orgy, an L, an honor.

My reading of that rule says I should have been invited to take advantage of *a unique* opportunity.

To solve usage questions such as these, you might want to keep handy a reference work such as *The Harper Dictionary of Contemporary Usage* or *Webster's Dictionary of English Usage*. Computer users might want to investigate software packages like Grammatik to see how helpful they can be in catching grammar problems. Cost: about fifty dollars. The final checker, of course, must still be *you*.

TWENTY RULES FOR GOOD WRITING

Writer's Digest School sends it students the following list of rules to use while revising manuscripts. Some of them may be useful reminders for your family history or memoir.

1. Prefer the plain word to the fancy.
2. Prefer the familiar word to the unfamiliar.
3. Prefer the Saxon word to the Romance. For example, here are some English words and their origins:

Romance	Anglo-Saxon
inebriated	drunk
espionage	spying
juvenile	young
terrestrial	earthly
imprudent	rash
dishonor	shame
inquire	ask
valiant	bold
meritorious	worthy

4. Prefer nouns and verbs to adjectives and adverbs.
5. Prefer picture nouns and action verbs.
6. Never use a long word when a short one will do as well.
7. Master the simple declarative sentence.
8. Prefer the simple sentence to the complicated.
9. Vary your sentence length.
10. Put the words you want to emphasize at the beginning of your sentence.

11. Use the active voice.
12. Put statements in a positive form.
13. Use short paragraphs.
14. Cut needless words, sentences and paragraphs.
15. Use plain, conversational language. Write like you talk.
16. Avoid imitation. Write in your natural style.
17. Write clearly.
18. Avoid gobbledygook.
19. Write to be understood, not to impress.
20. Revise and rewrite. Improvement is always possible.

SELF-HELP REMINDER ESSAY TO EDIT

The following imaginary family history essay has a number of writing and punctuation errors. You may wish not only to correct the existing ones, but rewrite the entire essay into a style of your own:

Nobody in either my husband's family or my own know where our ancestors were born. My mother's parents who died in an auto accident when I was very young and who I never knew when I was starting to talk and ask questions are Irish.

My father's sister, Aunt Helen told me this story about her family the William Johnson's.

"Grandfather Johnson said his father's name was really Johannson but when he immigrated from Sweden they spelled it the wrong way, everybody thought he was English.

I thought he should have changed it when he owned his own business in a Scandinavian community. "Why should I?" he said "everybody know who I really am."

Mary, your father's other sister agreed with me, we always had a much stronger sense of our heritage even after we were married and had other names to live by."

My mother's parents were born in this country but we don't know where when they moved to the midwest before my mother was born. Mother's father's name was O'Neal, he never spelled it like the playwright O'Neill. Her mother was a McGillicuddy. When that clan gathered on holidays the brogue and tall tales was thicker than Irish stew!

On the other hand father's mother was a very straight-lased English woman (she said her ancestors were in Burkes Peerage) and we tried not to invite both inlaws to dinner at the same time.

One holiday they all arrived at the same time with presents for we grandchildren. Grandmother Johnson always gave me books about English royalty. "Elizabeth" she would say "if you act like a princess, people will treat you like a princess." My class mates in third grade must read different books, they never treated me like a princess.

Grandmother O'Neal was partial to my brother Jack since he was named after her father John McGillicuddy. Grandfather O'Neal would always ask Jack about his soccer game because in this youth Grandfather was an outstanding player on an Irish team. That's when Grandmother Johnson would usually remind everyone that the first recorded soccer game was in England in the third century. That would bring a retort from James O'Neal "well maybe so and they haven't won a game since!"

Why can't families forget such old rivalries and get along? They used to say America was a melting pot but now it seems like we're all eggs in one of those partitioned cartons where we keep to ourselves less we bump each other and break into pieces like Humpty Dumpty.

Correction Sheet for Self-Help Reminder Essay

Our suggested changes are indicated by boldface and underlines.

Nobody in either my husband's family or my own **knows** where our ancestors were born. My mother's parents, who died in an auto accident when I was very young, and **whom** I never knew when I was starting to talk and ask questions, **were** Irish.

My father's sister, Aunt Helen, told me this story about **their** family, the William **Johnsons**.

"Grandfather Johnson said his father's name was really Johannson, but when he **emigrated** from Sweden they spelled it the wrong way; everybody thought he was English.

"I thought he should have changed it when he owned his own business in a Scandinavian community. 'Why should I?' he said. 'Everybody knows who I really am.'

"Mary, your father's other sister, agreed with me; we always had a much stronger sense of our heritage—even after we were married and had other names to live by."

My mother's parents were born in this country but we don't know where; **since** they moved to the midwest before my mother was born. Mother's father's name was O'Neal—he never spelled it like the playwright, O'Neill. Her mother was a McGillicuddy. When that clan gathered on holidays, **the tall tales and brogue** was thicker than Irish stew!

On the other hand father's mother was a very **strait-laced** Englishwoman (she said her ancestors were in **Burke's Peerage**) and we tried not to invite both **in-laws** to dinner at the same time.

One holiday they all arrived at the same time with presents for **us** grandchildren. Grandmother Johnson always gave me books about English royalty. "Elizabeth**,**" she would say "if you act like a princess**,** people will treat you like a princess." My classmates in third grade **must have read** different books. **They** never treated me like a princess.

Grandmother O'Neal was partial to my brother Jack since he was named after her father**,** John McGillicuddy. Grandfather O'Neal would always ask Jack about his soccer game**;** because in his youth Grandfather was an outstanding player on an Irish team. That's when Grandmother Johnson would usually remind every-one that the first recorded soccer game was in England in the third century. That would bring a retort from James O'Neal**. "Well, maybe so,** and they haven't won a game since**!"**

Why can't families forget such old rivalries and get along? They used to say America was a melting pot**,** but now it seems like we're all eggs in one of those partitioned cartons**,** where we keep to ourselves **lest** we bump each other and break into pieces like Humpty Dumpty **did when he fell off the wall.**(NOTE: Humpty Dumpty fell off a wall; he didn't break into pieces by bumping.)

Chapter Sixteen

Publishing Your Book

ow that you have completed your family history or personal memoir, how it will be published depends on several factors. Consider the following factors when deciding how your book should be published and marketed:

✔ Does it have national commercial sales possibilities with a regular trade publisher?

✔ Does it interest a specialty publisher because it has regional or other historical value?

✔ Do you plan to publish and market it yourself to a targeted audience?

✔ Is it only intended for family and friends?

Let's discuss the possibilities in each case.

A COMMERCIAL MARKET FOR YOUR BOOK

As you saw in earlier chapters in this book, some family histories became widely circulated Book-of-the-Month Club selections; others sell in the narrower, specialized circles of university presses. Whatever the marketplace, memoir books find commercial publishers because they accurately and interestingly reflect the people and attitudes of a particular generation as seen by a writer who was part of it.

Keep in mind, however, that in today's competitive book market, your family history or memoir must be unique to interest a commercial — or even a small press publisher. What would make it unique? Do you have access to some personal papers, diaries, documents about a particular aspect of American or regional history? Are you personally related to, or did you work with some well-known figure in American politics, sports, entertainment, education, science or medicine?

If you think your book has interest not just for your family but for the general public because of the special information or unique insight it offers, then you might want to query some potential trade book publishers.

Step one in this process is to get a copy of the latest edition of *Writer's Market*, which lists every major publisher that is currently looking for manuscripts. It will detail the specific subject matter each seeks, whom to contact, list some recent nonfiction titles it has published, tell what royalty it pays, and how long it will take the editors to answer your query.

You should also spend some time in the library studying the "New Nonfiction Books" stands, to see what kind of family histories or personal memoirs (other than those written by celebrities) are being published. Notice how recently they were published and by which companies.

Talk with the managers of bookstores in your area to see if they have handled any books like yours. Again, notice who the publishers were and the copyright dates.

Step two is to write to those publishers you think might be interested in your book based on what you read in *Writer's Market*. Request a copy of the publishers' catalogs, which you'll study to get a clearer idea of the kinds of books they publish and how yours might fit into their lineup. (The listings in *Writer's Market* will indicate if publishers will send their catalog for free or if you should enclose a specific-sized stamped envelope for their use in sending it).

Step three is to write a query letter to those publishers you've decided are likely prospects for your book. (Do not send your complete manuscript.) The query letter (no longer than one to one-and-one-half pages single-spaced) would describe how your book (give its title) fits into that specific company's publishing program, and what it has to offer that is unique and not currently available elsewhere. You may want to refer to a history or memoir book you've seen in the company's catalog. (You can check out your competition in the *Subject Guide to Books in Print* in your local library and by looking over current books on bookstore shelves.) Enclose an outline (a sentence or two describing the contents of each chapter), and ask the publisher if he would like to see some sample chapters. If you have previously published nonfiction articles or books, mention the most recent. If you have no publishing experience, say nothing about that; simply let your book idea and query letter speak for itself. Be sure to enclose a self-addressed, stamped envelope for reply.

Since, as you saw from reading *Writer's Market* listings, it sometimes takes publishers months to reply to a query, I'd suggest you send out all six of your query letters at the same time — personalized to each publisher, of course.

In the unlikely event more than one publisher asks to see some sample chapters, you can respond to each with photocopies. If one publisher wants to see the whole manuscript, send a complete photocopy. Only when one publisher offers you a contract and you agree to its terms do you need to withdraw your sample chapters from any other publishers who have received them. Just send a polite note to such publishers indicating that the manuscript is now under contract to another publisher.

A Selling Proposal

Here's the query letter that helped Dominic Caraccilo sell his book *The Ready Brigade of the 82nd Airborne in Desert Storm: A Combat Memoir*:

6920 Route 89
Ovid, New York 14521
31 March 1992

Mr. Robert Franklin
President and Editor-in-Chief
McFarland & Company, Inc. Publishers
Post Office Box 611
Jefferson, North Carolina 28640

Dear Mr. Franklin:

Desert Storm is most likely to be compared in history as one of the most destructive and successful military operations of modern times. A year has passed since the cease-fire and in that year a myriad of accounts have been written by leading analysts, media personnel, and other self-proclaimed experts. My question (and the question of my fellow soldiers) is, where are the first-hand accounts? The time has come where the "Big Hand-Little Map" explanation of how the Bush Administration and General Schwarzkopf won the war is rapidly becoming old news.

The book that I am suggesting is entitled "Invading Countries Makes Me Hungry." It is the unofficial and unabridged story of the soldiers of the 2nd Brigade, 82nd Airborne Division. This unit was the Ready Brigade sent by the National Command Authority to draw the "Line in the Sand" on 8 August 1990. I, as the Headquarters Company commander, have compiled a series of stories into a book that explains my experiences with the 82nd. We were the first forces into Desert Shield and subsequently fought under the command of the French Light Armored Division during the "Hail Mary" invasion in February 1991. Our eight-month deployment was not short of the type of military humor and drama that has yet to be captured in writing. I've attempted to portray these significant events in this book which brings the reader from our home in Fort Bragg, North Carolina, to the wadies of southern Iraq.

The unique idea about this book is that it is written as a firsthand account. Its substance is derived strictly from the log I kept for 227 days. I support my information with the many historical documents I have acquired throughout Desert Shield and Desert Storm (*i.e.*, the initial alert message deploying the 82nd). As opposed to a chronological step-by-step explanation of what actually took place, this book gives the reader an explanation of what was going on in the mind of the individual soldiers during each event of the crisis.

I have recently completed four chapters and a synopsis of the remaining 22. I anticipate to complete the book in two months. I envision it to be 90,000 words in length. I have photographs, maps and other inserts available that I plan on using to augment the text.

Having been an Army officer since my graduation from West Point eight years ago, I believe this kind of reading would not only benefit junior leaders within the military, but also attract the many curious military and history buffs. This book would particularly cater to the military enthusiasts audience with a fresh approach to a nonfiction topic that is still not exhausted. Competitive books on the market in this area include: Norman Friedman's *Desert Victory*, U.S. News' *Triumph Without Victory*, Peter David's *Triumph in the Desert*, and CNN's *War in the Gulf*. All of these books tend to be very general and focus mainly on the operational art of the war. To the contrary, my book is specifically focused on the individuals and their small units that tactically made the operation a success.

My military credentials include command of two companies in

the 82nd Airborne Division and I was decorated with a Bronze Star for actions in Iraq. I am currently a graduate student at Cornell University with a follow-on assignment as a professor at West Point. I have recently completed a manuscript, entitled, *A Battle Analysis: The Battle of Buna.* It is being marketed at this time.

Thank you for your consideration of this book proposal, Mr. Franklin. Upon request, I will provide you with the first four chapters and an outline/synopsis. I look forward to hearing from you. I have included an SASE.

> Sincerely,
> Dominic J. Caraccilo
> Captain, Infantry

Another Writer's Experience

John Egerton, whose book *Generations: An American Family*, was published in 1983 by University Press of Kentucky and later reprinted in paperback by Simon and Schuster, describes *his* marketing experience this way.

I felt the story I wanted to tell was not just one family's genealogy but a real slice of American social history reflected in the lives of about 140 people who were kin to one another. I was so confident of the book's commercial possibilities that I went to the trouble of writing an entire draft and submitting it to publishers. It was a disillusioning experience; I was turned down by more than twenty New York houses. They couldn't seem to get past the fact that I was writing about ordinary Americans, not famous people.

With magazine articles I was writing at the time, I asked editors to use an author's ident saying I was working on a social history based on a Kentucky family. An editor at the university press saw one of those pieces and contacted me. They liked the manuscript and wanted to publish it pretty much as it was, but I had decided that it needed more work, and I devoted several more months to a major revision. By that time, I had the better part of four years invested in the project — that meant expenses but no income — and I hated to have to go the university press route because there's generally no advance and the royalties are usually smaller and the marketing capabilities are more limited than at a commercial press. But I was able to negotiate a satisfactory royalty, and the book did well — it's still in print in both hard and soft cover — so what had the earmarks of a big disaster for me turned out to be one of my most successful books.

HOW TO FIND REPRINT AND SPECIALTY PUBLISHERS

As Egerton discovered, some publishers concentrate on books of interest to just certain regions of the country. Others concentrate on specific subject matter such as Americana or Ethnic or Military history.

You might want to find your library's copy of *Literary Market Place* to see who publishes books about the region of your book. Consult *Literary Market Place*'s Geographic Index which is a cross-reference to to the book publishers it lists.

Also, be sure to check the Nonfiction Book Publishers Subject Index in the back of *Writer's Market* for publishers interested in whatever subject categories your history or memoir covers.

Some publishers offer "co-publishing" arrangements. You pay part of the cost and they pay part. The publisher also handles marketing and distribution. This can be one avenue to publishing your book, but one that requires careful thought and reading of your contract. Listings of such "co-publishers" appear in *Writer's Market*.

If the publisher likes your subject matter and has no major editorial revisions to suggest, he still must consider whether it will sell enough copies to earn back the five-figure investment it would take to bring your book to market.

For example, he has typesetting, paper, printing, binding, shipping and marketing costs on even a limited pressrun of your book. He'll have to offer the bookstore an average of 47 percent discount on the retail price of the book.

To earn back his investment, he'll have to price the book anywhere from five to seven times his manufacturing cost. That means a high retail price on the book that may further limit sales.

And if potential readers don't buy the book within a certain time, bookstores will return the unsold copies to the publisher for credit, to make room for other books they think will sell better.

Is your book unique and appealing to enough people to overcome these hurdles?

SUBSIDY PUBLISHING

Some writers who are not successful in finding a commercial publisher to produce their book, will turn to a subsidy publisher. This is a company that edits, designs, typesets and prints your book, but passes the cost of those services along to you. In short, the author "subsidizes" the entire cost. Depending on your book's budget, the publisher may also send out press releases and review copies to selected book review publications and book distributors. The problem is, if your book is not unique enough to compete with the 40,000 to 50,000 books published each year for national consumption, your book may not be reviewed or taken by bookstores except the few in your hometown area. Sales likely will not cover your investment or even come close. How much would your investment be? It could be up to $40,000 depending on the book. If you can afford to give yourself that expensive a gift, fine.

Self-Marketing

"But," you say, "I'll do my own marketing and promotion."

Before you act, ask yourself if you have a large built-in audience for your book that will pay $14.95 for a short paperback or $20 to $30 for a longer hardcover book. Are you an expert in a certain subject who has speaking engagements regularly several times a year to groups of hundreds of people who would buy the book from you at a conference?

If not, what other marketing avenues would be open to you? For example, could you sell one thousand copies of your book by personally calling on hundreds of bookstores who might only be willing to try three or four copies each? Do you have the names and addresses of one thousand people who might be prospective buyers? Can you afford the cost of paper, printing and postage to mail your sales offer to them; and the cost of packing and shipping the books to those who buy?

If your answers to these questions are no, or your book is really only aimed toward your family and friends, then you may want to self-publish the book.

SELF-PUBLISHING

If your book is to be published only for your own family and friends, then you still have several questions to answer:

- ✔ How many copies do you want?
- ✔ Will it contain photographs or other illustrations?
- ✔ Will it be typeset from manuscript or reproduced in type from your own coded computer disk at less cost?
- ✔ What kind of binding will it have?

When you're buying a book printing job, you want to get bids just as you would if you were building a house or shopping for any other service.

To get a fair comparison of prices, make sure you give the same information to each company you're asking for a price quotation:

✔ What size book do you want? One standard size is 5½ × 8½ inches.

✔ How many pages? If the printer is setting type from your own typewritten manuscript, your book's page count will depend on the size type you select and the page size of the book. But if the printer knows the number of pages in your manuscript, he'll be able to make a quotation based on that. The average double-spaced typed manuscript contains 250 words to the page. Depending on the size of the type in the printed book, that may translate into 350 to 400 words per typeset page.

✔ If the book is being typeset, are there charges for author's proofs?

✔ What quantity do you want?

✔ How many and what kinds of illustrations will it include?

✔ Will the book be hardcover? Paperback? Spiral bound?

✔ If it is a hardcover book, will it have a book jacket? Printed in how many colors?

✔ What is the delivery time from the printer's receipt of manuscript or disk?

✔ What are shipping costs?

✔ Who keeps/owns the printing negatives? Most printers store negatives on the books they print for two to five years. If you decided to reprint the book before then and either weren't completely satisfied with the first printing job or got a better reprint price from another printer, you should be able to request the negatives be shipped to you. Check that paragraph in the printing contract. Of course, if you were just using a local photocopy chain to reproduce from your own camera-ready copy, those original pages are returned to you with the printed copies.

In any case, you want to be sure the book shows the copyright in your name.

If you want to learn more about what's involved in promoting and selling your own book, consult *The Complete Guide to Self-Publishing* by Tom and Marilyn Ross (see the Bibliography).

Desktop Publishing Your Own Book

If you've been thinking about buying a computer for your family's use, you could use it to "publish" your family history.

A computer with a basic operating system and monitor will cost about $1,000. (All costs represent those in 1994 at computer department stores like Micro Center.) An ink jet printer to produce the kind of dark print for a book (as opposed to the light computer type on a dot matrix printer) will cost about $300. A software desktop publishing program such as Microsoft Publisher for IBM compatibles or Aldus Home Publisher for Macintosh computers, will cost from $50 to $100. This program should contain, say, a dozen type fonts from which you can choose your chapter headings, subheads within the text and the text itself.

If you already have a computer and a wordprocessing program such as WordPerfect, but your printer only has the ability to produce bold or italics in the same type size, you have two options:

✔ Buy a simple publishing program like those mentioned above, or
✔ Use the services of companies (like Kinko's) that have self-serve computers with desktop publishing programs. You may want to just use them to type your front matter title page, contents page and the display heads for each of your chapters. These could be pasted in on the first text page of each chapter; your text would begin about one-third of the way down the first page of each chapter. Or, you could have Kinko's do that for you at a charge (in 1994) of about $9 per page.

PHOTOS IN YOUR FAMILY HISTORY

Some writers of personal stories use photographs rather than text to illustrate an important part of their own or their family's lives. Kenji Kawano, a Japanese photographer, was hitchhiking near Window Rock, Arizona, in 1974 during what was supposed to be a short visit to the U.S. That day, an old Indian man stopped and gave him a ride. As the Associated Press newspaper article reported:

> He was Carl Gorman, one of the original twenty-nine code talkers. Through that chance meeting, Kawano found his life's work.
>
> "When I told him I was Japanese, he told me he knew a little of my language, and that he liked sushi," Kawano recalled, "I didn't believe him! I didn't see how this could be. And when he told me about the code talkers . . . I have never heard of such a thing. I had to know more."

Early in the war, when the Japanese already had broken several U.S. codes, Navajo servicemen were asked to invent one based on their own complex language, which had no written equivalent.

They did — and then devised a code within the code. The Navajo language had no words for modern armaments, so they came up with substitute words for everything from dive bombers to battleships. The Japanese never managed to break the code.

Kawano stayed in the American Southwest for two decades living with the Navajo and taking pictures of the tribe's famous "code talkers" of World War II, in which Kawano's father had fought. Kawano's photographs of the Navajo went on display in a Tokyo gallery in 1994. About half the photographs depicted daily life on the Navajo reservation. The other half were portraits of the code talkers, now in their seventies.

Do you have some photographs that represent an important part of your family history or memoir? Incorporating them into your book can certainly provide another dimension to your book. How many copies of the book you plan to produce and the printing method you use, of course, will vary the cost.

Printers or national photocopy chains can incorporate reproductions of same-size, reduced or enlarged photographs into your text, which you indicate by an accompanying layout.

Keep in mind that there is a limit to what enhancement of a faded photograph is possible — even with advanced computer techniques such as the one described in chapter six in this book. If you have an old sepia-toned photo or faded black-and-white snapshot, don't expect its reproduction by orginary printing methods in your book to be better than the original. If you have a yellowed newspaper clipping containing a photograph, the yellow will reproduce as a mottled screen background. And if you enlarge a photograph from a newspaper clipping, the dots in the newspaper screen process will produce a patterned photograph. Reproducing an original photograph will not cause these problems.

Depending on your printing method, it may be a cost savings to group your photographs into a several-page photo portfolio, rather than scatter them throughout the book. Photos could carry identifying numbers, keyed to captions that appear on the page preceding those with photos.

Art in Your Family History

If you are an artist, your paintings or drawings are as much a personal memoir as your writings, and you may wish to incorporate copies of some of those into your personal story. Artists whose travels are beautifully illustrated in sketches or watercolors they created on site may have also documented other interests of theirs — whether it is the ever-changing view of nature from a kitchen window, a fox hunt or a sleeping child.

Some thoughtful artists, like Ede Schmidt, also take the time to think about the influences in their lives that have affected both their creative work and the people they have become. As a wife, mother, artist, horse-woman, businesswoman and traveler, Schmidt reflects on the variety of influences in her life:

> I see that my life has been built on several principles: 1. Love a lot. 2. Dream a lot. 3. Develop imagination. 4. Acquire knowledge. (I remember even at a young age listening in on my mother's literary club and noticing how they looked at things in their poetry.) 5. Build physical courage. (The first time I failed with a horse at a jump, two friends came back for me and encouraged me "You can do it!" and I learned that the horse has to sense that *you* really want to do it.) As I reflect on Who am I? I see that I'm the result of all my experiences and all that I have prayed about.

If you are only making limited copies for family and friends, national photocopy chains can make full-color reproductions of artwork at minimal cost (in 1994, an 8½ × 11-inch page was 99 cents.)

Some artists combine three or four small black and white sketches on a related theme for one 8½ × 11-inch page in their personal or family history.

THE DUMMY

"Dummy" is printer's lingo for the layout of how you want the text and illustrations in your book to be printed. The dummy is the guideline your professional photocopy shop or printer will use to print your book.

Depending on the binding method you will use, the inside margin of each page must be wide enough so that when the book is opened, type doesn't disappear into the binding. For example, the printing area for a 5½ × 8½-inch book is about 4 × 7 inches.

If you want certain photographs on certain pages near explanatory text, you should indicate in your dummy page layouts how you want the photographs placed on those pages. If you are grouping all photographs into a portfolio of certain pages, say, in the middle of the text, indicate on a layout of those pages which photos you wanted placed where.

Don't paste any photographs or other artwork into your dummy — just keep items separate and indicate on a blank page which photos or illustrations you want to be printed where.

PRINTING COSTS

If there are professional photocopy firms or small printers in your area, you'll want to get bids from them for printing your book from camera-ready typed pages or computer disk. Ask for samples of similar work they've done.

You might then want to compare those prices to those of firms that advertise as book printers or self-publishers in the display/classified advertising pages of magazines like *Writer's Digest*. Here, for example, are some prices quoted in 1994 from such advertisers.

Using a standard 5½ × 8½-inch book size and a page count of 176 pages, I asked a dozen printers/publishers to quote on print runs of 100, 250, 500 and 1,000 copies.

Depending on whether the manuscript had to be typeset, or was converted from computer disk into type, *typesetting prices* ranged between $3 and $10 per page; for 176 pages, that's between $528 and $1,760.

Preparation costs to include six black-and-white photos, one map and one family tree diagram ranged from $50 to $150 total.

Paper was usually specified as fifty-pound weight, but alternatives of more expensive or ecologically safe papers were offered. Printing costs (not including typesetting) for copies averaged as follows:

Paperback	No. of Copies	Hardcover
$1,000-1,800	100	$1,500-3,300
1,400-2,000	250	2,000-3,500
1,700-3,200	500	2,300-6,700
2,000-4,800	1,000	3,000-8,700

Paperbacks were perfect bound (glued); hardcovers had sewn bindings. Paperback covers were printed black and one other color. Hardback cover titles and author names were stamped in gold for the extra cost of a stamping die.

If your book was typeset from your manuscript and you plan to include an index, then of course you will have to develop that after you receive numbered page proofs.

Prior to receiving page proofs you may have received proofs for you to read for any printing errors. Keep in mind that any corrections you make at this stage — which are your own changes of mind and not "printers' errors" — will cause you to be charged for these "author's alterations."

PROOFREADING CHECKLIST

Sometimes we know the copy so well, we can't see the typos because we're so intent on reading for subject content. Here's a reminder checklist from *The Editorial Eye* newsletter to hang over your desk when you start to proofread typeset copy of your manuscript:

HOW DID THAT GET BY US?

Errors have the less-than-charming habit of creeping into plain view and hiding there. Remember that wherever one error lurks, another is likely in adjacent copy. Every pass through a document brings the possibility of new errors. We're only human. Busy editors often look right past omissions, duplications and typos. Here are some places to double check:

- ✔ headlines — read every letter
- ✔ titles
- ✔ the first line of a paragraph
- ✔ the first paragraph on a page
- ✔ the first page of a document
- ✔ the top lines of a new page
- ✔ the last lines of continuing copy
- ✔ the first lines of a runover (jumped copy)
- ✔ numerical sequences — page numbers, footnote numbers, outlines, lists
- ✔ alphabetical sequences — outlines, lists
- ✔ paired elements — brackets, parentheses, quotations marks, sometimes dashes
- ✔ numerals (figures, e.g., dollar amounts), dates, statistics, tables
- ✔ next to another error — the cluster syndrome
- ✔ in corrected copy — everything newly keyed or imported
- ✔ where copy has been cut — has *all* of it and *only* it been deleted?
- ✔ in copy that has been screened or has background graphics
- ✔ proper names — people, places, publications
- ✔ photo captions — more names than people? nameless people? named in order?

At the back of the book, you may want to leave a few blank pages to encourage you or other members of your family to make notes of events for future editions. Think of it as a Family Bible Supplement for the twenty-first century family tree keeper!

You may wish to title the pages "Notes for the Next Edition," and/ or include some suggestions for the types of records to keep.

IN CONCLUSION — CONGRATULATIONS!

The manuscript of your family history or personal memoir is a tangible asset that your relatives and friends will value for the contribution it makes to their lives. What they enjoy and learn from it will reward the self-discipline, detailed research, and literary skill you brought to the project. Even more important, you will have discovered some things about yourself and what you're capable of as a writer. You may have discovered some subjects you want to investigate further in a magazine article, a poem, a short story or a novel.

In the search for your roots, you have probably made some new friends, learned how to cope with frustrating fact-checking and overcome the biggest hurdle of all — sitting alone in a room with a typewriter, your memory, and a blank piece of paper.

Depending on the subject matter of your book, you may have been able to reach a broader audience than family and friends. Your effort has given to the region where you live or the profession of which you are a part a historical insight that only you could provide.

Whatever the initial motivations of family history or memoir writers, they all agree that the sense of accomplishment they felt on its completion far outweighed the long processes of research and writing.

Family members who were tiny tots at family reunions on Grandfather's farm now have children of their own who have a better understanding of where they come from and what their links are to the past.

In the epilogue to his self-published family history, C. Vincent Wright offers his assistance to other family members seeking forgotten twigs and branches on the family tree, but also says to readers:

> The rewards of this work are at least twofold. One, by learning more about my family, I appreciate and revere it more. Two, in the process of collecting the data, I have had the chance to get to know you through my letters, by telephone and personal visits.
>
> In the process of compiling the records of all of you, there is a very strong indication of the importance that our family has placed

on education — and, of course, the many career achievements that followed. You are a great tribe!

Dr. Eslie Asbury, whose eighty-five-year career as a practicing physician and thoroughbred breeding farm owner provided the personal experiences and humorous stories that resulted in his memoir *Horse Sense and Humor in Kentucky,* says

> Why would an old man, having renounced any possible revenue from it, bother to write a book, especially one featuring humor? I speak for myself and for others when I admit, without apology, it is for applause.
>
> Someone asked why I waited until old age to write this book. Two reasons: I had to accumulate the material, and I couldn't afford it while I was an active surgeon.
>
> .... I asked my friend how long I should make this book and what I ought to write about.
>
> "*About* twenty pages," he quipped.
>
> I persisted.
>
> "Well, just write what you know."
>
> "In twenty pages?"
>
> "Sure," he said, "that ought to do it."
>
> .... "You have convinced me," I said. "I'll make it thirty pages and include all we *both* know."

As mentioned in the introduction to this book, we hope you will share with us any advice on memoir writing, as a result of your experience, that we can pass along to readers of future editions of this handbook for writers.

BIBLIOGRAPHY

(See also publishers of excerpts on Permissions pages.)

America's Yesterdays, by Oliver Jensen. Copyright 1978. American History Publications Company, Inc., New York.

American Chronicle (1920-1989), by Lois Gordon and Alan Gordon. Copyright 1990 by Crown Publishers, New York.

A Century of Photographs 1846-1946, Library of Congress, 1980, Washington, D.C.

Chronicle of America. Copyright 1993. Chronicle Communications, Ltd., Farnborough, Hampshire, England.

Chronicle of the Twentieth Century. Editor, Clifton Daniel. Copyright 1987. Chronicle Publications, Inc., Mt. Kisco, New York.

The Complete Guide to Self-Publishing, third edition, by Tom and Marilyn Ross. Copyright 1994. Writer's Digest Books, Cincinnati, Ohio.

The Encyclopedia of American Facts and Dates, by Gordon Carruth. Copyright 1993. Harper/Collins, New York.

Families Writing, by Peter R. Stillman. Copyright 1989. Writer's Digest Books, Cincinnati, Ohio.

Family Names, How Our Surnames Came to America, by J.N. Hook. Copyright 1982. Macmillan, New York.

Finding Your Roots, by Jeane Eddy Westin. Copyright 1977. J.P. Tarcher, Inc., Los Angeles.

The Genealogist's Sourcebook and Companion, by Emily Anne Croom. Copyright 1994. Betterway Books, Cincinnati, Ohio.

Genealogy. Merit Badge Booklet. Copyright 1988. Boy Scouts of America, Irving, Texas.

Going, Going, Gone: Vanishing Americana, by Susan Jones and Marilyn Nessenson. Copyright 1994. Chronicle Books, San Francisco.

Guide to Genealogical Research in the National Archives, revised, 1985. National Archives Trust Fund Board, Washington, D.C.

The Handy Book for Genealogists, seventh edition, edited by George B. Everton, Sr. Copyright 1981. The Everton Publishers, Inc., Logan, Utah.

Harper Dictionary of Contemporary Usage. Copyright 1992. Harper and Row, HarperPerennial, New York.

How to Climb Your Family Tree, by Harriet Stryker-Rodda. Copyright 1977. J.B. Lippincott, New York.

How to Write Your Own Life Story, third edition, by Lois Daniel. Copyright 1991. Chicago Review Press.

Life Story: A Magazine of Writing Personal and Family History, editor, Charley Kempthorne. Letter Rock Publications, Manhattan, Kansas.

Life Writing: A Guide to Family Journal and Personal Memoirs, by William To Hofman. Copyright 1982. St. Martin's Press, New York.

Photographing Your Heritage, by Wilma Sadler Shull. Copyright 1988. Ancestry Publishing, Salt Lake City, Utah.

The Researcher's Guide to American Genealogy, by Val D. Greenwood. Copyright 1990. Genealogical Publishing Company, Inc., Baltimore, Maryland.

Searching for Your Ancestors, by Gilbert H. Doane and James B. Bell. Copyright 1992. The University of Minnesota, Minneapolis.

Shaking Your Family Tree, by Ralph Crandall. Copyright 1986. Yankee Publications, Dublin, New Hampshire.

Unpuzzling Your Past: A Basic Guide to Genealogy, second edition, by Emily Anne Croom. Copyright 1989. Betterway Books, Cincinnati, Ohio.

Webster Dictionary of English Usage. Copyright 1993. Merriam-Webster, Springfield, Massachusetts.

Write Tight: How to Keep Your Prose Sharp, Focused and Concise, by William Brohaugh. Copyright 1993. Writer's Digest Books, Cincinnati, Ohio.

The Writer's Digest Guide to Good Writing. Copyright 1994. Writer's Digest Books, Cincinnati, Ohio.

The Writer's Digest Guide to Manuscript Formats, by Dian Dincin Buchman and Seli Groves. Copyright 1987. Writer's Digest Books, Cincinnati, Ohio.

The Writer's Friendly Legal Guide, edited by Kirk Polking. Copyright 1989. Writer's Digest Books, Cincinnati, Ohio.

The Writer's Guide to Everyday Life in the 1800s, by Marc McCutcheon. Copyright 1993. Writer's Digest Books, Cincinnati, Ohio.

The Writer's Legal Guide, by Tad Crawford. Copyright 1977. Hawthorn Books, New York.

Writer's Market 1995, edited by Mark Garvey. Copyright 1994. Writer's Digest Books, Cincinnati, Ohio.

PERMISSIONS

In addition to those sources mentioned directly in the text, we thank the following for excerpt reprint permissions:

Memoir, by John H. Armour, edited by James C. Armour.

"Life with Mother," copyright 1987, essay by Russell Baker in *Inventing the Truth, The Art and Craft of Memoir*, edited by William Zinsser, Houghton Mifflin Company, Boston.

Do It Yourself, by Alan Bates.

Board for Certification of Genealogists.

Grover Buxton, Marietta, Ohio and the Montgomery County Historical Library, Rockville, Maryland.

Dominic J. Caraccilo, Captain U.S. Army Infantry, Assistant Professor, U.S. Military Academy at West Point, author, *The Ready Brigade of the 82nd Airborne in Desert Storm* and co-author of *Faces of Victory*.

"The Drowned Land," copyright 1993 by Arline Chase and Stoa Publications, Cambridge, Maryland.

"Skinner Hudson — Stowaway," by Skip Churchill, family historian and professional genealogist.

Memoir, by Diana F. Cooke, journal and fiction writer.

"Relationships: History Unites Old and Young," by Glenn Collins, copyright 1985 by The New York Times Company.

Memoirs, 1986 by Dot Darpel.

"To Fashion a Text," copyright 1987 by Annie Dillard, essay in *Inventing the Truth, The Art and Craft of Memoir*, edited by William Zinsser, Houghton Mifflin Company, Boston. Reprinted by permission of Blanche C. Gregory, Inc., agent.

The Writing Life, copyright 1989 by Annie Dillard. Reprinted by permission of Blanche C. Gregory, Inc., agent.

John Frederic Dorman, C.G., F.A.S.G.

Now You Know, copyright 1990 by Kitty Dukakis. Simon and Schuster, New York.

"Memoir 1952," by Ms. Sham (Gootman) Eden.

Generations: An American Family, copyright 1983 by John Egerton, The University Press of Kentucky, Lexington. Egerton's latest book is *Speak Now Against the Day: The Generations Before the Civil Rights Movement in the South* (Knopf, 1994).

Private Lives, copyright 1986 by Benita Eisler, Franklin Watts, New York.

"How Did That Get By Us?" from *The Editorial Eye*, copyright 1994, Editorial Experts, Inc., Alexandria, Virginia.

Changing Memories Into Memoirs, copyright 1984 by Fanny-Maude Evans, Harper and Row, New York.

Being Red: A Memoir, copyright 1990 by Howard Fast. Houghton Mifflin Company, Boston.

My Mother Worked and I Turned Out Okay, copyright 1993 by Garrett Press. Reprinted by permission of Katherine Wyse Goldman.

On the Way to Feed the Swans, copyright 1982 by Hannelore Hahn, Tenth House Enterprises, Inc., New York.

"Memoir," by Beth Mrea Hillerich.

"Trooper Bluegum at the Dardanelles" by Major Oliver Hogue. Reprinted by permission of his nephew, Jim Hogue.

Alice Hornbaker, "On Aging" columnist, excerpt reprinted from November 29, 1993 *Cincinnati Post*.

Book of the Hulls, by Oliver Hull, 1863. Printed by Peter Eckler, New York.

Memoir, copyright 1978 by Bella Briansky Kalter. Excerpt reprinted from the May 11, 1989, issue of the *Cincinnati Enquirer*.

The Writer's Art, copyright 1984 by James J. Kilpatrick. Andrews, McMeel and Parker, Kansas City, Missouri.

"Stringing Pearls: Making Heirlooms of Family Stories," copyright 1993 by Eileen Silva Kindig, excerpt from the October 1993 issue of *St. Anthony Messenger*. Kindig is also the author of *Goodbye Prince Charming*, Pinon Press, 1993.

V. Catherine Kozij, correspondence excerpt.

Memoir excerpt, Harriet S. Lazarus.

"The Floor Mopper," excerpt from "My First Job" article by Daniel R. Levine from the January, 1993, *Reader's Digest*. Reprinted by permission.

"Memoir," by Glory McLaughlin.

Memoir excerpt from *The Box Closet*, copyright 1987 by Mary Meigs. Talon Books Ltd., Vancouver.

The World Is My Home, copyright 1992 by James Michener. Random House, New York.

Jann Mitchell, "Relating" columnist for the *Oregonian* newspaper, Portland, Oregon. Excerpt on nieces and nephews, aunts and uncles.

Poem by Durward Morgan, Brown County, Ohio.

"Brand X" excerpt from the March 7, 1994, issue of the *New Yorker*. copyright 1994 by Terrence Rafferty. Reprinted by permission.

I Remember, by Dan Rather, Managing Editor and Co-Anchor of "The CBS Evening News." copyright 1991 by DIR Enterprises, Inc. Reprinted by permission of Little, Brown and Company, Boston.

The Hatfields and the McCoys, by Dr. Otis K. Price, Professor Emeritus of History, West Virginia Institute of Tehcnology. copyright 1978 by The University Press of Kentucky.

All Our Yesterdays: A Century of Family Life in an American Small Town, copyright 1993 by James Oliver Robertson and James C. Robertson. HarperCollins, New York.

The Story of the McGuffeys, by Alice McGuffey Ruggles. copyright 1950 by the American Book Company, New York.

Correspondence excerpt, Mary Gilpatrick Russell.

"Homecoming," short story by Irene L. Schwartz.

"Props," poem by Pollyanna Sedziol from the April 1994 issue of *St. Anthony Messenger*. Reprinted by permission.

"Reverence for Life," poem by Pollyanna Sedziol. Used by permission of the Judson Village Poetry Workshop.

INDEX